High Risk and Big Ambition

HIGH RISK and BIG AMBITION

The Presidency of George W. Bush

Edited by
Steven E. Schier

University of Pittsburgh Press

Published by the University of Pittsburgh Press, Pittsburgh, Pa., 15260

Manufactured in the United States of America
Printed on acid-free paper
10 9 8 7 6 5 4 3 2 1

Library of Congress Cataloging-in-Publication Data

High risk and big ambition : the presidency of George W. Bush / edited by Steven E. Schier.
p. cm.
Includes bibliographical references and index.
ISBN 0-8229-4234-8 (alk. paper) – ISBN 0-8229-5850-3 (pbk. : alk. paper)
1. United States–Politics and government–2001– 2. United States–Foreign relations–2001– 3. United States–Economic policy–2001– 4. Bush, George W. (George Walker), 1946– 5. Political leadership–United States. I. Schier, Steven E.
E902.H54 2004
973.931'092–dc22 2003027967

To Donald S. Schier,
with thanks for his continuing example

Contents

Tables

High Risk and Big Ambition

INTRODUCTION
George W. Bush's Project

Steven E. Schier

The unpromising circumstances surrounding the election of George W. Bush to the presidency in no way prepared Americans for the remarkable twists and turns of policy, politics, and events that characterized his early years in office. Elected with no public mandate whatsoever, Bush achieved surprising legislative success in his early months in the White House, winning passage of his two top priorities, a major tax cut and reform of education policy (Barshay 2001). His public support remained reasonably strong during this period, given that he had won only a minority of the popular vote. The defection of Senator James Jeffords of Vermont to the Democratic caucus in mid-2001, however, gave Democrats control of the Senate and heightened the tenor of partisan conflict in Washington.

Then came September 11, 2001, which refocused his presidency on national security concerns and drove his public support to unprecedented heights. The political opportunity granted by strong public popularity revealed the grand ambitions underlying the Bush presidency. Bush gained unprecedented supremacy over national security policy. Congress granted him war powers authority to initiate conflict with the rogue regimes in Afghanistan and Iraq, gave the administration extensive authority over domestic surveillance through the Patriot Act, and acquiesced to the administration's requests for additional military spending. Recurring partisan divisions in Congress in 2002 caused Bush to gradually adopt a more partisan approach in seeking congressional support. The president also took the unusual political risk of deploying his personal popularity during the 2002 midterm elections, with considerable success. The Republicans' two-seat gain in the Senate and six-seat gain in the House were a first for any president in his first midterm since the Roosevelt New Deal sweep of 1934. The Bush administration scored an important congressional victory in mid-2003 with the passage of a bill cutting taxes by $326 billion through 2013, aimed at spurring the flagging economy (Ota 2003a). Though the tax cut was less than half the size of the one his administration originally proposed, Bush claimed a policy victory. Congress also approved another administration priority, an ambitious plan for prescription drug coverage for Medicare recipients costing $400 billion over ten years (Toner and Pear 2003). Perhaps the greatest risk of his presidency, the 2003 war in Iraq, produced a swift military victory but also spawned much international opposition and a troublesome regime of military occupation.

The Grand Task of Regime Restoration

How to make sense of these zigs and zags? Presidential scholar Stephen Skowronek provides several concepts that help us to understand the project at the heart of the Bush presidency. To Skowronek, the presidency is an inherently "disruptive" institution; a sort of "battering ram" used by presidents to alter the actions and results issuing from permanent Washington, that thick encrustation of interest groups, legislative specialists in Congress, and careerist federal bureaucrats. Permanent Washington has evolved through "secular time," which Skowronek defines at the historical medium through which power structures grow and change (Skowronek 1997, 30). The rise of lasting power relationships beyond direct presidential control has proceeded apace throughout the twentieth century. This "institutional thickening" involved "an ever thicker" set of governmental and political arrangements in Washington that produce greater "institutional resilience" to attempts by presidents to alter established arrangements (1997, 413).

Presidents seek to create an alternative conception of government. Instead of merely acceding to the power patterns that develop in secular time, they often seek to rework those patterns to further their own purposes, as Nicol Rae notes in his chapter here placing Bush's presidency in historical context. In Skowronek's terms, presidents seek to create an alternative form of governmental operation by invoking "political time," the historical medium through which authority structures have recurred (1997, 30). That is to say, presidents frequently try to create political regimes supported by constitutional authority and popular approval. A successful political regime can order events according to its own schedule, displacing the ability of permanent Washington to order events through its residues of power. It is a battle between presidential authority and other traditional sources of power in Washington.

What constitutes a successful presidential "regime?" Robert C. Lieberman defines the various aspects:

> Regimes appear at a variety of levels, from formal institutions (such as the structure of Congress and the administrative state) to the social bases of politics (such as party alignments and coalitions and patterns of interest representation); from ideas (such as prevailing beliefs about the proper role of government) to informal norms (such as patterns of congressional behavior). Nested within these broadly defined institutional arrangements are commitments to particular policies that become the touchstone for political action and conflict for leaders and would-be leaders over the course of a generation or more. (Lieberman 2000, 275)

From this definition, it is not difficult to outline the regime the Bush administration seeks to entrench. Institutionally, the Bush administration seeks control of Congress by reliable, partisan Republican majorities and enhanced presidential control over the executive branch through reorganizations spawned by national security concerns, such as the creation of the Department of Homeland Security.

Politically, the administration seeks consistent Republican electoral majorities. The primary tactical imperative in this is maintaining high support among the party's core activists through strong national security policies and tax cuts. James L. Guth notes in his chapter how Bush also carefully cultivates Christian conservatives within his coalition by carefully emphasizing particular social policies. A second primary tactic is the wooing of key elements of the electorate—suburbanites, rural residents, white Catholics, Latinos, working-class males—through artful public statements and emphasis on issues of particular interest to them (accountability reforms in education, farm price supports, stem-cell research, judicial appointments, steel tariffs) (Brownstein 2002, 2). Key ideas of the regime include a recurrent emphasis on tax cuts as the preferred engine of economic management and an aggressive new foreign policy involving military preemption of potential terror threats and distrust of recent international agreements such as those on global warming and the International Criminal Court. Informal norms include a personal distancing of the president from micropolitical dealing and renewed emphasis on partisan unity in Congress.

What does all this constitute? The primary project of the Bush presidency is to complete the political reconstruction of national politics, government, and policy begun by Ronald Reagan in 1981. Examine the features of the second Bush regime, and you will find commitments, policies, and tactics consistent with those of Reagan and having as their ultimate end the lasting triumph of Reaganite rule in national government: military strength, tax cuts, enhanced executive power at the expense of Congress, and a stable electoral majority that prefers conservative Republicans. Bush is centrally engaged in a project of political restoration through tactically innovative means.

Skowronek identifies such presidents as "orthodox innovators" who seek to "articulate" the commitments of a previous regime "to fit the existing parts of the regime together in a new and more relevant way. . . . They galvanize political action with promises to continue the good work of the past and demonstrate the vitality of the established order to changing times" (1997, 41).

How has Bush sought to make the Reagan regime more relevant to the early twenty-first century? He has resurrected unsuccessful initiatives of the previous regime, such as the privatization of Social Security, a missile defense system, educational vouchers, and less-invasive environmental regulation. He has varied from the policy agenda by pursuing "magnet" issues that might broaden the regime's coalition of supporters through measures such as education reform and prescription drug coverage for Medicare recipients.

Bush has also gone beyond the Reagan regime in pursuing some of its original commitments. One example, assessed in detail in the chapter by Raymond Tatalovich and John Frendreis, involves the supply-side economics of tax cutting. Reagan and his vice president and successor, George Herbert Walker Bush, both signed tax increases (in 1982 and 1990) in the wake of budget deficits. As deficits grew in 2003, George W. Bush instead proposed large tax cuts totaling $726 billion through

2013, much to the delight of antitax advocates in his coalition like Grover Norquist, head of Americans for Tax Reform. Another example is his Iraq policy. The first Bush presidency strove to contain Iraq and hoped for a coup in the wake of the first Gulf War. George W. Bush pursued a more aggressive approach of "regime change" and invasion of the country. More broadly, as James M. McCormick notes in his chapter, Bush's foreign policy of military "preemption" toward international terror threats codifies in doctrine the earlier regime's pattern of situational uses of force overseas against perceived national security threats from Libya, Grenada, and Panama.

In his mission of regime articulation, Bush resembles previous orthodox innovators of American political history. These presidents' innovations often involved aggressive foreign policies given the constraints on domestic policy innovation presented by the established regimes with which they were affiliated. Democrat James K. Polk, a loyal Jacksonian Democrat nicknamed "Young Hickory," led the nation through a war with Mexico. William McKinley and Theodore Roosevelt, operating within the long-established Republican political regime of the era, greatly expanded America's diplomatic and military role in the world. Harry Truman and Lyndon Johnson, heirs of FDR's New Deal regime, committed American troops to long conflicts in Korea and Vietnam. George W. Bush, loyal to the commitments of the earlier Reagan-Bush regime, prosecuted international war on terrorism and invaded Iraq.

High Risk

The presidencies of many orthodox innovators came to a bad end because their innovations spawned dissension within the established political regimes with which they were affiliated. Polk's expansionist policies sparked controversies over the extension of slavery that he could not quell and would ultimately destroy the Jacksonian regime. Roosevelt's domestic progressivism caused a split in his party that led to the election of Democrat Woodrow Wilson in 1912. The interminable Korean War caused Truman to leave the White House as a highly unpopular president, succeeded by Republican Dwight Eisenhower. Johnson's disastrous Vietnam policy deeply split his party and helped elect Republican Richard Nixon as president in 1968.

The chief political strategist of the Bush White House, Karl Rove, looks for lessons in the presidency of William McKinley, the only orthodox innovator who presided over a major and lasting popular electoral realignment (Dubose, Reid, and Cannon 2003, 169; Dionne 2001, 1). Kevin S. Price and John J. Coleman note in their chapter how the Bush administration is pursuing partisan realignment as a governing strategy, hence McKinley's relevance for Rove. McKinley's term included a muscular new foreign policy and a popular foreign war (the Spanish-American War in 1898), as well as a domestic strategy that won additional working-class voters for Republicans through the promise of burgeoning industrial capitalism—the appeal of "the full dinner pail." Democrats veered away from the mainstream by nominating the strident populist William Jennings Bryan who ran against McKinley in both 1896 and 1900. No doubt, the Bush White House hopes the Democrats will similarly vacate the center in 2004.

Despite such hopeful analogies, the Bush White House faces great obstacles in its attempt to entrench the Reagan regime. First, as Skowronek notes, the political reconstruction attempted by Ronald Reagan was far from complete. He describes it as largely "rhetorical rather than institutional" (1997, 32) because "institutional thickening" in national government had become steadily more prevalent over time (1997, 422). The firm relationships among a Democratic Congress, sympathetic interest groups, and career bureaucrats made domestic policy innovation difficult for Reagan after his initial success cutting spending and taxes in 1981. These constraints encumbered his successor, George H. W. Bush, even more, leading him to raise taxes in a 1990 budget deal with the Democratic Congress, a move that splintered support among his conservative regime followers and contributed to his defeat in 1992. The Reaganite regime did reappear in the Republican sweep of Congress in 1994, led by the outspoken conservative Newt Gingrich (R-GA), who became House Speaker. But the Republican Congress had at best mixed success in dueling with Democratic president William Jefferson Clinton. From 1993 to 2000, elements of the Reagan regime contested but in no sense dominated national policymaking and political appointments.

Bush's accession to the White House despite his losing the popular vote and Republican losses of House and Senate seats revealed that the electoral coalition supporting a conservative policy regime had a far from secure grip on power. Consider the fragility of several regime components. The popular coalition that elected Bush amassed about 48 percent of the vote, half a million votes fewer than Al Gore received. Neither Congress nor the Supreme Court is securely under conservative control. Business and ideologically conservative interest groups do not continually prevail on major issues in Washington and are frequently outgunned on important issues by opposing liberal groups (Smith 2000; Berry 1999). Most major new ideas and policy commitments have come mainly from the Bush White House; other components of the Reagan regime seem content with a more conventional conservative agenda.

Given these limitations, Bush proved remarkably adept at winning approval for his top 2001 agenda items from Congress. One, the large tax cut, served to consolidate his base, and the other, a reform of education policy passed with the support of leading Democrats including Senator Ted Kennedy (D-MA), served to broaden his appeal among suburbanite voters not reliably part of his electoral coalition (Ornstein 2001). Bush's early success despite his controversial election victory lends support to Richard Pious's contention that adept use of the presidency's constitutional prerogatives is more central than short-term political factors "in determining what a president can accomplish" (Pious 1979, 16).

September 11 greatly boosted Bush's personal popularity and, for a time, public support for his party. John J. Pitney Jr. in his chapter discusses Bush's tactical exploitation of his status as a wartime president. But by 2002 the president faced a highly competitive midterm election. The savvy political tactics of regime leaders in the White House and the national Republican Party leadership, coupled with the president's risky decision to deploy his personal popularity on behalf of key Senate candidates, produced small but historically remarkable gains for Republicans. Republicans achieved narrow majorities in the House and Senate, but a close partisan division remained among the public. As the economy remained sluggish in 2003, a survey of statewide opinion polls revealed only the tiniest Republican edge in partisan identification (Cook 2003a, 1).

It remains far from clear, then, that Republicans have solidified a majority of voters around a conservative political regime. The GOP in recent years has made gains among rural voters, but they are a declining part of the electorate. It is true, as Price and Coleman note in their chapter, that the fastest-growing counties in America have voted increasingly Republican (Barone 2001, 31). Yet Democrats in the elections of 1992, 1996, and 2000 did quite well among female and professional voters. They maintain a huge advantage among African Americans. Latinos, the sleeping giant of American politics, also continue to favor

Democrats by a substantial margin. Analysts John B. Judis and Ruy Texeira find an emerging Democratic electoral majority in these trends that "reflects deep-seated social and economic trends that are changing the face of the country. . . . Today's Democrats are the party of the transition from urban industrialism to a new postindustrial metropolitan order in which men and women play equal roles and in which white America is supplanted by multiracial, multiethnic America" (Judis and Teixeira 2002, 6). Geographically, Democrats have done much better at aggregating electoral college votes in the last three presidential elections than have Republicans.

Bush's task, unlike that of previous orthodox innovators, involves finally installing a successful political regime, rather than merely maintaining its current dominance, the mission of his predecessors Polk, McKinley, Roosevelt, Truman, and Johnson. Despite astute political leadership by his White House, orchestrated by Rove, the conservative policy regime headed by Bush has yet to entrench its dominance in American politics. After the Iraq war in mid-2003, the Bush administration remained beset with a slowly growing economy, splits in congressional Republican ranks over mushrooming national budget deficits, and growing salience of an issue—health care—that has long worked to the electoral advantage of Democrats.

Another problem that makes Bush's task particularly difficult is the Washington politics endemic in an era of "institutional thickening." Benjamin Ginsberg and Martin Shefter describe it as "institutional combat" in which national politicians use weapons of institutional power to fight over governmental direction, rather than engage in risky and expensive mobilization of new voters in election campaigns (Ginsburg and Shefter 2003, 21). Electoral turnout remains low as parties and candidates "round up the usual suspects" through targeted activation using new communication technologies (Schier 2000). Elections are less conclusive, given the absence of an entrenched political regime, so incentives for obstruction grow among leaders of both parties.

The even partisan balance in government sharpens motivations to use institutional authority to disrupt opponents. Congress in recent years witnessed an abundance of such behavior. During the Bush presidency, party government has prevailed in the House, with the Speaker and the Rules Committee structuring the floor agenda to limit the potential of minority Democrats to prevail through amendments or procedural obstructions. When Democrats controlled the Senate in 2001 and

2002, then-Majority Leader Tom Daschle kept important administration initiatives, such as its energy plan and the homeland security reorganization bill, from reaching the Senate floor for a vote. Since then, a prime weapon of institutional combat during the Bush presidency has been the Senate filibuster. In recent years, ironically, Republicans were the first to employ it effectively—against Clinton's 1993 budget plan. Since 2001, Senate Democrats have derailed several judicial nominations through filibuster. The rancorous partisanship accompanying such tactics spilled over into foreign policy when many leading Democrats in early 2003 openly questioned the need for a war against Iraq and, after the war's official conclusion, challenged the evidence regarding weapons of mass destruction that the administration employed in arguing for the war.

Hence, the high risks for the Bush administration: it seeks to entrench a conservative regime among a public beset by even partisan divisions and without a stable Washington governing coalition. Journalist John Harwood aptly terms the Bush incumbency a "low margin, party-line presidency" (Harwood 2003, 1). The Bush administration has had limited room for maneuver, despite the windfall of public support after September 11. Bush played this national security "trump card" for maximum political effect from 2001 to 2003, but in terms of electoral and institutional politics, he faces considerable challenges as he completes his first term. His economic stewardship remains controversial, a troublesome military occupation of Iraq continues, and dissension within his own party has arisen over growing budget deficits (Cook 2003b, 1).

Clinton the Preemptor

All this suggests that at bottom, the Bush administration's political ambition of conservative regime restoration is still far from reality. As of 2003, Skowronek's politics of "permanent preemption" seems an apposite description of contemporary national politics, in which presidents face "the proliferation of interests and authorities throughout the government and the organizational resilience of the institutions that defend them" (1997, 443). In such a situation, regime construction or renewal is extremely difficult. The prudent presidential strategy in this situation is that followed by Bush's predecessor, Clinton, in which presidents "build new, personal bases of political support outside of regular political alliances and often outside of institutional politics altogether" (1997, 44).

Clinton was tactically nimble (after his many political mistakes of 1993–1994), announcing domestic policies poll-tested to appeal to swing voters and "triangulating" between Democrats and Republicans in his dealings with Congress. Clinton's project was not regime maintenance but rather, as is the mission of "preemptive presidents," tactically to master a difficult environment established by the hostile presidential regime that preceded him. The incomplete nature of Reagan's reconstruction lowered the cost of Clinton's improvisations until he laid himself low with scandal. Conservative forces in Congress and in the public forced him to pay the steep price of impeachment.

Bush's project is wholly different from Clinton's, but Bush confronts a political environment remarkably similar to the one Clinton encountered. The politics of preemption often involves personal attacks on presidents because no single regime is fully in control of government. Resurgent Republicans in the late 1990s, envisioning regime restoration, thus pilloried Clinton in harsh terms. Democratic politicians and activists have loudly announced their low esteem of Bush, particularly after his aggressive use of his office to win, narrowly, the 2002 elections. Politics in a preemptive era usually produces little regime construction and a reduced policy legacy for incumbent presidents. That seems a fair thumbnail summary of the Clinton legacy. Bush, however, seeks far more than the largely personal stamp on leadership and policy that Clinton pursued. As John F. Harris puts it in his chapter here, Bush is a "hedgehog" focused strongly on installing a conservative regime in contrast to Clinton, the nimble "fox" who scattered his energies widely. For Bush, conservative regime restoration through electoral domination and a strong policy legacy are the measures of presidential success. This is a big ambition, indeed, and, as we have seen, it brings many political risks.

Strategic and Tactical Prowess

The Bush presidency pursued its grand design with much adroitness in its early years. The initial task involved demonstrating presidential leadership in the absence of an electoral mandate. This Bush did very well, in part by adopting some of his predecessor's preemptive tactics. He came into office stating he wished to "change the tone" in Washington through pursuing personal, less partisan leadership. True to his word, he personally persuaded a handful of conservative Senate Democrats to pass his tax bill and worked well with liberal Democrats, including Senator Ted Kennedy (D-MA) and Representative George Miller (D-CA), to get his education bill passed into law. At the same time, Bush kept unvarying party unity among congressional Republicans.

In the wake of his great popularity after September 11, however, a more partisan style appeared. His 2002 campaigning was party-based and unusually aggressive. At the center of his 2003 agenda were orthodox conservative items—a large tax cut and possible war with Iraq—and an innovative proposal for Medicare prescription drug coverage for seniors. Bush's success in Congress in 2003, as Bertram Johnson notes in his chapter here, came primarily through party-line votes. The administration's 2004 reelection strategy also seems based on a central imperative of maintaining strong party unity behind the president. Evidently, his advisors expect a highly competitive election in 2004. The strategy, as one White House aide put it, "has to be to hold what you start with and then change the dynamics of 4 percent or 5 percent total. It's not like you're trying to build 60 percent of the vote, but rather build to 52 percent" (Brownstein 2002, 1). The primacy of regime maintenance puts a ceiling on Bush's likely vote, given the political weaknesses of the regime he seeks to restore.

Despite this emphasis on regime maintenance, Bush consistently employed some of Clinton's political tactics. Both White Houses sought to govern by campaigning, having the president "go public" in a "permanent campaign" seeking agenda domination (Kernel 1997; Mann and Ornstein, 2000). The Clinton presidency became famous for shaping its policy agenda according to poll results (Harris 2000b). Pollsters have a much less public presence in the Bush administration, and Bush pays much less personal attention to poll results than did Clinton. Still, Rove pours over polls and consults regularly with White House pollster Matthew Dowd. Poll results importantly shape the administration's tactics as they did those of the previous administration. Tactics informed by polls became essential given the harsh opposition each incumbent has faced. The close partisan balance in Washington since 1995 has subjected both presidents to the preemptive politics of personal vilification. Democratic congressional leaders in 2003 sharply condemned the Bush administration, much as Republican congressional leaders verbally assaulted Clinton in the later 1990s. The reasons for the vilification, however, differed greatly. Republicans expressed contempt toward Clinton for his success in "preempting" their agenda on issues such as welfare reform and balancing the budget. Democratic leaders attacked Bush for his attempt to restore a conservative political regime to political dominance. His 2003 agenda and aggressive partisanship during the 2002 elections fueled their anger.

Similar tactics, dissimilar ends. The Bush administration engages in a permanent campaign for public support, touts and trades on the personal popularity of the incumbent, targets swing voters in the electorate with its appeals, and tactically emphasizes issues that will boost its political prospects. The Clinton administration did the same. However, Clinton after 1994 was protecting himself in a hostile political environment and did little to tie himself publicly to his congressional Democrats or to create lasting political advantages for his political party, which at times split internally in response to his great flexibility on issues. Bush's pursuit of a lasting conservative policy regime is comparatively far more ambitious and risky a goal than that of his predecessor.

Bush's "regime" helps to explain his superior issue discipline compared with Clinton's more personal politics. Clinton's improvisational style, ranging from issue to issue, stands in stark contrast to Bush's dogged focus on a few issues. If the issues are well chosen, limited focus can be a great tactical asset to a president. Given the large regime task Bush has set for himself, such discipline is essential. Rove's short list of administration issues for 2003—winning the terror war, homeland security, faith-based initiatives, tax cuts, health care, and retirement reform—seem designed in the short term to secure the Republican base and appeal to selected groups of swing voters (Rove 2002). The Bush White House has had success on several issues by "taking them away" from Democrats—by achieving credibility with the public on a number of issues on which Democrats have traditionally been more trusted. The great example of 2001 was education. Bush's 2003 proposals on health care (a Medicare prescription drug benefit) and the environment (research support for hydrogen-powered cars) are more recent examples. His electoral success in 2004 will depend in large part on the effectiveness of such tactics.

Bush has demonstrated an impressive suitability for his office that brings his outsized ambitions within reach. Despite his thin experience in national politics before taking office, Bush has proven to be a temperamentally sound chief executive. Political scientist Donald Kettl, in a thorough analysis of Bush's administrative style, argues that Bush has manifested a strong aptitude for team leadership and effective management of the White House (Kettl 2003). Peri E. Arnold arrives at similar conclusions in his chapter here. Presidential scholar Fred Greenstein identifies several skills evident in Bush's presidential performance. On policy, Bush ably demonstrates an "aptitude for personal politics" and a "readiness to seek support on both sides of the aisle" (Greenstein 2002, 393). He adopts "policy positions to preempt his opponents as well as because of their appeal to him" (2002, 394). Though Bush has "ample native intelligence," he is not drawn to intellectual discussions or pursuits, but since September 11, his public rhetorical skills have steadily improved (2002, 392, 395). Bush's public persona, described by John Kenneth White and John J. Zogby in their chapter here as that of a "likeable partisan," has worn well with many in the public.

Bush has invested great authority in Rove, who dominates the political operations of the White House and frequently weighs in on domestic policy decisions (Lemann 2003). Rove has articulated the big ambitions motivating the Bush presidency. His formula for winning elections: "Have a robust domestic and foreign agenda. Don't trim your sails. Be bold. People want to hear big, significant changes. They don't want to be fed small micro-policy" (2003, 80). Rove's strategic innovation involves poaching traditionally Democratic issues to further Republican domination of national politics: "Do you weaken a political party, either by turning what they see as assets into liabilities, and/or by taking issues they consider to be theirs, and raiding them? Absolutely!" (2003, 83). Rove regularly pushes the administration to take risks on issues to meet its grand ambitions.

A Dangerous Opportunity

September 11 gave Bush considerable political capital. He spent much of it in the 2002 election, taking a risk that aggressive partisan campaigning would pay off. It did, narrowly. Still strongly popular in early 2003, Bush took three other risks. First, he proposed to cut taxes by $726 billion through 2013, despite short-term deficit forecasts—that did not include the costs of the war in Iraq—exceeding $300 billion per year. Second, he proposed a prescription drug benefit for Medicare recipients that required them to enter managed-care plans to receive the benefit. Third, he pressed a war against Iraq despite widespread opposition from major allies. All of these risks fit his role as an orthodox innovator. The Iraq war and tax cuts fit the aggressive foreign policy and supply-side economic policy of Reagan. The Medicare plan attempts to neutralize the Democrats' best domestic issue for 2004.

Not all risks pay off. The Medicare plan proved a nonstarter, and the administration then tried working with divided congressional Republicans on possible alternatives. The House and Senate passed greatly differing prescription drug plans in mid-2003 and slowly but successfully worked toward a difficult compromise. Only a much-reduced tax cut passed because moderate Senate Republicans rejected the scale of the Bush proposal. The quick military success in Iraq boosted public approval of Bush and the GOP, but the turbulent military occupation of the country produced fresh problems for the administration. Bush's uncertain prospects underline the difficulty of the task he has set for himself. He might have more success by operating as Clinton did, courting personal popularity in a Washington of even partisan balance and recalcitrant political institutions. But for Bush, personal popularity is merely a means to be used—and at times sacrificed—in the service of the greater end of restoring a conservative regime.

The Bush presidency thus involves a grand paradox. The president must garner personal popularity and often give precedence to personal politics in order to address other Washington institutions from a position of strength. Yet his fealty to a conservative policy regime requires him to expend his political capital in its service, which can put personal survival at risk. This will all turn out well if that regime is embraced by a majority of voters. However, if it is not, Bush will have taken risks and squandered political capital on a project that was unlikely to succeed in any event. If Skowronek is right, and Washington authority structures are so impervious to presidential change that regime construction is impossible, then political time—and the ability to build political authority structures that outlast any administration's time in office—has vanished. Bush is gambling that he can deploy the power of his office to resurrect political time. If political time has vanished, then so will his presidency.

I

Historical Perspectives

1 THE GEORGE W. BUSH PRESIDENCY IN HISTORICAL CONTEXT

Nicol C. Rae

George W. Bush's presidency has been contentious from the moment the Supreme Court confirmed his election as president in *Bush v. Gore*. The Court's decision meant that Bush joined John Quincy Adams, Rutherford B. Hayes, and Benjamin Harrison as one of four U.S. presidents who owed their elections to a victory in the Electoral College while finishing second in the national popular vote. The protracted and bitter postelection conflict over Florida's electoral votes and the various irregularities revealed in the Florida count also raised further initial questions about the "legitimacy" of the Bush presidency (Dionne and Kristol 2001).

Yet if Bush's political opponents believed that the circumstances of his election would temper his ambitions in terms of policy and conservative ideology, they were to be unpleasantly surprised by the course of his administration. Despite losing the popular vote, Bush from the outset has governed as if he had a clear mandate from the public for his strongly conservative economic, domestic, and foreign policy agenda (Frum 2003a,b). So integral to the presidency is the role of national agenda-setter and the notion of a policy "mandate" that these claims have been generally accepted by press and public, and several of the most significant items on the Bush agenda have actually been enacted (Cochran 2002).

The other distinguishing feature of the Bush presidency has, of course, been his reaction to the traumatic events of September 11, 2001. There is no question that the terrorist attacks on New York and Washington marked a significant turning point for Bush, not only in his popularity, which soared in the wake of the tragedy, but also in the focus and direction of his administration (Keller 2003a). The surprising Republican gains in the 2002 midterm elections seemed to indicate approval of Bush's conduct of the office after September 11 and provide the "mandate" lacking in the close election of 2000 (Nather and Cochran 2002)

So in the changed domestic and international political order subsequent to September 11 it fell to Bush, already a controversial president, to chart a course for America in a transformed international environment. The protracted domestic and international political debates surrounding Bush's decision to launch a "preemptive war" for the purpose of overthrowing Saddam Hussein's regime in Iraq in March 2003 were indicative of the potentially dangerous and uncharted territory this could be for any president. The United States won decisive victories on the battlefield in Afghanistan and Iraq, and the course of events in those countries as well as in the "war" against terrorism will play a large part in determining whether Bush secures a second term, an outcome denied to his father in 1992.

Problems of Presidential Legitimacy Since 1825

Bush's victory in 2000 was a reminder that American presidents are elected not by popular vote but by the 538-member Electoral College, composed of blocs of electors (roughly proportionate to the population of each state) awarded on a winner-take-all basis (except Maine and Nebraska) to the plurality vote winner in each state and the District of Columbia. The original intent of the aristocratically minded framers of the U.S. Constitution was that each state would select the "best and the brightest" among its political elite to elect the federal chief executive (Ceaser 1979, 41–87). With the advent of party competition, however, and the increasing democratic pressures within American society, states began to choose their electors at large by direct popular vote, leaving

South Carolina as the only holdout for legislative selection by 1832 (Wayne 2001, 14–15). The final passing of the founding generation's natural order of succession to the presidency in 1824 led to the Electoral College vote being splintered among four candidates. With no candidate achieving an electoral vote majority, according to the Constitution the House of Representatives then had to choose between the top three candidates, with each state delegation in the House casting one vote.

The House's choice of John Quincy Adams over the popular favorite General Andrew Jackson signaled the end of the Electoral College as an independent decision-making body. Four years later Jackson's supporters created a national electoral organization to corral voters behind slates of electors committed to voting for Jackson in the Electoral College. The Jackson slates prevailed and gave birth to the Democratic Party; the anti-Jacksonians similarly organized themselves into the Whig party by 1840 (McCormick 1975).

The post-1824 system made electing the president more of a popular contest but not completely, since states, rather than the national popular vote, remain the key unit of election. The system also left open the possibility that a candidate could prevail in the Electoral College with less than a majority of the popular vote and that in a very close election a candidate could be elected—through carrying enough states with significant numbers of electoral votes by narrow margins—who had finished second in the overall national popular vote. The final awarding of Florida's 25 electoral votes to Bush in 2000 (based on an official statewide popular plurality of 537 votes) enabled him to eke out a four-vote margin in the electoral college (271 votes, to Vice President Al Gore's 267) while losing the national popular vote by some 540,000 votes (0.5 percent) (see table 1.1).

In eighteen (40 percent) of the forty-five presidential elections from 1824 to 2000, the winner was elected despite his having won less than a majority of the national popular vote. (In ten of these cases, the presence of significant nonmajor party candidates effectively kept the winner of the electoral vote from winning a national popular vote majority.) The heavy or comfortable electoral vote margin of the winning candidate has probably helped to confer legitimacy on a plurality popular-vote winner, a function that has formed a major part of the defense of the Electoral College from political scientists and commentators (Wayne

Table 1.1

Presidents Since 1824 Who Failed to Win a Majority of the Popular Vote

Year	*President*	*Popular vote (%)*	*Margin (%)*	*Electoral vote (%)*
1824	**J. Q. Adams**	**30.5**	**–13.1**	**32.2**[a]
1844	Polk	49.6	1.5	61.8
1848	Taylor	47.4	4.9	56.2[a]
1852	Buchanan	45.3	12.2	58.8[a]
1860	Lincoln	39.9	10.5	59.4[a]
1876	**Hayes**	**47.9**	**–3.1**	**50.1**
1880	Garfield	48.3	0.1	58.0
1884	Cleveland	48.5	0.2	54.6
1888	**Harrison**	**47.8**	**–0.9**	**58.1**
1892	Cleveland	46.1	3.2	62.4[a]
1912	Wilson	41.9	14.5	81.9[a]
1916	Wilson	49.3	3.2	52.2
1948	Truman	49.5	4.4	57.1[a]
1960	Kennedy	49.7	0.1	56.4
1968	Nixon	43.4	0.7	56.0[a]
1992	Clinton	42.3	4.9	68.8[a]
1996	Clinton	49.2	8.5	70.4[a]
2000	**G. W. Bush**	**47.9**	**-0.5**	**50.4**

Source: Mieczkowski 2001.

Note: 1824 is the first election with accurate data on the national popular vote. Boldfaced entries are popular vote losers elected president.

[a]Minor party candidates with over 5 percent of the national popular vote.

2001, 13–21; Polsby and Wildavsky 1996, 291–99). Plurality popular vote victories have also not precluded presidents such as James K. Polk and Woodrow Wilson from successfully pursuing ambitious legislative agendas, indicating that presidential "mandates" are not made by election tallies but by astute politicking by presidents once in office.

In four of the eighteen elections won with less than a majority of the national popular vote (almost 10 percent of the total number of elections since 1824), presidents were elected despite their having *lost* the national popular vote: John Quincy Adams (1824), Rutherford B. Hayes (1876), Benjamin Harrison (1888), and George W. Bush (2000). In a nation that takes its democratic credentials extremely seriously, the legitimacy issue may be particularly troublesome for presidents who have lost the popular vote.

John Quincy Adams, 1825–1829

In addition to being losers of the popular vote, George W. Bush and John Quincy Adams share another distinction: they are the only presidential offspring to ascend to the office in their own right. While Bush's governmental experience was limited to two terms as Texas governor, Adams came to the office with an extremely distinguished resume. He had served as ambassador to the Netherlands, Prussia, Russia, and Great Britain; as a U.S. senator (1803–1808); and as secretary of state in the administration of his predecessor, James Monroe (1817–1825), in which he was primarily responsible for the famous "hands off America" doctrine that bears Monroe's name (Hecht 1972; Nagel 1997).

While Adams may have appeared to be the natural successor to Monroe, his candidacy for president in 1824 was swept up in the new democratic fervor and political controversy sweeping the nation as the so-called Era of Good Feelings came to a close (Wood 1992, 287–305). The Jeffersonian Democratic Republican Party had become meaningless in the absence of serious competition, and the nomination of its congressional caucus ("King Caucus") was no longer decisive, as the caucus nominee Treasury Secretary William Crawford of Georgia attracted opposition from Adams (Massachusetts), House Speaker Henry Clay of Kentucky, and General Andrew Jackson of Tennessee, hero of the 1815 battle of New Orleans and champion of the frontier and states rights against the federal government (Remini 1999, 99–117). Adams finished second behind Jackson in both the electoral vote (receiving eighty-four votes to Jackson's ninety-nine) and the popular vote (receiving 32 percent to Jackson's 43 percent), but since no candidate had gained a majority in the Electoral College, according to the Constitution the House of Representatives—with state delegations voting as units—had to choose the president from among the top three contenders: Jackson, Adams, and Crawford (who had forty-one electoral votes). Clay (with thirty-seven votes) had been eliminated, but in the House, the Speaker threw his decisive support to Adams, who won thirteen states to Jackson's seven and Crawford's four. Three days later it was announced that Adams would appoint Henry Clay to be his secretary of state (Milkis and Nelson 1999, 108–12).

Adam's move infuriated Jackson's supporters, who accused Clay and Adams of having made a "corrupt bargain" to deny the presidency to the popular favorite, Jackson (Remini 1999). Although Clay and Adams both strenuously denied the accusation, Adams was never allowed to escape the controversy over his election, and the notion that a corrupt Washington political elite had robbed Jackson of the presidency only seemed to enhance popular enthusiasm for the general and his states' rights agenda.

The Jacksonians were further provoked when President Adams pursued an ambitious policy agenda utterly opposed to their objectives. The agenda was based on internal improvements by a vigorous federal government and was designed to promote economic growth and development of the West (Skowronek 1997, 110–27). Dogged by his election controversy and lacking political skills commensurate with his formidable intellect, Adams was unable to advance his legislative program. After the rampant Jacksonians took over Congress in 1826, his administration's agenda-setting capacity essentially ended (Milkis and Nelson 1999, 108–11; Hargreaves 1985), and he was easily defeated by Jackson in 1828. The circumstances of Adams's election undoubtedly undermined his authority as president from the start, and once in office Adams lacked the political ability or good fortune to ever escape the shadow of illegitimacy that hung over his presidency.

Rutherford B. Hayes, 1877–1881

In contrast to Adams, Hayes, while losing the popular vote to Democratic candidate Samuel J. Tilden, actually did win a majority in the Electoral College. He did so only after the House of Representatives intervened to resolve disputed electoral votes in his favor following another infamous political "deal" that had much more long-lasting ramifications for American politics than the so-called corrupt bargain of 1824.

Hayes was a typical Republican presidential nominee of the post–Civil War era. He had served as a major general during the war and as a congressman and three-term governor of his home state, Ohio, a decisive battleground in presidential elections during this period (Hoogenboom 1995; DeGregorio 1997, 279–91). Hayes also had a reputation as a reformer, endearing him to the Republican Party bosses who controlled party nominations at this time, because he was unassociated with the scandals that had marred the administration of incumbent Republican Ulysses S. Grant (Sproat 1968, 88–103). The Democrats selected another reformer, Governor Samuel J. Tilden of New York, conqueror of Tammany Hall and the notorious "Tweed Ring" in New York City, as their candidate. Tilden won the popular vote with a narrow but decisive margin on election day (51 percent to Hayes's 48 percent), and he led Hayes in electoral votes (184 votes to Hayes's 165). But he remained one vote short of an Electoral College majority because of disputed election returns in four states: Florida, Louisiana, South Carolina, and Oregon, the first three being former confederate states still occupied by federal forces. If Hayes could win all twenty electoral votes at stake in these disputed contests, he would win the Electoral College and the presidency by a vote of 185 to 184 (Mieckzkowski 2001, 63–64).

With the outcome in doubt, the Republican-controlled House of Representatives decided to create a committee of ten members of Congress and five Supreme Court justices to resolve the issue. Coincidentally, this commission had an 8–7 Republican majority, which just happened to resolve all the disputed states in favor of Hayes, thus giving Hayes the 185 electoral votes sufficient for victory. To overcome potential Democratic resistance and filibustering, the Republicans conceded that in exchange for allowing the election and inauguration of Hayes to proceed, federal troops would be withdrawn from the former confederate states and Reconstruction brought to an end, which duly came to pass after Hayes was inaugurated (Ayers 1992).

Having been elected in such circumstances, it is no surprise that Hayes' legitimacy as president was clouded—Democrats referred to him as "Rutherfraud B. Hayes" (Mieckzkowski 2001, 64). But no matter how cynical the deal making that led to his occupying the White House, he turned out to be serious in his commitment to civil service reform (Hoogenboom 1995). And this commitment set him on a collision course with the bosses in his party both in Congress (particularly the Senate) and back in the states and cities who relied on federal patronage and spoils to sustain their political machines. His first run-in with the Senate occurred when he refused to consult with Republican senators on cabinet nominations. He appointed a former confederate as postmaster general and Carl Schurz, the nation's leading civil-service reformer, as interior secretary—both key patronage positions (Sproat 1968, 100).

Hayes then proceeded to appoint an independent commission to investigate corruption in the New York federal customs house, where tariffs on imported goods (the main source of federal government revenue at the time) were collected. Hayes subsequently decided to remove the top three officials in the customs house, even though all three were important figures in New York Republican politics (including Chester A.

Arthur, who would himself be elected president in 1880 and succeeded the assassinated James A. Garfield as president the following year) (Milkis and Nelson, 1999, 173–76). The struggle over the New York customs house used up what little political capital Hayes possessed, and his administration achieved little else. Having alienated the party bosses, Hayes would not likely have been renominated in 1880 even had he wished to run for a second term.

For all the murkiness surrounding his election, Hayes did succeed in restoring some integrity to a federal government sullied by the scandals of the Grant administration and thereby dissipated some of the questions of legitimacy surrounding his election. In an era of limited federal government and a generally weak presidency, Hayes was not notably weaker than any of his contemporaries who occupied the office during this period and whose elections were uncontroversial.

Benjamin Harrison, 1889–1893

Like Hayes, Benjamin Harrison was a Republican president in an era of very limited presidential power. The so-called Gilded Age (1876–1896) was a period of intense party competition and extremely close presidential elections. In the five presidential elections from 1876 to 1892 presidential "winning" margins in the popular vote were: -3.1 percent, 0.1 percent, 0.2 percent, -0.9 percent, and 3.2 percent, respectively (see table 1.1). With the parties so closely matched and possessing an unprecedented capacity to mobilize the electorate, it is hardly surprising that half of the four instances in U.S. history of popular vote losers winning in the Electoral College took place during this period. It is also probably not entirely coincidental that both winners were Republicans. While the Democrats piled up popular votes in the South, more often than not Republican candidates eked out narrow margins in the key northern states heavy with electoral votes.

The Republican Congress elected in 1886 had blocked incumbent Democratic president Grover Cleveland's tariff proposals, rendering him highly vulnerable in his bid for reelection in 1888 (Milkis and Nelson 1999, 180–83). The Republican candidate—former Indiana senator Benjamin Harrison (1881–1887)—had not enjoyed a particularly distinguished political career up to that point, but he had a nearly ideal background and profile for a Republican presidential candidate of the period. He was the great grandson of Benjamin Harrison, a signer of the Declaration of Independence, and the grandson of the ninth president,

William Henry Harrison. And he had served as a brigadier general under William Sherman during the Civil War. Harrison led a united Republican campaign against Cleveland on the tariff issue, which also stimulated a high level of support from the northeastern business community for the Republican ticket (Marcus 1971, 101–150). Although Cleveland secured a narrow popular vote plurality of 0.9 percent—ironically more than four times his winning margin in 1884—he lost the Electoral College vote 233–168 to Harrison primarily because he narrowly lost the thirty-six electoral votes of his home state of New York (Mieckzkowski 2001, 71–72).

Harrison was not as bedeviled by questions over his legitimacy as president as Adams and Hayes had been, perhaps because he held such a passive view of the presidential role and subordinated himself to Congress in terms of setting the national political agenda (Sievers 1968; Socolofsky and Spetter 1987). The archetypal Gilded Age president, Harrison was by and large content to sign the bills and dole out the federal patronage to party regulars. Indeed, the presidency appeared to be so ineffectual at this time that the issue of his legitimacy hardly seemed relevant, and real national political leadership lay in the hands of House Speaker Thomas B. Reed of Maine (Strahan 1998; Peters 1990, 52–91).

In the 1892 rematch between Harrison and Cleveland, again fought largely over the tariff issue, Cleveland won a comfortable Electoral College victory, 277–145–22 (the third candidate was Populist James Weaver) and a popular vote plurality over Harrison of over 3 percent, although Cleveland's winning percentage (46.1 percent) was lower than in 1888 (48.7 percent).

George W. Bush: A Minority President in the Modern Era

Perhaps the major difference between Bush's presidency and that of those who lost the popular vote during the nineteenth century is the vastly changed nature of the modern presidency in its scope and political power. A century of expanded federal government in the domestic sphere and the United States' rise to global superpower status have made a contemporary presidency along the lines of Hayes's or Harrison's not only impossible but inconceivable. The modern president is the lynchpin and dynamic element of the American system of government. The contemporary president is expected to claim an electoral mandate from the voters and use it to set the national policy agenda in

Washington (Ceaser 1979, 170–212). The president is the most visible symbol of the United States at home and abroad and is expected to display immediate and decisive leadership during national calamity or crisis. Of course, this power to deal with national emergencies—particularly in the foreign-policy sphere—was latent in the powers conceded to the president in the 1787 Constitution, but because the United States was a peripheral power for most of the nineteenth century, this potential went untapped. When the United States rose to global power and then superpower status in the twentieth century, the extent of the presidency's power became evident (McDonald 1994).

In the domestic sphere, presidential power remains more circumscribed, particularly by Congress's strong constitutional powers over the federal budget (Wildavsky 1975). The president is nevertheless expected to set the national agenda on the budget as with most other domestic political issues. Indeed, the president has almost come to resemble an institutionalized "charismatic leader" in Weberian terms, expected to render shots of democratic energy and adrenalin to a political system that is largely inert and incremental most of the time (Weber 1970, 245–52). The president roams the modern American political system like a "magnificent lion," to use Clinton Rossiter's colorful phrase (Rossiter 1957, 52). By contrast, Richard Neustadt's classic *Presidential Power* emphasizes the persisting constitutional constraints on presidential power in a separated system of government, even in the modern era (Neustadt 1990). Yet Neustadt's purpose is to demonstrate how presidents can effectively exercise their power, because he is convinced that the modern American political system absolutely requires strong and effective presidential leadership (Neustadt 1990, 152–63).

Following the failures of the Johnson, Nixon, and Carter presidencies, a recurring theme in presidential scholarship has been the growing gap between the actual powers of the presidency and public expectations—as well as the president's—about what the holder of the office can realistically achieve (Lowi 1985). At least since the time of Woodrow Wilson—who first thoroughly articulated the theory—presidents have claimed that their election constitutes a "mandate," that is, an expression of the will of the American public regarding the course of public policy. Moreover, according to this view, as the sole nationally elected office-holder, the president is best placed to interpret and shape that popular will once in office (Tulis 2003). This in turn has given rise to an increasingly "plebiscitary" presidency that constantly campaigns for public support or "mandates" against the other branches of the system: a tendency that, some scholars have argued, undermines the spirit and the authority of the Constitution and the American system of separated government (Lowi 1985; Dahl 1990; Kernell 1997).

One implication of enhanced presidential power contingent on popular support is that the authority of a contemporary president elected after losing the national popular vote might well be seriously undercut from the beginning of the president's administration, with potentially deleterious consequences for a governmental process that has become so dependent on presidential power and authority. In short, how can a president who fails to win the national popular vote claim any kind of mandate or authority to advocate policy change?

The Bush administration set out to deal with this problem by denying its existence. Not wishing to concede the legitimacy issue and be on the defensive from the start, his administration simply proceeded as if it had a mandate and began to advance a highly conservative Republican policy agenda (Frum 2003a,b). Doing so appears to have been an inspired political move, and the idea of presidential leadership is so endemic to the modern American political process that the circumstances of Bush's election appear to have had little long-term relevance to voters outside the ranks of hardcore Democrats.

In fact, Bush was able to implement a significant $1.3 trillion tax cut with the support of several Senate Democrats, although they were largely able to block the Bush policy agenda on other domestic issues in the spring and summer of 2001, particularly after the Democrats regained control of the Senate in May 2001 following the defection of Vermont Republican James Jeffords. While the conservative Bush strategy might have alienated moderates like Jeffords, it did give direction and energy to his presidency and enabled him to solidify his support among the conservative Republican base, which had become estranged from his father's administration prior to the 1992 election (Keller 2003a). Before September 11, then, it appeared that Bush would be a highly partisan Republican president and that his administration would be characterized by the legislative gridlock and ideological partisan warfare typical of American politics at the end of the twentieth century. But even with his legitimacy still questioned by Democrats, it was by no means obvious that Bush would lose this struggle if he chose his issues carefully and kept his base mobilized (Brownstein 2002).

September 11 tilted everything in favor of the president. The attacks on New York and Washington demanded a firm presidential response, and Bush provided it with the successful American military operation against the Taliban regime in Afghanistan. Remaining doubts about Bush's legitimacy faded into the background, and, since a national security crisis is the primary raison d'etre for the presidency, the public rallied behind him (Cook 2001). America's vulnerability to national security crises since becoming a global superpower has given modern presidents (regardless of how they got to the White House) a potential political advantage denied to most of their nineteenth-century predecessors. There were no comparable crises on which Adams, Hayes, or Harrison, for example, might have capitalized politically.

Bush parlayed the effectiveness of his response to September 11 to a surprise victory for his party in the 2002 midterm elections, and the Republicans regained control of the Senate and strengthened their grip on the House. Following the election, Bush submitted another huge tax cut proposal ($726 billion) to the new Congress (Brownstein 2003). The president ended up getting only $326 billion in tax reductions from Congress in May 2003, but he could still claim a success in achieving another substantial federal tax reduction (Ota 2003a). In April 2003 Bush, in defiance of several of America's traditional allies and the United Nations Security Council, led the United States into a successful "preemptive war" against Saddam Hussein's Iraq (McManus 2003): a new foreign policy doctrine that surely implies another dramatic increase in presidential power and initiative.

In the modern era, where "democracy" has an even stronger place in American political culture than it did a century ago and the presidency has become the most powerful branch of the federal government, one might have assumed that one instance of a popular vote loser securing the presidency would bring about the fairly immediate demise of the Electoral College in favor of direct popular election of the president. In the aftermath of the 2000 election, however, there has been remarkably little popular momentum for this radical but obvious solution to the constitutional problem. Perhaps the concentration of the antagonists and the media on the electoral shenanigans in Florida in November 2000 distracted public attention from the broader constitutional issue. It is also apparent, however, that the presidency has become so integral to American government and society, and the demand for effective presidential action in response to crises at home and abroad is so ubiquitous, that contemporary America cannot afford to indulge in prolonged uncertainty over the electoral legitimacy of the chief executive and commander-in-chief.

The extent of presidential power today has given Bush an advantage in the struggle to establish himself as a legitimate president that was denied to his three predecessors who came to office in similar political predicaments, and his administration appears to be fully aware of this fact. Even prior to the tragic events of September 11 Bush was using the power and authority of the office with some success to establish a governing "mandate." The ongoing crisis atmosphere at home and overseas since that date, has, of course, elevated his authority to an even higher plane and rendered moot any lingering doubts about his legitimacy. Like all modern presidents, however, Bush remains vulnerable to the "expectations gap" discussed earlier. Having raised public hopes concerning the effectiveness of pre-emptive war in neutralizing the dangers from international terrorism and rogue states, as well as large tax cuts as the remedy for the sluggish domestic economy, the administration needs to produce substantive results on both fronts or face the prospect of losing legitimacy from another and more electorally significant direction—policy failure.

Bush and "Political Time"

Dissatisfied with analyses that focus on individual presidential characteristics such as political skill, character, or emotional intelligence (Neustadt 1990; Barber 1992; Greenstein 2000) or that emphasize the gulf between the powers of the contemporary presidency and that of the nineteenth century, Stephen Skowronek has suggested that presidents should be viewed from the perspective of their place in the development of a specific political regime, or what he refers to as "political time" (Skowronek 1993; 2003). These regimes reflect the balance of power between political forces during a particular period, define the roles of political institutions, and set the national policy agenda. Skowronek classifies presidencies as those of "reconstruction" (founding a regime); "articulation" (maintaining the regime); or "disjunction" (signaling the end of a regime and beginning the transition to a new one). He also has a fourth category, "preemption," where peculiar short-term circumstances might lead to the election of a president from outside the regime, though one who is ultimately unable to change it substantially (Skowronek 1997, 3–58).

Are there any early indications where the presidency of George W. Bush might be placed according to this scheme? If we take Ronald Reagan as the founder of the conservative Republican regime beginning in 1980, then the most obvious way to classify Bush's presidency is "orthodox innovation" or "articulation" (Skowronek 2003, 153–54). Bush has made no secret of his admiration for Reagan and adherence to Reaganite values of a smaller federal government, major tax cuts to stimulate growth, social conservatism, and "standing tall" in defense of American interests abroad. Indeed, it appears that Reagan has been more of an ideological and political model for Bush than is his own father, whose electoral defeat in 1992 helped instigate the son's political career, and whose alleged mistakes in office he has striven to avoid (Keller 2003a; Nagourney 2003a). Of course, as the elder Bush demonstrated, a presidency of articulation—or what Skowronek refers to as the "faithful son" (Skowronek 1997, 430)—does not guarantee political or electoral success, particularly if the president is being forced by the exigencies of political time into a role contrary to his personal political inclinations, as was the case with the first President Bush (Parmet 1997). The upshot for the elder Bush was a presidency torn between moderate instincts harking back to the New Deal era and the need to conciliate the new conservative base of the Republican party created by Reagan. In the end George H. W. Bush lost the enthusiasm of the base with his support for tax increases to deal with the deficit and then overcompensated by sounding shrilly and inauthentically conservative in his failed 1992 reelection campaign against the agile Democratic preemptor Bill Clinton and populist outsider H. Ross Perot (Frum 1994).

If the younger Bush appears most apt for the role of articulator, however, his place in the political regime is not ultimately in his own hands. While preceding political regimes have been of at least thirty years duration, Skowronek has also spoken of the waning of political time, due to wider changes in the American political universe, such as the decline of traditional party loyalties and the rise of the mass communications media as the primary political intermediary institutions in the modern era. As a result, politics is more fluid, political regimes less durable, and under the greater power of short-term forces, preemptive politics—à la Clinton—becomes more prevalent (Skowronek 1997, 49–58). If the conservative Republican regime has exhausted itself intellectually and its nostrums seem irrelevant to the changed circumstances of the nation at home or abroad, then Bush also might find himself as a president of "disjunction" with a failed presidency representing the last gasp of a dying political regime. The end of the Cold War that was so integral to the Reagan regime certainly appeared to have eroded the Republican grip on the presidency during the 1990s. And Bush's own slender and contentious election victory in 2000 by comparison with the Republican landslides of the 1980s might be adduced as additional evidence for regime decay. Finally, if the Bush administration tax cuts send the U.S. economy into long-term deficit and recession, and his post–September 11 foreign policy doctrine of "preemptive war" against rogue states leaves America isolated internationally, still vulnerable to international terrorism, and enmeshed in civil strife in Iraq, then defeat in 2004 would likely bring about the final demise of the post-1980 conservative Republican political regime.

But it is obviously too soon to pronounce the end of the "Reagan era," and there is compelling evidence for an alternative conclusion. The Republican majorities in Congress since 1995 after over half a century of largely minority party status hardly indicate the political demise of conservative Republicanism. Moreover, Bush's politics of orthodox innovation—Reagan-style tax cuts and social conservatism tempered by "compassionate conservativism" on issues like Medicare coverage of prescription drugs—are intended to bring new constituencies such as seniors and Hispanics into the Republican electoral coalition. Similarly, Bush's preemptive war doctrine may also provide an effective substitute for "standing tall" against the Soviets during the Cold War as a new conservative Republican national security policy. Thus Bush's articulation and innovation may actually succeed in reinvigorating the precarious regime (certainly the conservative Republican Party base is more energized behind him than it ever was behind his father), and the Republican successes in the 2002 midterm elections may indicate that these tactics are working, at least to some extent.

The Skowronek framework is useful in placing the Bush presidency in historical perspective, but as yet we cannot definitively answer whether he is a Theodore Roosevelt (an effective articulator and innovator) or a Herbert Hoover (a classic disjunctive leader). Skowronek's allusion to the "waning" of political time and rise of preemptive politics in recent times might also shed some light on the factors underlying the volatile and bitter partisan conflict of the past decade in American politics. The rise of George W. Bush and his conduct of the presidency also needs to be placed in the context of this changed American political environment.

A Partisan President in a Partisan Era

Bush's presidency is taking place during one of the most partisan periods in American history. In fact, contemporary American politics is regularly compared to the Gilded Age (1876–1896): the period between the Civil War and the Progressive Era when party loyalties were strongest, party machines mobilized unprecedented numbers of voters to go to the polls, and the major political parties were extremely evenly matched nationally, as evidenced by the exceedingly close presidential contests of the period (Silbey 1991). Most of the twentieth century has been characterized by party decline, and political scientists and historians have well documented the erosion of the party machines, the erosion of party loyalty in Congress, the rise of the primary system for choosing presidential candidates, and the loosening of party ties among voters (Burnham 1982; McGerr 1986; Wattenberg 1984).

The major parties were at their nadir from 1952 to 1980, when they appeared to be irrelevant to the dominant concerns of the country such as civil rights and the Vietnam War (Nie, Verba, and Petrocik 1979). The civil rights revolution and the political turmoil of the 1960s, however, also generated a gradual realignment of electoral forces so that the two major parties gradually became ideologically homogeneous with particular reference to issues involving cultural cleavages, such as abortion, the relationship of church and state, affirmative action, gun control, the environment, and gay and lesbian rights. With the dramatic erosion in the numbers of "liberal northern Republicans" and "southern conservative Democrats," party loyalty rates in Congress have risen dramatically, and the two congressional parties have strengthened their leadership in an effort to implement a partisan policy agenda (Rohde 1991; Sinclair 1995). This process began under Democratic House Speakers Thomas P. "Tip" O'Neill and Jim Wright and continued under the Republican House majority led by Speaker Newt Gingrich (Fenno 1997). While this development has been less evident in the Senate, the movement toward greater party loyalty and interparty acrimony has also characterized that chamber (Rae and Campbell 2001).

Much of the driving force for this new partisan politics in Congress lies in the electoral process. Most congressional districts are drawn to favor one or other major party and thus the decisive contest becomes the primary election where ideologically oriented party activists have disproportionate influence due to low voter turnout (Burden 2001). Single-issue and ideological groups aligned with the major parties increasingly provide the funds, infrastructure, personnel, and electoral base for each of the major parties in most areas of the country (Schier 2000). In presidential primary elections the same rules apply although somewhat mitigated by the higher turnout of independents in early presidential primaries such as New Hampshire. It is still generally the case, however, that a presidential candidate who is seriously "out of sync" with the activist base of his or her party is highly unlikely to be nominated in today's political environment.

Party competition in the United States today has become not only increasingly shrill but also remarkably evenly balanced of late. The Republican dominance of the presidency and the Democratic control of Congress that prevailed for most of the 1952–1992 period have been replaced by competitiveness at all levels since the early 1990s. Margins of victory have been slight and tenuous, and elections have increasingly become a game of mobilization—getting one's own faithful troops to the polls—rather than a battle for the broad center ground of American politics (Schier 2000). And while the number of "ticket-splitting" voters have declined from the high rates of the 1970s, there were still enough of them to lead to situations of divided government with different parties controlling the presidency and at least one chamber of Congress, for all but a few months in the 1995–2002 period (Jacobson 2000). From the 1950s to the mid-1970s, the congressional parties were so amorphous and broad that divided government could be mitigated by cross-party coalitions—such as the one that passed the 1964 Civil Rights Act. By contrast, the congressional parties of today are so polarized and ideologically homogeneous, and the margin of control is so slight, that there is little incentive for cooperation on either side. Thus the last six years of the Clinton presidency were characterized by bitter partisan warfare, leading to a shutdown of the federal government in the winter of 1995–1996 and the impeachment of the president over the Lewinsky affair by the Republican House in December 1998 (Rae 1998; Rae and Campbell 2003).

As has already been noted, the 2000 presidential election was characteristic of the preceding decade: exceedingly close and exceedingly partisan, with a highly controversial aftermath in Florida that left the parties more embittered and polarized than ever. George W. Bush's rise to the presidency took place within the context of this new polarized politics. Conservative activists who dominate the Republican Party needed a fresh face who was ideologically sound enough to enthuse the Republican base but would not frighten independent voters. Bush, who had pioneered a "compassionate conservatism" as governor of Texas, seemed to fit the bill perfectly, and he became the clear Republican frontrunner early in the 2000 nominating campaign by securing the necessary money, endorsements, and activists from the party base (Ceaser and Busch 2001, 49–76). The only serious challenge to Bush came from the maverick Arizona senator and Vietnam War hero John McCain. On most issues the Arizonan's policy positions were akin to Bush's, but McCain emphasized his differences on two issues—campaign finance reform and putting a balanced federal budget ahead of big tax cuts (2001, 77–107). McCain enjoyed some successes in early primaries largely due to the help of Independents and Democrats in states where they could vote in the Republican presidential primary, but the more he courted them by emphasizing his differences with Bush, the more he alienated the conservative Republican base that held the key to the nomination, and in the end Bush easily overwhelmed him in the primaries on Super Tuesday 2000 (Mayer 2001, 34–37).

For the remainder of the 2000 campaign season, Bush did nothing to distance himself from conservative Republicans. While electoral strategy might have dictated the choice of a northeastern moderate as his vice-presidential running mate, Bush instead chose a reliable Republican conservative, former Congressman and Defense Secretary Richard Cheney (Ceaser and Busch 2001, 137–41). The risk of estranging the Republican base by choosing a running mate with deviating positions on one or two major issues (such as abortion) was too great in an age when electoral success has become so contingent on ideological mobilization. Bush's gestures toward the center in the 2000 campaign were mainly cosmetic and rhetorical—such as the staging of the anodyne 2000 Republican convention—and at no point did he make a point of distancing himself publicly from a major conservative position. However, in an effort to reach out to Independents and Democrats, the Bush campaign did devote more attention to some traditionally Democratic issues such as education (Ceaser and Busch 2001, 116–17).

Governing as a partisan president in a partisan era when your party has only a tenuous control over Congress—and even that was forfeited after the Jeffords defection and the Senate switch to Democratic control—is a skill that requires some degree of political dexterity. Clinton demonstrated how it might be done in the last six years of his presidency through the agile use of the "triangulation" strategy pioneered by his 1996 reelection strategist, Dick Morris. The trick here was to do enough to keep the devoted loyalty of your own party's core voters while making strategic departures on certain selected issues—such as the 1996 welfare reform and the Defense of Marriage Act—calculated to appeal to centrist and more moderate Republican voters (Rae 2000).

Even so deft a politician as Clinton was only able to make "triangulation" work intermittently, and, as the events of 1998 proved, it did nothing to reduce the intense Republican hostility toward him. Yet as Skowronek has also noted, this strategy of preemption might provide a more effective means of presidential governance in a political universe where the velocity of political information and the inability of parties to mobilize voters beyond the hard-core ideologues has eroded the natural "life cycle" of political regimes and the constraints of "political time" (Skowronek 1997, 442–46).

Since Bush is evidently not a "preemptive" president in the Clinton mould and his personal authority has clearly benefited from his response to September 11, he has not been required to demonstrate the same degree of political agility. Yet while Bush's main political strategist, Karl Rove, publicly eschewed the idea of a Republican version of "triangulation" (Crabtree 2003), the Bush White House has at least been pursuing a strategy that can be described as "base plus": seeking to reach out to key Democratic constituencies while fortifying the GOP's conservative base. As already mentioned, during most of the first six months of Bush's presidency, he adhered to a clear conservative line but strove to avoid a rhetorical tone that might disconcert more moderate voters, and he continued to emphasize his reform proposals on traditionally Democratic issues such as education and health care (Brownstein 2002). On the highly controversial issue of stem-cell research, for example, Bush found a position that simultaneously pleased most Republican conservatives and public opinion more generally. The dominance of national security issues after September 11 also enabled Bush to move the national political debate to new terrain where it was easier to accommodate both Republican conservatives and the political center (Frum 2003a,b). Democrats also found it extremely hard to oppose the president vigorously in such an ongoing crisis atmosphere. This was demonstrated dramatically in the 2002 congressional elections when Democratic senators and Senate candidates suffered at the polls after the president and the Republicans had attacked them for failing to support legislation establishing the new Homeland Security Department (Nather and Cochran 2002).

Bush has not departed from a strict conservative Republican agenda in terms of budget policy, abortion, affirmative action, or in the highly vexed areas of court appointments, but his loyalty to the Republican base diminishes the probability of debilitating intraparty challenges in 2004 (Nagourney 2003a). At the same time he has made inroads into the political center by choosing his issues and his rhetoric carefully (as in his address in August 2001 on stem-cell research) and practicing his own version of "triangulation" on Democratic issues like education and prescription drugs. And while the word *triangulation* was singularly absent from the vocabulary of the Bush White House, the president earned plaudits for his political astuteness from the architect of the practice, Dick Morris (Morris 2003). September 11 and the subsequent wars in Afghanistan and Iraq, however, have also made it easier for Bush to govern in a partisan era since that catastrophic event and its aftermath have focused political debate on an area—national security—where the president has all the advantages.

In a national crisis, American presidents almost inevitably rise to heroic status (at least temporarily) in the eyes of the American public because they are expected to take on the enemy, win, and "save the nation." George W. Bush has found that the mantle of defender of the nation has enabled him to transcend polarized ideological party politics without conceding any substantial ideological territory to his political opponents in a highly partisan era characterized by narrow and electorally vulnerable presidential and congressional majorities. The strategy is contingent, however, on his continued ability to "deliver the goods," in terms of economic recovery and the global war that Bush himself has declared against terrorism and rogue states. A major setback in these endeavors would surely leave his presidency vulnerable to Democratic preemption in 2004.

2

POLITICAL WARFARE DURING WARTIME

George W. Bush and the Democrats

John J. Pitney Jr.

"Politics is battle," wrote Richard Nixon, "and the best way to fire up your troops is to rally them against a visible opponent on the other side of the field. If a loyal supporter will work hard for you, he will fight twice as hard against your enemies" (Nixon 1991, 285). When George W. Bush took office, national Democrats faced an administration seeking to entrench Republican power. Their strategic challenge involved not merely faulting President Bush's policies but attacking the GOP's legitimacy. Their foes were digging in deep, so Democrats thought they had to hit deep. During his 2001 farewell address to the Democratic National Committee, outgoing chair Joe Andrew thundered: "We're going to fight 'til hell freezes over and then we're going to fight on the ice" (Thomma 2001).[1]

At first, the murky outcome of the 2000 election promised to supply the firepower. Not since the nineteenth century had a president faced such strong suspicions of election fraud. As we shall see, the issue fizzled in the barrel, except with Democratic activists and African American voters.

The Democrats still had ammunition. One may strike at a party's legitimacy by charging it with corruption, and the model for this line of attack has long been the Watergate scandal. Since the 1970s, aggressive strategists have tried to follow this model in such political battles as Koreagate, Irangate, Travelgate, and Whitewatergate. None of these controversies ended as dramatically as the original. In the early Bush administration, Democrats tried to find the next "-gate," but they came up short.

Ideology provides another weapon against legitimacy. That is, one side may say the other's policies are not just mistaken but beyond the pale of American politics. Under George W. Bush, Democrats focused on this line of attack. Even before the 2001 inauguration, they were accusing the incoming administration of an extremist agenda. They seized on the nomination of John Ashcroft as attorney general to suggest that President Bush would "turn back the clock" on social issues. To mobilize African Americans, they stressed civil rights.

Hard-core Democrats did indeed burn with hatred for Bush. Most came from the "blue states," so we may dub them the "blue-hots."[2] Yet anti-Bush sentiment did not catch fire beyond their ranks. The percentage of Americans who saw Bush policies as "too conservative" dropped from 29 percent in June 2001 to 20 percent in November 2002 (Blanton 2002). And in the midterm election that month, Republicans gained seats in both the House and Senate. Blue-hots blamed their party's leaders, saying that they had scarcely resisted Bush, much less fought on the ice.

Such criticisms overlooked two deeper sources for Democratic frustrations. First, circumstances blunted the attacks. The most obvious hitch was Bush's unexpected status as a wartime president. Leaders of the opposition party must pause before going after the president, lest they seem to undercut the war effort. The months after the September 11 attacks followed the historical pattern. President Bush's approval ratings went up, and Democrats toned down their criticisms. Similar phenomena occurred during the invasion of Iraq.

While military conflicts may reshape political warfare, they do not stop it for long. A rally can vanish, as the first President Bush learned after the Gulf War. And criticism may resume long before the last soldier fires the last bullet. Franklin Roosevelt's wartime administration was not immune from attack, and neither was George W. Bush's. In the months after the end of major combat in Iraq, casualties continued to mount, and Bush's poll numbers began to dip.

The Democrats' second obstacle lay in the Bush administration itself. The president and his supporters often proved skillful in cooling, co-opting, and containing his opposition. As John Harris's chapter suggests, Bush resembled his immediate predecessor in this way. Senator John McCain once compared the GOP's relationship with Clinton to Wile E. Coyote and the Road Runner. Every time Republicans thought they had trapped Clinton, said McCain, "the dynamite goes off or we run over the cliff or the train runs over us" (*Online Newshour* 1999). Several years later, journalist Richard Benedetto (2003) used similar terms for Bush. A growing line of political foes had "misunderestimated" Bush, wrote Benedetto, "But like Wile E. Coyote of 'Road Runner' cartoon fame, Democrats remained undaunted." In a more serious vein, Carl von Clausewitz (1976, 149) reminds attackers that their will "is directed at an animate object that *reacts*."

The Aftermath of 2000

In war and politics, enmity deepens when one side thinks the other has won through treachery. A recurrent theme in warfare is the thirst to avenge a "stab in the back." The tight 1960 election ended with reports of vote fraud. Richard Nixon chose not to contest the results, citing the Cold War as his reason: There would be no worse example for the Free World, he said, than "wrangling over the results of our presidential election and even suggesting that the presidency itself could be stolen by thievery at the ballot box" (Nixon 1968, 447). Skeptics also speculated that an investigation might have found GOP ballot shenanigans.

In the days after the 2000 election, some observers urged Al Gore to follow Nixon's example (Caldwell 2000). Without the restraint of the Cold War, Gore chose to fight. The Republicans quickly gained the offensive, however. As Bush aide Joe Allbaugh said, they realized that besides the legal war, "you had a PR war and you had a political war" (Political Staff 2001, 73). Whereas Democrats questioned the legitimacy of the original tally, Republicans attacked the legitimacy of recount procedures. When Democrats sought to invalidate military ballots, Republicans seized the opening. Said Montana governor Marc Racicot, a Bush spokesman and future chair of the Republican National Committee: "The vice president's lawyers have gone to war, in my judgment against the men and women who serve in our armed forces" (Political Staff 2001, 129). The Gore legal team retreated. For every Democratic complaint about a partisan U.S. Supreme Court came a Republican complaint about a partisan Florida Supreme Court. In the end, the GOP denied the high ground to the Democrats, and most Americans seemed ready to accept the result.

Democratic activists still tried to turn the outcome against Bush. During the counting of electoral votes, Democratic House members raised symbolic objections. Representative Peter Deutsch of Florida said, "Mr. Vice President, there are many Americans who still believe that the results we are going to certify today are illegitimate" (*Cong. Rec.* 147, January 6, 2001, H32). A few weeks later, Terry McAuliffe, incoming chairman of the Democratic National Committee, proclaimed, "We will transform the anger about Florida into energy about politics" (Coile 2001).

News organizations planned their own recounts, and Democrats hoped that the results would prove their case. The final tallies doused these hopes. Bush would still have won under certain ballot-counting standards, while Gore might have won under others. Either way, the margins were so thin that no one could say what would have happened in an actual recount (Elhauge 2001). While liberal authors could turn out works denouncing the Bush victory, conservatives could still plausibly make their own case. *Washington Times* reporter Bill Sammon published a book titled *At Any Cost: How Al Gore Tried to Steal the Election.*

After the September 11 attacks, McAuliffe and most major Democratic leaders toned down their rhetoric about the 2000 election. In general, so did rank-and-file activists. "Soon after George W. Bush took office, I'd occasionally see someone with a 'Hail to the Thief' poster, referring to Election 2000," wrote journalist Martha Brant in the spring of 2002. "But during the height of the war in Afghanistan, I rarely saw any protesters outside 1600 Pennsylvania Avenue" (Brant 2002).

The election issue still angered African Americans, however. Bush won only 9 percent of the black vote in 2000, and because many of the disputed Florida ballots came from minority precincts, the recount controversy only deepened his unpopularity in the black community. After the Supreme Court decision, a CNN/*USA Today*/Gallup poll showed a racial difference in reactions. Fifty percent of African Americans said that Bush "stole the election," and 68 percent said they felt "cheated." The comparable figures for whites were just 14 percent and 28 percent (Holland 2000). In June of 2001, the Democratic majority on the U.S. Commission on Civil Rights charged Florida with "widespread voter disenfranchisement." The Justice Department's Civil Rights Division found procedural problems but no intentional misconduct. Black leaders assailed the head of the division, an African American: "I guess he's the modern-day Uncle Tom," said Democratic Representative Corrine Brown of Florida (Washington 2002).

Bush's support among blacks did rise after September 11 but never approached the level he enjoyed among whites. As we shall see, other issues reinforced the racial divide.

In Search of the "-Gate"

A regime loses legitimacy if the people think it is corrupt. Psychological warfare operations typically stress the enemy leadership's dishonesty, in hopes of draining internal support. Political warriors sometimes take a similar approach.

For a while, it seemed as if corporate accounting scandals might hand President Bush's foes a Watergate-scale issue. Skullduggery at Enron and other companies hurt thousands of employees and millions of shareholders. President Bush had close ties to Enron CEO Kenneth Lay, whom he had called "Kenny Boy." And when Senator Jim Jeffords switched parties, he gave Senate Democrats a crucial weapon of scandal warfare. Control of committees now enabled them to hold hearings and issue subpoenas. Democratic strategists James Carville, Stanley Greenberg, and Robert Shrum wrote, "Enron has the potential to shape the entire political environment for 2002" (Carville, Greenberg, and Shrum 2002). It never materialized. In an election-eve poll by *CBS News*, only 4 percent of respondents cited "corporate reform" as their key voting issue (Pollich 2002). After the midterm, columnist Walter Shapiro wrote that the Enron collapse should have triggered dramatic Senate hearings. "Instead, the high-energy Enron hearings took place in the GOP-controlled House, which allowed the Republicans to adroitly distance themselves from this corporate debacle" (Shapiro 2002).

So what became of the battle? The corporate-accounting issue resembled the savings-and-loan controversy that came to a head in 1989–1990 under the elder Bush. There were several reasons why neither event took casualties from the president's party. The first and most obvious was the absence of serious wrongdoing by major administration officials. In both cases, people close to the president did have links to the businesses in question. Neil Bush, another son of the elder Bush, was a director of a troubled S&L, and several officials of the George W. Bush administration had owned Enron stock. But in neither instance could anyone prove undue influence. When Kenneth Lay asked cabinet members for help in averting Enron's bankruptcy, they turned him down (Bumiller 2002a). Securities and Exchange Commission Chairman Harvey Pitt took flak from Democrats, but for ineptitude rather than corruption. In any case, Pitt quit on Election Day 2002.

Second, both messes were bipartisan. Democrats and Republicans alike had taken S&L contributions. Democratic Speaker Jim Wright of Texas and Majority Whip Tony Coelho of California both resigned in 1989, in part because of questions about their S&L dealings. Although Enron executives favored the GOP, they gave significant sums to Democrats, including Senate Majority Leader Tom Daschle. In the election cycles between 1990 and 2000, six of the top ten House recipients of Enron money were Democrats (Center for Responsive Politics 2002). Enron also had a strong bond with the African American community and contributed to members of the Congressional Black Caucus. The company backed affirmative action and gave money to such groups as the United Negro College Fund (Yardley 2002).

Republicans noted that Robert Rubin, secretary of the treasury under Clinton, had unsuccessfully contacted his old department on Enron's behalf. They also tweaked Democratic National Committee Chair McAuliffe for making millions from his stock in Global Crossing, another troubled company. And among the alleged corporate tricksters, the most famous name was Martha Stewart, a major Democratic donor. Democrats thus worried that the issue could result in "friendly fire," that is, attacks wounding their own troops. "It's not a clean hit," acknowledged one Democratic strategist (York 2002).

Third, both problems led to passage of reform legislation before the midterm. In 1989, the elder Bush signed the Financial Institutions Reform Recovery and Enforcement Act (FIRREA). Thirteen years later, the younger Bush signed the Oxley-Sarbanes bill, the Corporate Responsibility Act of 2002. He further softened the issue when he signed campaign finance legislation banning soft money. Ironically, early data suggested that the new law was helping the GOP by shifting the fundraising battlefield to hard money, where Republicans have always had an advantage (Edsall 2003).

Fourth, both in 1990 and 2002, impending war with Iraq diverted media attention from corporate scandals. Moreover, the war on terror raised the chance that the United States could find itself in military conflict overnight. Any all-out ethics war against the administration could have ended up coinciding with real combat. In 1998, Operation Desert Fox showed how such a scenario would play out. President Clinton launched missile strikes against Iraq just as the House was taking up impeachment. Senate Majority Leader Trent Lott initially raised questions about the timing of the attack, but backed off under criticism. During floor debate, House Democrats struck hard:

> Rosa DeLauro (CT): "Thwarting the public's will, they do so even as the president commands our troops in battle against Iraq. . . . This debate amidst those bombs more than anything else symbolizes the madness that has inflamed the partisan fires on the other side of the aisle" (*Cong. Rec.* 144, December 18, 1998, H11781).
>
> Alcee Hastings (FL): "Our military, under the aegis of our president, is attempting to downgrade weapons of mass destruction in Iraq and we are en masse as a body degrading the institution of the presidency" (H11823).
>
> Martin Frost (TX): "We are sending the ultimate mixed message to Saddam about our national resolve. We may be encouraging him to resist longer by our actions in the midst of war. Starting this proceeding today may wind up costing American lives. The majority may well have blood on its hands by starting this proceeding today" (H11779).

One may speculate that in 2002 Democrats feared that Republicans would fire these words back at them.

Extremism and Quadrangulation

Political and military warriors rally their troops by depicting the enemy as an "other" who flouts the rules of acceptable thought and behavior. American politicians have often accused their foes of sympathy with foreign powers. Partisan newspapers charged that Thomas Jefferson would import the terrors of the French Revolution and that John Adams would bring back British rule. In their famous 1858 debates, Stephen Douglas implied that Abraham Lincoln had committed treason: "Whilst in Congress, he distinguished himself by his opposition to the Mexican war, taking the side of the common enemy against his own country" (Douglas 1858). During the Red scares of the twentieth century, the most frightful political weapon was an allegation of communist links. In this context, religion has also been a political battleground. Stephen Douglas objected to the efforts of clergy to abolish slavery. "It is an attempt to establish a theocracy to take charge of our politics and our legislation," he said. "It is an attempt to make the legislative power of this country subordinate to the church" (*Congressional Globe,* Senate, 33rd Congress, 1st sess., March 14, 1854, 621). In the Hoover-Smith campaign of 1928 and the Kennedy-Nixon campaign of 1960, a Catholic candidate battled rumors that he would put pope above country. And, of course, a generic line of attack is to accuse the other side of extremism. Lyndon Johnson's 1964 campaign against Barry Goldwater was a vivid case. Thanks to Democratic attacks—and Goldwater gaffes—many voters thought that Goldwater was an extremist who would scrap Social Security and start nuclear war.

Attacks against Bush drew on the 1964 model. Early in 2001 GOP strategist-turned-nemesis Kevin Phillips suggested a battle plan: "The electorate that voted for Gore and Nader represents a loose majority opposed to Bush's incredible $1.3-trillion tax cut plan and to the GOP drive to privatize Social Security. Bush is nevertheless now pushing ahead on both. But his illegitimacy as well as lack of mandate should underscore the cavalier behavior of campaigning for such extremes" (Phillips 2001).

Democrats also went after social issues. Bush's choice for attorney general was John Ashcroft, a social conservative with ties to the Christian Right. Though liberal Senate Democrats lacked the votes to defeat him, they made a spirited fight. "It's a shot across the bow," said Charles Schumer of New York, using a military metaphor. "I think we have helped set the tone for many of the upcoming issues that will face us" (Kennedy 2001). Democrats meant to warn Bush against changing the judicial branch by filling it with conservatives. Two years later, Senator Orrin Hatch returned to Schumer's words when complaining of a Democratic filibuster against judicial nominee Miguel Estrada. "This is a shot across the bow right now—that you had better darned well conform to a particular ideology or you are just not going to make it" (*Cong. Rec.* 149, February 12, 2003, S2328).

A few Democrats alluded to Bush's own religiosity. Representative Zoe Lofgren of California suggested that GOP opposition to cloning had an illegitimate basis. "Our job in Congress is not to pick the most restrictive religious view of science and then impose that view upon federal law. We live in a Democracy, not a Theocracy" (*Cong. Rec.* 147, July

31, 2001, H4919). And California representative Fortney "Pete" Stark said that the Bush administration was paying less attention to prescription drug coverage for seniors than to faith-based drug-abuse treatment programs. "This is a president who has cut back on the social safety net for the poorest and most vulnerable people in our country. Then he's saying: 'let's take money and give to the churches.'" Stark attributed the proposal as "fanaticism to force (Bush's) right wing Christian religion on the rest of the country" (Sandalow 2003).

The boldest line of attack likened the Christian Right to Islamic fundamentalists. Julian Bond, former Democratic politician and national chair of the NAACP, said early in 2001 that Bush "has selected nominees from the Taliban wing of American politics [and] appeased the wretched appetites of the extreme right wing" (Abrams 2001). Carville, Greenberg, and Shrum (2001) linked the war on terror to the liberal fight against the religious right. "We are defending America, which means for most people in the context of the current attack, we are defending the freedom of choice and religion. Religious fundamentalism and fanaticism are uncomfortable with the life choices and gender roles at the center of American life."

Such charges drew little blood. Allegations of GOP extremism focused on domestic issues, but national and homeland security came to overshadow such concerns. The fight against terrorism bolstered Ashcroft's public stature. Between the fall of 2001 and spring of 2003, Harris surveys consistently showed strong majorities rating his performance as "excellent" or "pretty good" (Taylor 2003). And the "Taliban" attack became obsolete with the U.S. victory in the Afghanistan military campaign. Bush avoided the Goldwater mistake of sounding extreme, and he picked his fights carefully. His nuanced position on cloning offended few people, and as for the delicate matter of abortion, he concentrated on late-term, or "partial-birth," abortions, where public opinion was in his corner.

Bush also distinguished himself from the Democrats on one side and the congressional GOP on the other. During the 2000 campaign, he ran as a "different kind of Republican." He spoke of compassionate conservatism and avoided the personal attacks that many had come to associate with Hill Republicans. During his presidency, he sometimes parted company with House Majority Leader Tom DeLay, a hard-edged conservative. By taking different positions on issues such as tax breaks for the poor, Bush made himself look more moderate. Said a House GOP staffer, "It's a good cop, bad cop thing" (Hook 2003c).

President Clinton took a similar approach—which political adviser Dick Morris called "triangulation"—but it hurt his relations with congressional Democrats. Bush largely escaped such resentment. By consulting with conservatives and taking their side on key issues such as taxes, he won some maneuvering room (Nagourney 2003a). And whereas Hill Democrats blamed Clinton for losing their majorities, Hill Republicans credited Bush's campaigning for their 2002 gains. If occasionally playing "bad cop" was a cost of holding control, the congressional GOP was willing to pay it. Moreover, Rove sometimes served as an in-house "bad cop." Whenever conservatives grumbled about excessive concessions, they could blame Rove instead of Bush himself. In 2001, for example, the administration announced an end to bombing runs on the Puerto Rican island of Vieques, a major issue for Latino political activists. Oklahoma Senator James Inhofe said, "It was Karl Rove who made the decision. It was politically motivated" (Berke and Bruni 2001). So, at various times, Bush could define himself against liberal Democrats, conservative Republicans, and even his own adviser. Call it "quadrangulation."

The Special Case of Race

African American voters typically support Democratic candidates over Republicans by a margin of at least nine to one. In mixed-race constituencies, therefore, Democratic success hinges on high black turnout (Black and Black 2002, 29–30). Standard get-out-the-vote drives can only go so far, so it is helpful to have a galvanizing issue. In the 1998 midterm, many analysts believe, resentment about the Clinton impeachment effort drove African Americans to the polls and helped Democrats score unexpected gains.

Bush tried hard in his 2000 campaign to avoid offending blacks. The Republican national convention pushed images of diversity to the point of self-parody. Bush downplayed affirmative action, instead praising "affirmative access." Democrats dwelt on the issue, and in their last joint debate, Gore tried to goad Bush into a clearer stance. In broadcast advertisements by the NAACP National Voter Fund the daughter of a hate-crime victim said, "When Governor George W. Bush refused to support hate-crime legislation, it was like my father was killed all over again"

(Lawrence 2000). Such mobilization efforts boosted black turnout and were a major reason for Gore's strong showing in Florida.

In an effort to appeal to social conservatives, Bush nominated Linda Chavez to be secretary of labor. A foe of racial preferences, Chavez might have aroused strong black opposition. But she had to withdraw because of a controversy surrounding an undocumented immigrant in her household. Bush then picked Elaine Chao, former Peace Corps Director and CEO of the United Way. Chao was conservative but less confrontational than Chavez.

Another cabinet choice offered another target. While attacking the GOP "Taliban wing," NAACP chairman Bond also scorned "cabinet officials whose devotion to the Confederacy is nearly canine in its uncritical affection" (Abrams 2001). He was referring to John Ashcroft, who had once given an interview to a neo-Confederate magazine. House Majority Leader Dick Armey (R-TX) complained of "racial McCarthyism," but Bond repeated his attack, word for word, the following summer (Russell 2001). In 2003, 55 percent of blacks rated Ashcroft as "only fair" or poor," compared with 35 percent of whites (*National Journal* 2003).

The war on terrorism led to a truce on the racial front, with polls showing increases in black approval of Bush's performance. Bond said that Bush had gained because the war on terrorism had "driven most of the radical conservative agenda both out of the headlines and out of present-day politics" (Sack 2001). And for most of 2002 racial issues had a low profile.

During the midterm election campaign, Republicans stepped up minority outreach efforts, buying ads on black radio stations to tout GOP ideas and attack the Democratic record. Liberal commentator John Judis offered a cynical but accurate explanation: "The idea is not so much to win votes but to deprive the opposition of a bogeyman against whom they can turn out the vote" (Judis 2002). Though the causal link is uncertain, there was no upsurge in black turnout as there had been in 1998.

Then came Trent Lott. At a hundredth birthday celebration for Senator Strom Thurmond (R-SC) late in 2002, Senate Republican Leader Lott said that he was proud that Mississippi had backed Thurmond in the 1948 presidential election. "And if the rest of the country had followed our lead, we wouldn't have had all these problems over all these years, either." Thurmond ran as a states' rights Democrat ("Dixiecrat") in support of racial segregation, though he later changed his views. Though reaction was muted at first, attacks soon mounted. Representative John Lewis (D-GA), a civil rights marcher in the 1960s, asked, "Is Lott saying the country should have voted to continue segregation, for segregated schools, 'white' and 'colored' restrooms?" (Edsall 2002b). Foreseeing that Lott would become the villain that the Democrats needed, Republicans and conservatives began turning their backs on him. Bush himself publicly criticized Lott's comments.

Democrats belittled the GOP efforts. Former president Clinton said, "How can they jump on him when they're out there repressing, trying to run black voters away from the polls, and running under the Confederate flag in Georgia and South Carolina. . . . He just embarrassed them by saying in Washington what they do on the backroads every day" (Fram 2002). Senator Hillary Rodham Clinton said that the Lott affair was an example of the Republicans' "constant exploitation of race." She cited allegations about Bush's 2000 primary fight against McCain: "The campaign for then-Gov. Bush in South Carolina had a huge outreach effort to say they [the McCains] adopted a black baby" (Lisi 2002).

With tacit White House encouragement, Senate Republicans moved to oust Lott as leader. After failed attempts to defend himself, Lott stepped down in favor of Bill Frist of Tennessee, a conservative with a nonsegregationist past. But the partisan war was back on. When Sonny Perdue, the new Republican governor of Georgia, proposed a nonbinding referendum on whether the state flag should include a Confederate symbol, the Democratic Leadership Council said that Perdue had the same problem as Republicans in general: "They may not be racists, but they are cheerfully ready at the drop of a hat to exploit racist sentiments, no matter what the cost" (Democratic Leadership Council 2003).

Early in 2003, the Bush administration filed amicus briefs in a prominent pair of affirmative-action cases before the Supreme Court. The briefs argued against racial-preference admissions policies at the University of Michigan but did not contend that consideration of race is always unconstitutional. White House counsel Alberto Gonzales reportedly modified tougher antipreference arguments by Solicitor General Theodore Olson. Despite its narrow scope, the administration's position drew Democratic fire. Representative Lewis denounced President Bush's statement on the briefs. "Five times Bush used the word 'quota' to denounce the University of Michigan's admissions policy. . . . Five times Bush uttered racial code words that appeal to the worst within us. Five times he divided our nation into 'us' and 'them'" (Lewis 2003).

The Supreme Court struck down a point system for undergraduates but upheld a less explicit version of racial preference in the university's law school. Conservative scholar Robert George said that the decision must have pleased Bush and Rove. "Many Republicans believe that 1989's Casey Supreme Court decision putting restraints on abortion may have fired up feminists and suburban women in 1992. The last thing Republicans wanted was minority Democrats having a passionate desire to come out and vote in droves in 2004. This decision will not drive Democrats to the polls" (George 2003). Bush's reaction confirmed George's observation. Said the president, "I applaud the Supreme Court for recognizing the value of diversity on our nation's campuses. Diversity is one of America's greatest strengths. Today's decisions seek a careful balance between the goal of campus diversity and the fundamental principle of equal treatment under the law" (Bush 2003d).

The Khaki Mandate

As long as a war remains popular, a president has the "khaki mandate," an implicit go-ahead from the people to lead the fight without the friction of domestic political combat. During wartime, however, the president and opposition may differ on the scope of the mandate. The president will try to stretch it as much as possible, deeming a variety of foreign and domestic policies as vital to the war effort. To the president's supporters, criticism of these policies is of dubious legitimacy. The opposition will define the mandate more strictly, forgoing attacks only on the most basic elements of war policy. Under the narrowest interpretation, the president's opponents will maintain that their only obligation is to voice support for the troops.

In late 2001, some commentators compared the political atmosphere in the country to that of the early 1940s. Their assumption was that the World War II had created a bipartisan consensus on a very broad khaki mandate (Kilgore 2001). Not quite. After Pearl Harbor, Republicans did unify behind the war's basic aims, but they also reserved the right to criticize aspects of foreign policy and military management. On December 19, 1941, Senator Robert Taft (R-OH) said, "I believe there can be no doubt that criticism in time of war is essential to the maintenance of any kind of democratic government . . . . The maintenance of the right of criticism in the long run will do the country maintaining it a great deal more good than it will do the enemy, and will prevent mistakes which might otherwise occur (History News Network 2003).

Conservative Republicans in Congress did fault the Roosevelt administration for shortchanging General MacArthur in the Pacific theater and for using the war as a pretext for expanding the New Deal (Darilek 1976, 32–35). Liberal Republicans were less critical, but one of their leaders came close to all-out political war. In 1944, Republican presidential nominee Thomas Dewey concluded that American code breaking should have enabled Roosevelt to anticipate Pearl Harbor. Learning that Dewey might raise the issue, Army Chief of Staff George C. Marshall sent a War Department analyst to ask Dewey to stand down. The analyst said that publicizing the issue might provide information to the Japanese. Though angry and skeptical, Dewey gave in. His advisors also feared that the Democrats would counterattack him for helping the enemy (Smith 1984, 425–30).

The Dewey camp had reason to be afraid, because Democrats did not hesitate to go after Republicans over the war. The Ohio Congress of Industrial Organizations issued a pamphlet titled "He Wanted to Do Business with Hitler and Hirohito—The Amazing Story of Senator Taft." It said that Taft's pre–Pearl Harbor isolationism had "brought joy to the hearts of fascists and despair to thousands suffering in the dungeons of Europe" (Patterson 1972, 275). Taft barely won reelection.

If Dewey's near-attack raised ethical issues for the out-party, assaults on the opposition raised issues for the in-party. Despite their criticisms, Republicans generally backed the Roosevelt war effort. Later, as World War II shaded into the Cold War, Senator Arthur Vandenberg posed a rhetorical question about the administration's political response: "Having been the beneficiary of minority cooperation . . . what is its ethical and essential attitude when election time rolls around? What does it do—as a practical matter—in respect to the candidates of minority leaders whose indispensable cooperation has made this successful 'foreign policy' possible?" (Darilek 1976, 180). On the day that President Truman named Vandenberg as a delegate to the United Nations, he recalled ruefully that the Democratic National Committee "sends two of its most prominent orators . . . into Michigan to seek my Party's defeat in general and my defeat in particular. Bang!" (Darilek 1976, 181).

The same tensions arose decades later. Disagreements about the extent of the khaki mandate started to surface just weeks after the terrorists' attacks in Washington and New York City. Just as Democrats in 1943 had called for renewing the Trade Agreements Act in the name of wartime unity (Darilek 1976, 67), Republicans in 2001 made the same case for restoring "fast track" trade negotiating authority. Said House Speaker Dennis Hastert (R-IL): "This Congress will either support our president, who is fighting a courageous war on terrorism and redefining American world leadership, or it will undercut the president at the worst possible time" (*Cong. Rec.* 147, December 6, 2001, H9012). In both cases, the opposition grumbled about the linkage while the president's position prevailed.

In the spring of 2002, Representative Cynthia McKinney (D-GA) made the kind of attack on President Bush that Dewey had planned against FDR: "What did this administration know and when did it know it, about the events of September 11th?" she asked during a radio interview. "Who else knew, and why did they not warn the innocent people of New York who were needlessly murdered? . . . What do they have to hide?" (Eilperin 2002). The remark drew the reaction that Dewey's advisors had feared fifty-eight years earlier. Republicans damned her, and most Democrats kept their distance. Backlash from her constituency led to her defeat in the Democratic primary.

In the fall of 2002, Democratic concerns about labor provisions were stalling the president's proposal to establish a Department of Homeland Security. During the debate, Senate Democratic Leader Tom Daschle made a floor speech that echoed Arthur Vandenberg's complaints about the Democrats:

> The Vice President comes to fundraisers, as he did just recently in Kansas. The headline written in the paper the next day about the speech he gave to that fundraiser was: Cheney Talks about War: Electing [GOP House candidate] Taff Would Aid War Effort. And then we find a diskette discovered in Lafayette Park, a computer diskette that was lost somewhere between a Republican strategy meeting in the White House and the White House. Advice was given by Karl Rove, and the quote on the disk was: "Focus on war.". . . The President is quoted in the *Washington Post* this morning as saying that the Democratic-controlled Senate is "not interested in the security of the American people." Not interested in the security of the American people? You tell Senator Inouye he is not interested in the security of the American people. You tell those who fought in Viet-

> nam and in World War II they are not interested in the security of the American people. That is outrageous—outrageous (*Cong. Rec.* 148, September 25, 2002, S9187).

Republican Leader Lott yielded no ground: "Who is the enemy here? The President of the United States or Saddam Hussein? That is who was attacked this morning here on the floor of the Senate. I think we would be better served debating Saddam Hussein and the threat he poses for the world" (*Cong. Rec.* 148, September 25, 2002, S9203). Lott said that Bush had been "referencing the current debate over management flexibility of the Department of Homeland Security not the war on terror in Iraq" (S9204). He also argued that Cheney has simply praised the Republican candidate as one who "'will make a fine partner for us in the important work ahead.' What is the problem with that?" (S9204).

Republicans kept up the heat. Reprising the 1944 attacks on Robert Taft, Georgia Republican Senate candidate Saxby Chambliss ran ads with photos of Osama Bin Laden and Saddam Hussein, which faded into a photo of incumbent Democrat Max Cleland. In October, House Majority Leader Armey (R-TX) blamed Democrats for stalling the creation of a Department of Homeland Security: "Americans must be wondering why it is that al Qaeda, this ragtag bunch of terrorists scattered all over the globe, can reorganize themselves . . . and the United States cannot reorganize itself. Al Qaeda doesn't have a Senate. Al Qaeda doesn't have a Senator Daschle that has another focus" (Dewar 2002). Conservative commentators picked up the theme, with emphasis on Daschle.

After the GOP triumph in the midterm election, Daschle vented his frustration. Blaming the attacks for unspecified threats against his family, he briefly revived the "Republican Taliban" theme. "You know, we see it in foreign countries, and we think, 'Well, my God, how can this religious fundamentalism become so violent?' Well, it's that same shrill rhetoric, it's that same shrill power that motivates" (Bash 2002). Conservatives counterattacked, and even some moderate commentators criticized Daschle for overreacting. He did not repeat the accusations.

Daschle, along with House Minority Leader Dick Gephardt, did support a resolution authorizing the use of force in Iraq. The issue split their party. Senate Democrats backed the resolution 29–21, while House Democrats opposed it 81–126. Many blue-hots were angry that their congressional leaders had not put up a fight. Perhaps in response to their concerns, leading Democrats grew critical in early 2003. Shortly before the invasion, Daschle said that diplomatic failures had brought the country to the point of war. Massachusetts senator John Kerry compared the Democratic struggle to the war in Iraq. : "What we need now is not just a regime change in Saddam Hussein and Iraq, but we need a regime change in the United States" (Johnson 2003).

Republican responses were biting. John Kerry "looks French," said a Bush adviser, alluding to France's opposition to the attack, which angered Americans (Nagourney and Stevenson 2003). Tom DeLay (R-TX), the new House Majority Leader, said Daschle was "emboldening Saddam Hussein" (VandeHei 2003c). Nancy Pelosi (D-CA), who had succeeded Gephardt as House Minority Leader, came to Daschle's defense by quoting Taft: "'Criticism in time of war is essential to the maintenance of any kind of democratic government.'" She added, "In expressing his views, Tom Daschle is being patriotic. The Republican leaders are being partisan" (Coile 2003). Daschle himself argued for a narrow khaki mandate: "We support strongly the troops, but there's a difference between the troops and the administration of a war" (Lakely and Dinan 2003).

Mayberry Machiavellis and the Unknown Unknowns

By midsummer of 2003, the khaki mandate appeared vulnerable. With no major domestic incidents of terrorism since the fall of 2001, the issue of homeland security seemed less urgent. The invasion of Iraq was over, but American troops continued to die. And questions about prewar intelligence enabled Democrats to attack Bush's credibility.

They had earlier raised the credibility issue. During the 2000 campaign, Jesse Jackson dismissed Bush's "compassionate conservatism" as "wolf's politics in sheep's clothing" (Hurt 2000). Al From, head of the Democratic Leadership Council, said shortly after Bush took office, "His rhetoric may be compassionate, but his actions are conservative" (From 2001). "Between [this administration's] rhetoric and the reality is a credibility gap," said Senate Democratic Leader Daschle in January 2003. "And it's growing with each new broken promise, each new misleading claim, and each new case of bait and switch" (Office of Senate Democratic Leader 2003). Daschle and other Democratic leaders said that Bush had failed to follow through on education reform and was dissembling on the impact of tax cuts (Fournier 2003).

Democrats liked to quote former Bush aide John DiIulio, who referred to jaded White House staffers as the "Mayberry Machiavellis" (Suskind 2003, 104). The "Mayberry" reference, however, pointed up an inconsistency in Democratic attacks. Ever since Bush first ran for governor of Texas, his opponents had mocked him as a simpleton. Now some were suggesting that he was a mastermind of sophisticated deceptions. Could they convincingly portray him as Richard III after years of painting him as Gomer Pyle?

They also had to contend with GOP skill in strategy and tactics. Republicans understood Clausewitz's definition of defense "not as a simple shield but a shield made up of well-directed blows" (Clausewitz 1976, 357). In 2003, they took criticism of judicial nominee William Pryor as a wedge to split off a Democratic constituency. When Democratic senators took exception to Pryor's strong opposition to abortion, Republicans suggested that they were actually opposing his Catholicism (Toner 2003b).

But reality beats strategy. In other words, changing circumstances can overwhelm even the cleverest political operation. In guessing what those circumstances might be, we should recall the famous words of Defense Secretary Donald Rumsfeld: "There are things we know that we know. There are known unknowns. That is to say, there are things that we now know we don't know. But there are also unknown unknowns. There are things we don't know we don't know" (Rumsfeld 2002). In mid-2003, the "known unknowns" included the election-year economy and the progress of the war on terror. And the "unknown unknowns" included all the potential issues and scandals that could catch political warriors by surprise.

So Democrats continued to fight on the ice, hoping that fate would deliver them some fresh ammunition.

3 THE PARTY BASE OF PRESIDENTIAL LEADERSHIP AND LEGITIMACY

Kevin S. Price and John J. Coleman

Elected under controversial circumstances, George W. Bush entered office facing a legitimacy crisis. A significant proportion of the American public viewed Bush as a false president, in part because he was outpolled in popular votes by the losing candidate, and in part because his road to the White House took several legal detours through the Florida courts and finally through a contentious Supreme Court decision. His legitimacy crisis may have ebbed when the events of September 11 recast his presidency, but it did not disappear. Just as the president was declaring victory over Iraq in late April 2003, Democratic presidential candidate Bob Graham, U.S. Senator from Florida, was declaring that the legitimacy of the Bush presidency was in question because of the circumstances in Florida in November 2000. Moreover, the broader leadership question encased in the legitimacy question remained: how can this president lead? His second-place popular vote finish certainly, most observers thought, made any claim to a mandate irrelevant. Accordingly, when Bush entered office, these observers expected that the president would have tremendous difficulty enacting his legislative agenda and leading the government.

These analyses, however, ignored the possibilities inherent in the

American party system for presidents to establish legitimacy and exert leadership. Presidents seek to establish identities and political strengths independent of their party, but they remain dependent on party members to achieve many of their goals. Presidential leadership is connected to the party system in two important ways. First, the historical trajectory of the party system may be more or less favorable for the establishment of presidential leadership; that is, some presidents are simply in a more difficult position historically because of the strength or weakness of current party alignments. Second, a president whose own victory was very narrow may face extra leadership challenges when his party's majority is also paper thin, but this situation can also create opportunities.

In these respects, President Bush was in a strong position regarding the first point, the historical trajectory of the party system. Simply put, the basic dynamics of the party system—realignment, economic conditions, and loosening ownership of issues by the Democratic Party—were favorable for establishing leadership claims. On the second point, Bush faced a challenge of legitimacy and leadership similar to that faced by many other presidents we classify as "plurality presidents," but his situation was sufficiently different from theirs that he had advantages that they did not. Therefore, despite some similarities in their election victories, Bush started his term in a stronger position than these presidents. This is not to minimize the challenges Bush faced but, rather, to say that we should not exaggerate them either. The ingredients were in place for Bush to establish both legitimacy and leadership, even without the intervening events of September 11.

The Republican Ascendancy

President Bush inherited a party system well situated for his leadership efforts. Although Bush did not have an electoral mandate, the trends in the party system were largely, though not entirely, favorable toward his party and his presidency. First, although this is a matter of some controversy (Mayhew 2002), it is plausible to say that the party system has realigned in a manner favorable to Republicans.

Partisan realignment is an umbrella term covering distinctive varieties of political change. These varieties include secular realignment and critical realignment. Uniting these terms is an attempt to understand changes in the party system and how it moves from one type of competition to another. In effect, realignment theory takes "before and after" photographs of the party system. The "before and after" might be from a period in which one party dominates to a period in which the other party does, or from a time when a party has a particular coalition to a time when that party has a different supporting coalition, or from a period in which one party dominates to a period in which neither party does. Whichever change it is, significant policy departures accompany the party realignment.

Our analytical eye is often drawn to the dramatic and disruptive, but V. O. Key (1959) alerted scholars to the fact that significant political change often occurs after the cumulation of small, incremental, gradual developments. This type of realignment is known as secular (that is, gradual) realignment. As a social group becomes more affluent, for example, its members might find the policy appeals of a conservative political party more to their liking. As one particular social group becomes better represented within a political party, other groups might gradually pull out of that party. Scholars have suggested that both of these developments have occurred in the party system over the past few decades. For example, as Catholics moved steadily into the middle class, they became less reliably Democratic. As blacks gained a louder voice in the Democratic Party, whites, especially southern whites, increasingly supported Republicans. As religious and social conservatives played an increasing role in the Republican Party, Republican moderates found themselves increasingly likely to vote Democratic. Evangelical Christians moved from Democratic voting to Republican voting over time.

In the 1990s, secular realignment moved in a direction that tended to favor Republicans. Groups that were considered part of the Democratic New Deal coalition—organized labor, agricultural interests, urban ethnic groups, Catholics, Jews, the less educated, southerners, industrial blue collar workers, liberals—tended to support Democrats less strongly in the 1990s than in the 1940s (Mayer 1998). Indeed, if these groups were still voting for Democrats at their traditional levels, Democrats would not have lost control of Congress, state legislatures, and governorships in the 1990s. Still, Stonecash (2000) and Stonecash, Brewer, and Mariani (2003) have shown that class-based divisions between the parties were on the upswing in the 1990s, so the idea that Republicans represent the better-off economically and Democrats the less well-off still rings true. And certainly the groups that one would think of as typically Democratic have not necessarily become majority Republican—they have become less Democratic but, for the most part, still lean Democratic.

In the 1990s, the New Deal coalition could no longer cement Democratic victories, and that works to the Republicans' advantage. By the 1990s a Democrat, particularly a Democratic presidential nominee, could no longer plan on winning by simply rounding up the old coalitional suspects. Even a candidate who found that he did well with these traditional New Deal coalition groups—and most Democratic candidates did do reasonably well with them—would find that he needed to reach outside this cluster to ensure victory (Bartels 1998). This provided an opportunity for Republicans in general and George H. W. Bush in particular. Although Bush fared miserably among African Americans, he defused some of the Democratic advantage with other groups, such as women, and defused some of the issues that were typically seen as owned by Democrats, such as Social Security and education. The upshot is that the Republicans were poised to strengthen their majority status when Bush entered office, and his fellow partisans knew it. That gave them great incentive to cooperate with Bush, which they did at very high levels in roll-call votes. Unlike Bill Clinton, who many Democrats suspected did not hold the key to future Democratic victories, Bush seems to have had his fellow partisans believing he had unlocked the code to Republican dominance. Regaining control of both houses of Congress with the 2002 elections only reinforced that impression among Republican elites. As Davies (2003, 146) puts it, reviewing the results of the national and state 2002 elections, "it is almost a statistical tie—a shift of a few votes here and there would have changed the results. But the Republicans won this tie. In every case the small majority lies with the Republicans, and the combination is to give that party a very considerable, and interlinked, foundation for national political authority."

The old New Deal coalition is not dead, but it is not sufficient for Democratic victories, and with secular realignment, Republicans are at worst co-equal with the Democrats or arguably the clear majority party. It has been a long time since Republicans controlled the presidency, House, and Senate simultaneously, as they now do, and an even longer time since they have won and maintained control of Congress for five consecutive elections, as they have now done. Bush's presidency, though the result of an unusual election, has benefited from occurring at this point in history. His fellow partisans in Congress have proved willing to let him lead. This does not mean that he has the unconditional support of his party nor that he hasn't faced trouble from the more moderate members of his party. It does mean that, unlike Clinton, who seemed to many Democrats to preside over and perhaps, in their view, cause the dissolution of the Democratic majority, Bush is seen by his Republican friends as the person who can make the Republican majority durable. To be sure, the Republicans' majority has been thin by historical standards, but it is nonetheless a majority (Barone 2002; Brooks 2003; Meyerson 2002; Teixeira 2003).

Another form of historical change is known as critical realignment. Elaborated most importantly by V. O. Key (1955) and Walter Dean Burnham (1970), realignment theory posits that some elections (either a single one or a series of two in sequence) have enduring consequences for the party system. Rather than the gradual change at the heart of secular realignment, critical realignment focuses on sharp, quick transformations of the political landscape that have effects for a generation or longer. Typically, critical realignments bring a new majority party to power and have effects at the local, state, and national level. Among scholars, the 1800 (Jeffersonian Republicans), 1832 (Jackson and the Democrats), 1860 (Lincoln's Republicans), and 1932 (Roosevelt and the Democrats) elections fall into this category. Other realignments might keep the same majority party but create a new supporting coalition for it, as in 1896 (McKinley and the Republicans).

Looking back, scholars such as John Aldrich (1995) and Walter Dean Burnham (1996) have argued that the 1968 election marked a critical realignment of a different type. This realignment was notable for its dealigning features: members of the public pulled away from their party loyalties, turnout began to drop, and control over government was usually divided between the two major parties. With this shared power, policy began to move in a more conservative direction. The dramatic victory of Ronald Reagan in 1980, in this view, solidified the ongoing system rather than marking a realigning election in its own right. The Republican Party strengthened by gaining control of the Senate from 1981 through 1986, and policy moved more clearly still in a conservative direction. But control of government in Washington remained divided and the Democrats remained the majority party in the states and cities.

The 1994 electoral earthquake had all the hallmarks of a traditional partisan critical realignment: issues were highly prominent, the political atmosphere seemed unusually energized, the election results tilted almost universally toward one party, institutional reorganization (especially in the House) was extensive, policy changes (or attempts at policy changes) were numerous and, for the most part, ideologically consistent (Burnham 1996). It seemed that at last the Democratic era was over.

Unfortunately, history is hardly ever as neat and tidy as our models. In this supposed new Republican era, a Democrat won the presidency in 1996, and in the midterm election of 1998 the Democrats achieved the historical anomaly of gaining seats. Much of the conservative Republican agenda either failed or was watered down to ensure passage and the signature of the Democratic president.

Nonetheless, it is fair to describe 1994 as a critical realignment akin to the 1896 realignment. The 1896 realignment did not create a new majority party, but it created a new supporting coalition for the existing Republican majority. Similarly, the 1994 realignment continued the possibility of divided control of government that was typical of the 1968 realignment, but it changed the balance of power within that division. With 1994, the Republican Party achieved parity with the Democrats throughout the country and at all levels of government. Although a case could be made for the Republicans as the new majority party, it would be a shakier case than one could make, for example, for the Democrats after the realignment in 1932. The Republicans did not become the undisputed majority party following 1994, but the realignment had a clear partisan direction. The period from 1968 to 1994 featured divided government that leaned toward Democratic control at most levels and in most offices; the period after 1994 seems likely to continue the closely contested balance of party power but now with the balance tilting more toward the Republicans. As mentioned above, the fact is that the Republicans through 2003 had remained the majority party in Congress for five straight terms (with a brief deviation following the defection of Senator James Jeffords), something the party had not accomplished in nearly seventy years. Moreover, of the nineteen states that had population growth from 1990 to 2000 that exceeded the national average of 13.2 percent, Bush won fourteen. Republicans are doing best where the population—and the electoral votes it provides—is growing most. Bush won 271 electoral votes in 2000 to Al Gore's 267, but winning those states in 2004 would garner Bush 278 electoral votes for a more comfortable seventeen-vote margin. Moreover, albeit from a vantage point about a year before the election, the chances for Republicans not only to hold onto Congress but also to gain seats in the 2004 races look strong. Democrats have more senators up for reelection than do the Republicans, and more of these appear to be vulnerable seats. Remarkably few House seats appear competitive and, on the whole, Republicans emerged in a solid position after the redistricting induced by the 2000 census. The political soap opera in Texas in mid-2003 eventually resulted in a Republican-leaning redistricting in that state—Republicans, unhappy with a judicially created redistricting map, opened a special session of the legislature to draw a new map, leading Democratic representatives to flee and go into hiding in Oklahoma, and then New Mexico, in protest—and an estimated additional seven seats may go to the Republicans, which is a very large number in the current environment.

The 1990s also witnessed the partial demise of ideas that the American electorate was dealigning at the national level. In the 1970s and 1980s, a number of scholars pointed out that Americans seemed to be losing their partisan moorings, that attachments to the parties were not as deep or as permanent as they had once been. Rather than realignment, these scholars suggested, *dealignment* best described the new American electorate. To a large degree, these accounts were compelling descriptions of the electorate of those two decades. In the 1990s, however, this trend bottomed out and, to some degree, reversed. Most notably, the percentage of voters splitting their tickets between the two major parties—for example, voting for a House candidate of one party and a presidential candidate of another party—declined throughout the 1990s and in the 2000 election: in 2000 the percentage (14 percent) was the lowest it had been since 1964. Similarly, the percentage of districts electing a House member of one party while supporting a presidential candidate of another party in 2000, 20.2 percent, was at its lowest level since 1952. To be sure, these trends are just one side of the story. Voting turnout continues to be low and the strong showing of third-party presidential candidates in 1992, 1996, and to a lesser extent 2000 suggest an electorate that is not fully satisfied with the options presented by the major parties. And even if voting is highly partisan within a particular election, there might be a share of voters who split their votes in one election but not the next, or who might even vote straight party but for different parties in different years. The point here is not that the partisan electorate of the nineteenth century, or even the 1950s, has been restored, but that the continuing dealignment feared by some scholars has been stemmed and partially reversed.

Both in the sense of secular and critical realignment, then, the historical position of the party system was advantageous for George W. Bush. Republicans had, for the first time in many decades, a clear opportunity to become the majority governing party on a stable basis. Viewing the aggressive tactics of Newt Gingrich in the 1990s to have been a failure, the party was open to a different approach and somewhat different message. Bush capitalized on these openings and garnered tremendous loyalty from Republicans in Congress. Coming to office when he did, Bush was able to leverage his leadership opportunities to an unusual degree, certainly to an extent greater than his thin victory would suggest. His ability to exercise leadership, his Republican colleagues realized, would enhance his legitimacy credentials.

We will mention other features of the historical trajectory—political time, economic conditions, changing issue ownership, and social trends—only briefly. First, Bush's leadership benefited among Republicans because of his place in political time. As is explained elsewhere in this volume, Bush's presidency is one of the politics of articulation or the orthodox innovator. Expectations are relatively low for this kind of president, and his ability to lead is also tied to the perceptions of the presidency he is linked to. In Bush's case, that would be Ronald Reagan. The reverence for Reagan among Republicans is substantial, and Bush found himself in the role of fine tuning and adjusting the Reagan legacy and agenda, not discarding it. For this, he was given substantial leeway to lead among Republican politicians and activists. His early passage of a large tax cut and his insistence on additional cuts proved his Reaganite bona fides to both groups.

Second, Bush inherited an economy that had grown strongly for years and generated budget surpluses. This allowed him to make the case for his tax cuts despite, initially, any clear economic reason the economy required such stimulus. Early into his term, however, the economy began to slide and the tax cut that once seemed to be economically unnecessary could now be defended as reasonable and stimulatory. He could use the continuing troubles of the economy to push additional rounds of tax cuts in 2002 and 2003. Obviously, at some point the president would need economic conditions to improve to enhance his reelection prospects, but he was able to leverage those conditions in pursuit of his ideological beliefs in a manner most satisfactory to his base. By the third quarter of 2003, the president was seeing precisely the strong gains in economic growth he had desired. Even if those outside his base thought tax cuts unnecessary, it is difficult to mobilize strong opposition among the public to the idea of keeping more of its money.

Third, Bush also rode the wave of the nationalization of the education issue, particularly as the link between education and financial well-being became ever more strongly entrenched in public assumptions. Both of these developments proved helpful for passage of major parts of the Bush campaign agenda. Because of Bush's personal efforts, the Democratic ownership of the education issue had diminished markedly when he took office. The same was true of Social Security, though the collapse in the stock market prevented Bush from making any headway on his campaign promise to reform the pension system. And while Bush had weakened some of the Democratic ownership of key issues, he was able to reinforce issues on which Republicans had been strong. The tragedy of September 11, in particular, provided a means to reinforce Bush's arguments during the campaign that American military and security readiness needed to improve. Lastly, Bush entered office at a time when many important indicators seemed to be pointed in the right direction. In the late 1990s, crime was down, educational achievement was moving up, out-of-wedlock births were declining, the abortion rate was dropping, and so on. Simply put, Bush inherited a very favorable policy environment. He did not take office in an environment swirling with crisis—other than the circumstances surrounding his election.

Close Matters . . . But It's Not the Whole Cigar

We believe that "close matters," but it does not fully determine presidential success and public acceptance. For most Americans, the legitimacy of Bush's presidency would ultimately depend on his achieving some measure of policy success, and that success would depend on his ability to master the difficulties inherent in his controversial victory. Even after September 11, it was not obvious or inevitable that Bush would escape from questions about the legitimacy of his presidency, even if these questions might be asked in hushed tones. We are not suggesting that policy success can overcome every legitimacy problem a president faces—Richard Nixon's policy success was substantial even as his legitimacy eroded—but that for Bush policy achievement would help dissipate lingering doubts about his victory.

Through most of the 2000 campaign, many Americans appeared unmoved by the leading presidential candidates and unconvinced that the upcoming election would make much of a difference in their lives. Indeed, Ralph Nader grounded his insurgent candidacy in the premise that a President Gore would differ from a President Bush only in the smallest details of program and rhetoric. Amid the unfolding drama of election night, however, many formerly disinterested citizens began to suspect that something vitally important was at stake. By the time the Supreme Court ended the suspense five weeks later, committed partisans on both sides had adopted scorched-earth tactics in pursuit of their preferred outcomes, and many of those who yawned their way through the official campaign now seemed certain that the overtime selection of their next president would be very consequential indeed (Dionne and Kristol 2001).

As subsequent events have made abundantly clear, the 2000 contest was not a *Seinfeld*-style "election about nothing." Indeed, the effort to resolve the controversy in Florida raised a number of significant concerns: the effectiveness of our voting procedures, not only in Florida but around the country; the effects of the Electoral College on campaign strategies and outcomes; the role of state and local governments in conducting federal elections; and the role of courts in answering explicitly political questions. In addition to all of that, one problem raised by the election of 2000 was truly fundamental: the political and constitutional legitimacy of an incoming president.

Politically submerged by the many remarkable developments of the Bush years, the problem of our forty-third president's legitimacy has now receded beyond recognition. Our purpose is not to judge the legitimacy of the Bush administration; after all, reasonable people can disagree about the post-election process that yielded the Texan's narrow victory in the Electoral College. Instead, the point is to explain the rapid disappearance of legitimacy as a politically contentious characteristic of the Bush presidency. Credible questions of legitimacy could have plagued this president in the early months of his administration, perhaps even throughout his term. That they did not requires an explanation that situates George W. Bush in the ongoing flow of American party politics.

Plurality Presidents

We begin with the simple notion that elections provide political information to winners and losers alike.[1] Generally speaking, winners—and the journalists who play a central role in establishing the conventional wisdom after each election—will credit the victorious side's savvy tactical decisions, the general brilliance of the triumphant candidate, or, at times, the inevitability of the outcome. Losers, on the other hand, engage in postmortem analysis not simply to apportion blame but to develop a strategic plan for future contests. Not all presidents are elected in the same circumstances. Some win landslides. Others win comfortably. Others manage close wins. Some win despite having received less than half the vote. In this category, some win largely because of the implosion of the opposition party. Presidents like Richard Nixon and Bill Clinton won, to a significant degree, because of the internal fractures within the opposition party that led to third-party candidates. It is this last type of president that we refer to as the plurality president.

The central intrigue of the plurality presidency is that it fuses the analytical frames of the winner and the loser into a single act of political interpretation. After all, a plurality winner has indeed triumphed, and he is thus entitled to use the authority of the presidency, but the unconvincing nature of his victory compels him and his team to search for more reliable footing in the shifting sands of American politics. This prospective project—a fusion of the winner's rationalization and the loser's retooling—captures the basic outlook of the plurality presidency. Moreover, this dynamic process connects elites and voters in an ongoing process of party definition in which elites offer voters a choice, voters choose, and elites interpret that choice with an eye to the next round of electoral competition.

As party politicians assess their prospects, the best guide to an upcoming election is the most recent one. In other words, potential candidates (including incumbents) look ahead by looking back. In search of a winning formula, candidates in the just-defeated party assess the political terrain and build an electoral blueprint based on the best available information.[2] A defining characteristic of a plurality election is that its winner must engage in effectively the same analysis as the losers of most other elections. The key difference is that the winners of these elections conduct such assessments from the White House. To put it another way, plurality presidents engage in something like a loser's analysis from a winner's position of power.

To understand the plurality presidency, one must understand what it is not. It is not an automatic result of multiparty elections. Third- and fourth-party insurgencies have played significant roles, but other notable multicandidate contests have not produced plurality presidencies as we define them. Consider the 1948 election, in which Democrat Harry Truman fell just short of a popular majority.[3] We do not regard Truman as a plurality president because the minor-party candidates who held him short of a majority broke from the Democratic orbit.

A president like Truman won *despite* a split in one of the major parties. Plurality presidents, on the other hand, win in part *because* of a split in one of the major parties. Elites will derive little political information from the simple fact that a candidate does not reach 50 percent. Instead, elections that reveal the winning side's persistent weakness in the party system generate useful political information. If Truman can succeed even when his party suffered two breakaway movements, he may perceive electoral vindication for the orthodox Democratic formulas of the New Deal and Fair Deal. Such a victory would thus embolden its winner, suggesting little need to revise basic party positions.

Now consider the contrasting message of the 1912 election, in which Woodrow Wilson won largely—if not exclusively—because of Theodore Roosevelt's challenge to incumbent Republican William Howard Taft. In nearly eight years as president, Roosevelt forged a distinctly progressive identity for himself and, by extension, for the Republican Party. By siphoning substantial progressive support from Taft's Republican coalition, Roosevelt effectively guaranteed Wilson's victory. The political upshot of this election turned on what Wilson would do with the information conveyed by his election. In practice, Wilson's plurality election compelled him to pursue a new direction for the Democratic Party, which remained tied to the conservative impulses of the Bourbon South.[4] The important point here is that plurality presidents (a category for which the winners in 1856, 1860, 1912, 1968, and 1992 clearly qualify) win under conditions that encourage them to reformulate their parties' respective identities.

If the plurality presidency is not just a function of multicandidate campaigns, neither is it a simple consequence of close races. The more relevant question is, what does a close election suggest about the underlying state of party competition? It certainly suggests that it is *close*, and that any given election can go either way. But it does not necessarily indicate that the winner prevailed in spite of his party's persistent electoral weakness. In turn, it does not necessarily recommend that the winner and his party move in any particular ideological or programmatic direction in order to generate additional support in future contests.

All of this leads us back to the election of 2000. Does George W. Bush qualify as a plurality president? He may be the most difficult historical case to categorize. The 2000 election was indeed quite close. By winning nearly 48 percent of the popular vote, Bush did well enough to suggest that his party remains competitive, if not dominant, in national politics. In addition, continued Republican control of Congress suggested that the party remained viable at that level. Nevertheless, on one count—the nature of significant minor-party insurgencies—the 2000 results suggested that Bush would confront the challenges and opportunities of plurality leadership.

Given the razor-thin margins in key states where Ralph Nader hurt Al Gore, Bush may have won because of Nader's willful departure from the Democratic fold. The presence of Pat Buchanan in the race further complicated matters, but his limited impact rendered his candidacy more or less irrelevant in most observers' postelection interpretations. During the campaign of 2000, at least, Bush fused appeals to his ideological base with self-conscious departures from party orthodoxy, which is a hallmark of savvy plurality leadership. The notion of "compassionate conservatism" fits comfortably within the basic premise of plurality leadership, which recommends subtle revisions to the presidential party's identity.

Two Points of Comparison: The Elections of 1824 and 1992

To get a clearer sense of Bush's legitimacy and leadership situation in historical perspective, we briefly look back to two other presidents. In early 1825, John Quincy Adams prevailed in the House of Representatives after no candidate in the effectively partyless contest of 1824 received a majority of the votes in the Electoral College. Immediately, a defeated Andrew Jackson railed against the "Corrupt Bargain" allegedly struck between Adams and the fourth-place finisher, Speaker of the House Henry Clay.[5] Jackson had won the popular vote by more than 10 percent, and he did not let Adams or the rest of the country forget it. In the ensuing four years, Jackson assembled a potent set of electoral claims rooted largely, though not exclusively, in the presumptive illegitimacy of the Adams's presidency. Ultimately, those claims propelled

Jackson to victory in 1828 and finally secured the enduring connection between the constitutional office of the presidency and the extra-constitutional domain of party politics.

One should not strain the comparison with more than it can bear, but the events of early 1825 are at least roughly analogous to the events of late 2000. In both cases, a popular vote winner was stymied not only by the Electoral College but by the intervention of a co-equal branch of government, and was ultimately forced to concede the election to a bitter rival. For our purposes, however, two key distinctions are more instructive than the similarities between the cases. First, where Andrew Jackson protested his defeat unrelentingly in the mid-1820s, the defeated Al Gore did nothing of the sort in 2000. Second, where John Quincy Adams had no viable, reliable party organization to which he might turn for support, George W. Bush enjoyed the effectively unanimous backing of a vigorous Republican apparatus before, during, and after the Florida controversy. Though it is tempting to think of the latter as a matter of course, the unbridled enthusiasm with which Republican elites advanced Bush's claims in the postelection period requires some elaboration and explanation. Moreover, Gore's dignified concession attracted substantial praise at the time, but, following Jackson's (admittedly remote) precedent, he might have protested a bit more loudly. Why did all of this turn out the way it did? Why, in other words, did Bush encounter so little trouble with the problem of legitimacy in the aftermath of such a hotly contested, highly controversial victory? To begin to answer these questions, one might turn to a more recent election for a second point of comparison.

In 1992, Bill Clinton won a classic plurality election. With a comfortable majority in the Electoral College, the Arkansas governor was the first Democrat to win a presidential election in sixteen years. After more than a decade in the presidential wilderness, many Democrats anticipated a productive era of harmonious unified government. Lost amid the celebration was the essential characteristic of Clinton's triumph: He carried only 43 percent of the popular vote. Like other plurality presidents before him, he won in spite of his party's continuing weakness in presidential politics.[6] More to the point, his election confronted him with three related dilemmas.

First, he encountered an *abstract dilemma of legitimacy.* This is admittedly an expansive concept, and it lacks clear empirical referents, but Republican Senate Minority Leader Bob Dole seemed to know it when he saw it. As soon as the day after Clinton's 1992 election, Dole offered a telling interpretation of that victory: "Fifty-seven percent of the Americans who voted in the presidential election voted against Bill Clinton," Dole intoned from the Senate chamber, "and I intend to represent that majority on the floor of the U.S. Senate." Dole soon adopted a more conciliatory tone (in his public rhetoric, at least) after critics objected to his "rancorous" partisanship, but one can scarcely imagine a more resounding declaration of plurality politics.

Second, he faced a *practical dilemma of governance.* Notwithstanding his lifelong ambitions, Clinton ran in 1992 for reasons larger than his own power prospects. He had in mind a number of means to improve the performance of the national government and, of course, the lives of American citizens. But he recognized that the constitutional system separates institutions and distributes lawmaking authority horizontally among branches and vertically between the federal government and the states. He hoped to enact measures that might give practical meaning to his rhetorical vision, but his limited victory rendered that task uncertain. How would Clinton make this fragmented system do what he wanted it to do? If nearly every member of Congress won a larger share of the popular vote than he did, how might he lead the national legislature with any authority?

Third, he confronted a *political dilemma of reelection.* Perhaps he ran for reasons larger than simple ambition, but the old congressional maxim that one needs to save one's seat before one can save the world applied nicely to Bill Clinton as he assumed the presidency. Clinton clearly intended to run again in 1996, but he could not assume that the peculiar circumstances of his initial victory—especially the significant minor-party insurgency of Ross Perot—would prevail during his bid for reelection. Clinton had to wonder: If he won only four in ten voters the first time, how might he expand his support on the road to reelection?

Though each of these dilemmas related to a specific dimension of presidential politics, they combined to encourage Clinton—and each of his plurality predecessors—to swim upstream against the prevailing ideological and rhetorical currents of his party. In Clinton's case, of course, this incentive structure confirmed the incoming president's inclination to pursue the identity of a "New Democrat." One should note, of course, that Bill Clinton was present at the creation of the centrist Democratic Leadership Council in 1985, later chaired the group, and invoked the New Democrats' holy trinity of opportunity, responsibility, and community as a central theme of his 1992 candidacy (Baer 2000). In a sense, then, the election of 1992 did not turn the incoming president into a New Democrat. But what it did was hugely important: It made a would-be New Democrat the incoming president, placing him at the vital center of the American party system. In addition, it set the stage for an intraparty struggle between Clinton and his centrist allies on the one hand and an array of unreconstructed liberals in Congress and their supporters on the other.

The relationship between Clinton and the Democrats on Capitol Hill is thoroughly fascinating—and worthy of a searching examination—but here we will simply recount the story in outline form to motivate the ensuing discussion of the Bush presidency. As Clinton set out to forge a New Democratic identity, a stable of decidedly Old Democrats—including but not limited to congressional barons such as Senate Majority Leader George Mitchell, Speaker of the House Tom Foley, and House Majority Leader Dick Gephardt—had a rather different party project in mind. On political reform, welfare, trade, and crime, among other issues, the established center of Democratic gravity complicated Clinton's reformist effort. Given the institutional characteristics of the Democratic majorities on Capitol Hill, this is not particularly surprising. After all, Democrats had been winning congressional majorities—often very large ones—for decades. With the exception of the six-year break in the Senate during the early 1980s, the Democrats had enjoyed uninterrupted dominance in Congress since the Eisenhower years. In light of those simple facts—the size and durability of the Democrats' congressional majorities—it is not hard to understand the difficulty Bill Clinton encountered as he sought to push his party toward a new formula for electioneering and governing (Price 2002).

Contrast Clinton's treatment after the 1992 election—outright claims of his illegitimacy from conservatives who could not abide the new president and an uneven welcome from liberals who were unmoved by all the talk of New Democratic politics—with the reception George W. Bush received after his 2000 victory. In the latter case, the incoming president encountered congressional Democrats who were relatively docile and congressional Republicans who were both deeply supportive and broadly unified. Why the difference?

First, and most important, Bush encountered a Republican majority in the 107th Congress that was both narrower and shorter-lived than its Democratic analog of the 103rd. Where many congressional Democrats resisted Clinton's reformist party project, in part because they had little reason to suspect in 1993 that their own electoral prospects turned on the success of that project, many Republicans in 2001 had plenty of reason to believe that preserving their tenuous congressional majorities would depend on the new president's vindication in office. One might note here that the Democrats had gained House seats in every congressional election since 1994; in the Senate, meanwhile, the Democrats had forged a fifty-fifty tie by erasing the Republicans' four-seat advantage in the elections of 2000. In this context, what would demonstrate Bush's legitimacy more clearly than a congressional majority rallying immediately to his side?

The key point here is that the congressional Republicans of 2001 interpreted Bush's 2000 election differently than the congressional Democrats had interpreted Clinton's 1992 election. In the earlier case, Clinton's party was certainly pleased that he had prevailed, but many of his putative allies remained largely unmoved by the New Democratic formula through the 103rd Congress. In Bush's case, on the other hand, Republican elites moved quickly to bolster the new president. One can now place the Bush experience in context alongside these two points of comparison. Where Adams had no real party to which he could turn in 1825, and where Clinton could only turn to a divided (in some ways downright recalcitrant) party in 1993, Bush found in his fellow Republicans just what he needed in 2001.

Second, one might reasonably suspect that Republican elites endowed Bush with the legitimacy that flows from unified partisan support in part because the outcome of the 2000 election was so indeterminate, because the Court's decision in *Bush v. Gore* was likely to be perceived as baldly partisan, and because the entire episode had manifested such willful cynicism on all sides. Because potential charges of illegitimacy were so plausible, and thus the risk of illegitimacy so acute, Bush and the Republicans moved quickly to nullify such charges before the Democrats could get them off the ground. In the aftermath of *Bush v. Gore*, in other words, the Republicans may have suspected that the Democrats would hammer away at the uncertain legitimacy of the incoming Bush administration. To counter that would-be challenge, they circled the partisan wagons and denied that anyone could question the legitimacy of the outcome without treading on treasonous ground.

But a third element in this story remains to be explained: neither Al Gore nor most elite Democrats questioned, at least publicly or loudly, the legitimacy of the Bush presidency. The only notable elite-level protest of the election's outcome took place when members of the Congressional Black Caucus walked out on the vote-counting ceremony in the House of Representatives. Unlike Adams, who faced a bitterly determined Jackson and a budding Democratic juggernaut in the 1820s, and unlike Clinton, who faced a conservative movement that simply never accepted his legitimacy, Bush encountered a relatively quiescent Democratic opposition. Democrats had mobilized behind Gore during the Florida recount, of course, but once the Court stopped that process, they folded the battle flag in a magnanimous spirit of reconciliation. Why were the Democrats so reluctant to depict president-elect Bush—once he officially became such, that is—as somehow less than fully legitimate?

When Gore conceded the election in a nationally televised address on December 13, 2000, he enjoyed a generous reception in the political press. At the conclusion of the wrenching process in Florida, the conventional wisdom suggested that the country could not take any more scorched-earth politics. If the country suffered from Florida fatigue, this line of thinking went, Gore had only one choice once the game was up: concede like a gentleman and move on. Indeed, we suspect that the weight of journalistic opinion, which implied that the only thing less legitimate than a Bush presidency would be an ongoing Democratic protest of it, led Gore and his fellow partisans simply to concede. They decided that playing the legitimacy card would prove more costly than beneficial, in part because establishment opinion simply would not tolerate it.

Another factor in the Democrats' relative quiescence after *Bush v. Gore* was the electoral success of some congressional Democrats in states and districts where Bush had done quite well, and with the balance of power in Congress so precarious, "some" equals "a lot." These Democrats had little trouble in deciding that they had little to gain from a sustained challenge of the fundamental legitimacy of the Bush presidency. Again, the contrast with Adams and Clinton is instructive. In the former case—where Adams won only 31 percent of the popular vote—members of Congress who might challenge the president's legitimacy had little to fear in their own states and districts. In the latter case—where Clinton won with 43 percent of the popular vote—few Republicans hailed from states or districts where Clinton had outpolled them in

1992. In 2000, however, Democrats such as Senators John Breaux of Louisiana, Ben Nelson of Nebraska, Tim Johnson of South Dakota, and Max Baucus of Montana had more to lose than to gain from aggressively partisan charges of illegitimacy against the new administration.

Finally, one must consider a third explanation for the opposition's official reticence after *Bush v. Gore:* Might Democrats simply not play hardball politics as energetically or effectively as Republicans? Consider the aggressive tactics of Newt Gingrich and Tom DeLay, whose nickname—"The Hammer"—just about says it all. In the Clinton years, these Republican leaders not only issued explicit and implicit charges of illegitimacy against the president but also exercised iron-fisted leadership of their fellow partisans in the House of Representatives. We do not want to make too much of this distinction, but it seems that contemporary Democrats simply do not operate with the same tooth-grinding determination. Whether this is a function of the contemporary political cultures in the two parties, of idiosyncratic personalities of partisan leaders in the last several years, or some other set of factors, it strikes us as plausible that the Republicans would have taken a different, much more aggressive approach if *Bush v. Gore* and the recount process had produced a Gore presidency. In that counterfactual event, The Hammer and his allies may not have hesitated to play the legitimacy card for all it was worth.

Two Paths Taken?

We have suggested that George W. Bush entered office facing significant challenges of legitimacy and leadership. We have argued, however, that Bush was well positioned to make the best of these challenges despite his controversial victory and, we suggest, this would have been true even without the events of September 11. Our argument has essentially been that Bush, given his dilemma, benefited from being on favorable historical ground. First, the currents of partisan realignment were favorable to Bush and gave him the kind of support from congressional Republicans that he dearly needed. Second, although Bush's victory resembled those of other plurality presidents, he has only one foot in that category and thus has escaped some of the difficulties facing other presidents who more clearly had both feet in the plurality category. In some ways, Bush seemed to inherit some of the same problems Clinton did eight years earlier, but his election victory was sufficiently different that he was able to read different meaning from his victory than Clinton could divine from his.

In general, then, these two historical stories were parallel and reinforcing regarding the party base for Bush's legitimacy and leadership. Over the course of his term in office, however, they could have pushed Bush down different paths. Were Bush to be more influenced by the realignment story, he might well pursue a bold agenda that seeks to create a solid conservative majority. Certainly one influence here was Karl Rove, Bush's chief campaign strategist and his senior political adviser in the White House. Before the election, Rove was ruminating that the 2000 election could parallel the 1896 election for Republicans. Clearly, he saw signs of potential realignment. By mid-2003, Bush himself was echoing Rove's analysis, telling Republicans around the country that he did not want a "lonely victory" in 2004 but a clear, partisan mandate. Of course, all presidents say something to the same effect, but not all presidents have a chief adviser whose strategy is so guided by the notion of realignment. If he saw himself more in the mold of a plurality president, however, he might be more tempted to straddle party lines, capturing Democratic issues and reshaping his party's identity. Bush's Texas history might push him in this direction. Though clearly conservative, Bush very effectively received support from Democrats on major initiatives and received the votes of many Democrats in his gubernatorial bids. Or he might well attempt both these paths simultaneously.

Surely there are signs that Bush has traveled the first path. The early months of the Bush presidency revealed a president more committed to solidly conservative positions than to the synthetic project he seemed to promise in his campaign. And since the events of September 11, 2001, Bush has pursued a genuinely conservative identity rooted in a worldview grounded in the notion of good versus evil and us versus them, substantially lower taxes, higher defense spending, an increased role for faith-based organizations, eliminating "partial-birth" abortions, arguing against same-sex marriage, pushing for market-oriented reforms of regulation, and promoting a more competitive environment for Medicare and, in potential future action, Social Security. The Bush vision is not the comprehensive or far-reaching conservative vision offered by House Speaker Newt Gingrich and exultant congressional Republicans in 1995, but in its essentials, this approach echoes the formula established by Reagan in nearly every important sense.

Bush has also followed the plurality strategy, taking issues the Democrats had long considered their own and using them to his advantage. This began in the 2000 campaign with Bush's heavy emphasis on the issues of education and Social Security reform. Although the condition of the stock market prevented much movement on the Social Security issue, Bush did sign an education reform bill that received Democratic support, including from Senator Edward Kennedy, perhaps the leading Democrat on this issue. To the consternation of conservatives who denounced it as a huge new welfare-state entitlement program, Bush also energized support behind a version of Medicare reform that, when passed and signed into law, added a prescription drug benefit to the program. The reform is the most substantial in the program's history, costing an estimated $400 billion over ten years, and for the first time Republicans are seen as leading the effort. This was on top of federal spending that had already been increasing during Bush's tenure—midway through his third year, Bush had yet to veto any legislation, spending or otherwise. "Compassionate conservatism" and a pitch to minority voters jelled when Bush pushed for $15 billion of assistance to fight AIDS in Africa. Finally, in expressing acceptance of two Supreme Court decisions in 2003—one of which upheld the use of race in the college admissions process, the other striking down a Texas law concerning homosexual sexual conduct—Bush again surprised conservatives. That the *National Review*, the stalwart periodical on the right, printed an editorial in its July 23, 2003, issue titled "Left Turn: Is the GOP Conservative?" gives some sense of conservative unease at these developments. The *Review* noted that it never expected Bush to be a solid conservative on issues like small government, racial preferences, or immigration, but assumed that he would act conservatively on most matters. Granting Bush a passing grade for national security, judicial appointments, and tax cuts, the *Review* viewed him as unable to deliver on the rest of the conservative agenda.

Which strategic impulse will carry the day as Bush moves through a fourth year and possibly a second term? Will he seek a durable realignment along boldly partisan lines, or will he trim his sails in accordance with our notion of the plurality presidency? We suspect that Bush, Rove, and others at the center of this political project see something like a full-blown realignment as both desirable and plausible. But we expect him to use a variant of plurality leadership to attempt to attain that realignment in 2004 and beyond. In making a few strategic feints to the middle, Bush will not seek to redefine his party, as a classic plurality president would, but will accommodate the Center and the Left as a tactical means of achieving his strategic partisan ambitions. In this process, as in his successful initial efforts to escape his legitimacy problem in 2001, Bush should enjoy the indispensable, though hardly inevitable, support of a broadly unified, deeply committed Republican Party.

II

Popular Politics

4 THE LIKEABLE PARTISAN
George W. Bush and the Transformation of the American Presidency

John Kenneth White and John J. Zogby

Popular presidents get what they want, and unpopular ones don't.

ANONYMOUS U.S. SENATOR

Ever since the horrific events of September 11, 2001, George W. Bush has ranked among the most popular American presidents. Americans admire his strong leadership, especially in the tension-filled days following the terrorist attacks. Just three weeks after Osama bin Laden and his al Qaeda network recreated a twenty-first-century Pearl Harbor on American soil, Bush's job-approval rating in one Gallup poll soared to an astronomical 90 percent, exceeding the previous record of 89 percent posted by George H. W. Bush during the Persian Gulf War (Moore 2001). His high numbers lingered long after September 11 became a day of infamy. One Gallup poll study found that Bush's overall two-year approval rating (2001–2002) averaged 69.3 percent. Only John F. Kennedy registered a higher score with 70.1 percent (Jones 2003).

It was not supposed to be this way. Bush's controversial election gave every indication of introducing another four years of partisan backbiting and gridlock. A poll conducted in the aftermath of the Florida fracas found 58 percent of those surveyed saying the election shambles would make it harder for the new president to keep his campaign promises (*Los Angeles Times* poll, December 14–16, 2000). And a poll taken immediately after the Supreme Court's pronouncement in

Bush v. Gore found an alarming 37 percent who believed that Bush was *not* a legitimate president (Reuters/NBC/Zogby International poll, December 13, 2000). Democratic partisans remain embittered by the manner in which Bush became the nation's forty-third president. Early polls of likely Democratic voters in the all-important 2004 contests in Iowa, New Hampshire, and South Carolina found respondents evenly divided as to whether they liked Bush "as a person" (Zogby International polls, spring 2003).

History teaches that controversial elections usually doom the "winner" to failure. Back in 1824 John Quincy Adams, son of another president, won a bitter contest in the House of Representatives over popular-vote winner Andrew Jackson. Adams's victory came after a deal that Jackson famously derided as a "corrupt bargain" when Adams named former rival Henry Clay to be secretary of state in return for Clay's support in the House. Forty-eight years later, Rutherford B. Hayes prevailed by a one-vote margin in the electoral college over popular-vote winner Samuel J. Tilden. Hayes made his own corrupt bargain for support by removing federal troops from the Old Confederacy.[1] The troops had been stationed there in order to protect the constitutional freedoms granted to its former black slaves after the Civil War. In 1888, Benjamin Harrison, grandson of former president William Henry Harrison, beat Grover Cleveland in the electoral college, even though Cleveland won the popular vote. In this case, only backroom deal-making made Harrison's victory possible. Celebrating on election night, Harrison declared, "Providence has given us the victory." At this, one Republican party boss exclaimed: "Think of the man! He ought to know that Providence hadn't a damn thing to do with it" (Lorant 1951, 405). Of Benjamin Harrison's tenure, the best that can be said is that like so many other ignominious presidents, he, too, once called 1600 Pennsylvania Avenue home.

From the outset, George W. Bush was determined *not* to be one of these forgettable presidents. Fiercely ignoring the election deadlock, Bush governed as though he had won in a landslide. Undoubtedly, Bush was persuaded by political advisor Karl Rove's strongly held view that the 2000 election represented a pivotal turning point that would usher in a new Republican majority. Rove believed the country was overdue for a so-called realigning election. Indeed, most party scholars believe that such political realignments occur once every twenty-eight to thirty-six years, and the last one was the three-way Nixon-Humphrey-

Wallace contest of 1968 (Burnham 1970, passim). Between 1968 and 1988, Republicans won six of the seven presidential elections.[2] Bill Clinton's back-to-back victories broke the Republican lock in the electoral college. But some saw an early precursor of a new era in the 1994 Newt Gingrich–led congressional landslide, which resulted in a GOP takeover of both houses of Congress for the first time since 1952. The Gingrich Revolution also saw Bush defy the odds and win the Texas governorship over a popular incumbent. Bill Clinton's 1996 defeat of Bob Dole—considered by many to be a weak and ineffectual presidential candidate—was judged by Rove to be an aberration in what was increasingly becoming a Republican era. If the political scientists and Rove were correct, then a realigning era should have begun as early as 1994 and crested in 2004.

While political scientists quarreled over whether these elections represented the demarcation of a party realignment that favored the Republicans, Rove saw to it that no matter what happened at the ballot box his boss would govern as a fierce partisan. Rove was determined that, unlike George H. W. Bush, the younger Bush should do nothing to alienate the core Republican base on domestic issues—especially taxes. At the same time, Rove made sure that while Bush would be a tough partisan behind closed doors, he would not strike a harsh tone in public, as Speaker Gingrich had. Indeed, Bush's public persona was friendly. During the 2000 campaign, Bush presented himself as a "compassionate conservative"—the suggestion being, of course, that there was a different type of hard-line, hard-headed conservatism represented by the unpopular Gingrich. As Bush frequently stated in his stump speeches, "I'm a uniter [*sic*], not a divider."

Yet, while Bush presented a friendly public face, he was able to maintain a strong bond with the Republican base. Bush's persona helped, but it was his policies that drove core Republicans so strongly into his camp. During his first few months in office, Bush won approval for a tax cut that was more comprehensive than that achieved by the conservative icon Ronald Reagan twenty years earlier. At an early stage in the tax debate, Bush stubbornly resisted an urge to compromise with congressional Democrats, telling White House Director of Legislative Affairs Nick Calio, "Nicky, we will not negotiate with ourselves, ever" (Brownstein 2003). Conservatives willingly accepted Bush's formula for political success: be a compassionate talker in public, but in private concede nothing when it comes to making policy.

When Vermont senator James Jeffords switched from Republican to independent in May 2001 and control of the Senate fell into Democratic hands, Bush intensified his partisan approach. He frequently got the Republican-controlled House to pass his legislative initiatives without revision, only to see them stymied in the Democratic-controlled Senate. According to a *Congressional Quarterly* analysis of roll-call votes held during Bush's first two years in office, Republicans voted with their party nearly 90 percent of the time, whereas Democrats were nearly as cohesive with an 86 percent solidarity rating (Brownstein 2003).

While Bush solidified his relationship with the Republican base, Americans continued to express doubts about his domestic agenda. His health-care, environmental, and economic proposals were negatively rated by a skeptical public. According to a July 2003 poll, only 36 percent of respondents gave Bush positive marks for his handling of health care, whereas 61 percent expressed a negative opinion. His marks on other domestic issues were hardly better: environment, 31 percent positive, 65 percent negative; taxes, 45 percent positive, 54 percent negative; jobs and the economy, 33 percent positive, 66 percent negative (Zogby International poll, July 16–17, 2003). Even as Bush succeeded in getting Congress to pass a second round of tax cuts in 2003, there were growing doubts as to whether these reductions would do much to improve a sluggish economy. According to a June 2003 poll, just 8 percent said they would benefit "a lot" from another tax cut; 51 percent answered "only a little;" and 34 percent said "not at all" (Harris poll, June 10–15, 2003).

Thus, Bush's brand of "compassionate conservatism" was hardly producing the kind of political revolution either at the ballot box or in the polls that the party realignment theorists expected. On the eve of the September 11, 2001, terrorist attacks, the country remained as divided as it had been in the Bush-Gore contest. In an August 2001 poll, only 50 percent gave Bush positive marks, whereas 49 percent rated his performance as fair or poor (Zogby International poll, August 27, 2001). Seen from another perspective, Bush received 48 percent of the vote in the 2000 election, and after just eight months in office he added only two points to his score, whereas Gore (if you count Bush's disapproval numbers as likely Gore votes) toted one additional point. Furthermore, an August 2001 poll found that if the 2000 election were rerun, the outcome would be another dead heat: 48 percent for Bush, 48 percent for Gore (CNN/*USA Today*/Gallup poll, August 3–5, 2001). Finally, when asked whether the country should go in the direction Bush wanted to lead it or take the course offered by congressional Democrats, the result was another deadlock: 42 percent liked Bush's direction; 43 percent preferred the Democratic road (*ABC News / Washington Post* poll, July 26–30, 2001). Realignment advocates notwithstanding, Bush had done little to unite the country around his governing agenda. He was likeable, but not many agreed with him on key issues.

A Presidency Transformed

September 11 changed everything. After the smoke cleared and the ashes from the World Trade Center and Pentagon were swept away, Bush's approval ratings zoomed. Henceforth and forevermore, Americans were hardly in a mood to look back at a controversial election that paled in insignificance to the trauma the country had suffered. Even the vanquished Al Gore now referred to Bush as "my commander-in-chief," telling a muted audience of Iowa Democrats: "Regardless of party, regardless of ideology, there are no divisions in this country where our response to terrorism is concerned" (Balz 2001). The country needed a strong president, and following a dramatic appearance at the ruins of the World Trade Center, along with a powerful address to a joint session of Congress, Bush filled the role. Few had feelings of buyer's remorse. A poll taken less than a week after the terrorist attacks found 67 percent saying they did *not* believe the nation would be better served if Al Gore were president (Zogby International poll, September 17–18, 2001). Similar percentages were happy that Clinton was no longer in office and that Dick Cheney rather than Joe Lieberman was vice president (Zogby International poll, October 8–10, 2001). Looking ahead, one poll found Bush trouncing Gore in a hypothetical 2004 match-up by a gargantuan 26 percentage points (Gallup poll, November 2–4, 2001).

For Bush, the terrorist attacks thrust his heretofore unremarkable (and, according to Bush speech writer David Frum, failing) presidency deep into the long arms of history (Frum 2003b). Like other presidents whose tenures have been defined by historic challenges, Bush realized that his response to this new strain of international terrorism would define his presidency. Publicly, he declared that overcoming the dangers posed by Osama bin Laden and his cohorts "is the purpose of my administration" (Bruni 2001c). Indeed, the shedding of so much blood on American soil gave Bush an unparalleled opportunity to seize Theodore

Roosevelt's famed "bully pulpit." No longer would *Time* issue a cover with the headline, "The Incredible Shrinking Presidency," as it did in the waning days of the elder Bush's presidency (*Time* 1992). The transformation of the chief magistrate from insignificance—recall Clinton's response when an inquiring MTV reporter wondered what sort of underwear Clinton wore, "Briefs, usually" (Kerbel 1995, 1)—into near-imperial status was well suited to Bush's *Father Knows Best* persona. Conservative commentator Andrew Sullivan once likened the Bush-Cheney governing style to a 1950s Hallmark card: "The model of their masculinity is definitely retro—stern dads in suits and ties, undemonstrative, matter-of-fact, but with alleged hearts of gold" (Sullivan 2001). The secrecy needed to pursue the Afghanistan war, along with the demise of any opposition from the Democrats, accentuated this aspect of Bush's personality and dampened his instinct to stiffen when challenged.

Americans embraced Bush's *Father Knows Best* persona in the immediate aftermath of the terrorist attacks. The two nations that were so evident on election night 2000—as seen in the red states supporting Bush and the blue states that sided with Gore—mutated in the days following the attacks into the red, white, and blue of the American flag. A Democratic consultant captured the prevailing bipartisanship: "I actually went into church and knelt down and prayed that [Bush would] be successful. He's ours. He's all we've got. Pray God that he's going to do what's best for our country" (Dionne 2003). That Bush could achieve this sense of national unity around his persona surprised both pundits and voters alike. Leaving the polls on election day 2000, just 55 percent thought Bush could handle a world crisis, whereas 64 percent thought Gore capable (Voter News Services exit poll, November 7, 2000). By February 2003, 69 percent believed Bush showed "good judgment in a crisis"—numbers buoyed by a strong performance in the days following September 11 and by Bush's subsequent decision to go to war with Iraq (*Los Angeles Times* poll, January 30–February 2, 2003). In a July 2003 poll, Bush continued to enjoy high marks for his handling of the terrorist threat: 59 percent gave him a favorable rating; 40 percent were negative (Zogby International poll, July 16–17, 2003).

As Bush cast the war on terror as a fight to preserve freedom, individual rights, and equality of opportunity, the public came to identify him as a guardian of these sacred American values. According to a February 2003 poll, 58 percent agreed with the statement that Bush "shares the values that you hold important" (*Los Angeles Times* poll, January 30–

February 2, 2003). Moreover, a June 2003 poll found that 57 percent of respondents agreed with the statement, "He cares about the needs of people like you" (CNN/*USA Today*/Gallup poll, June 27–29, 2003). This is a remarkably high number, given that the Great Depression gave the Democratic Party a lock on the "he/she cares" partisan dimension of politics and that the economy was performing so poorly (*Los Angeles Times* poll, January 30–February 2, 2003).

Republicans benefited from Bush's hold on the public imagination. A poll taken just prior to the 2002 midterm elections found 52 percent chose the GOP as the party best able to deal with terrorism; only 20 percent picked the Democrats (*CBS News/New York Times* poll, October 27–31, 2002). These favorable numbers—coupled with Karl Rove's decision to make the midterm contest a referendum on Bush's handling of homeland security—translated into a historic Republican victory and rekindled hopes of a party realignment. Republicans added seven seats to their majority in the House, and won 53 percent of the popular vote to the Democrats' 47 percent (Sailer 2002). The Republican victory was made even sweeter in the Senate, where the GOP returned to power with a fifty-one to forty-eight majority. Even at the state level, Republicans defied the pundits by winning 53 percent of the votes cast in gubernatorial contests. Democratic pickups—which had been expected in light of the poor economy and several unpopular Republican incumbents—were limited to three statehouses. Equally impressive were the 180 state legislative seats the Republicans gained—thereby expanding to twenty-one the number of state legislatures under their control, while Democrats' held onto seventeen.

Although the Democrats had won a surprising midterm victory four years earlier—thanks to a backlash against the Republicans at the height of the Clinton-Lewinsky scandal—the GOP victory in 2002 was more impressive, because it was centered on issues—terrorism and homeland security—that were likely to dominate politics for years to come. Indeed, not since 1934, when the Democrats won additional congressional seats during the New Deal party realignment led by Franklin D. Roosevelt, had there been such a resounding triumph. Bush was buoyed by the results because these cumulative Republican victories signified belated ballots that ratified his "election" as president. Unlike the scorned presidents of yesteryear who had won controversial victories, Bush was now a political colossus and a man to be reckoned with in the newly Republican-dominated Capitol. One anonymous senator summarized the situation: "Popular presidents get what they want, and unpopular ones don't" (Dewar 2003a). But it quickly became apparent that Bush would be constrained by the reemergence of the "two presidencies."

The Return of the Two Presidencies

During the 1960s, political scientist Aaron Wildavsky developed a concept that became known as the "two presidencies." This idea maintains that there is a foreign policy president, who presides over a vast defense and national security apparatus and is fairly unfettered, and a domestic president, who succumbs to the frustrations of having high-priority initiatives rejected by a recalcitrant Congress. The Cold War gave ample proof to Wildavsky's claim that the foreign policy president had a monopoly on the flow of information, could at a moment's notice move vast numbers of U.S. troops around the globe, and was aided by late-twentieth-century technological advances that enhanced his ability to act decisively. Wildavsky noted that given these superior resources presidents often used their otherwise scarce powers to achieve long-lasting foreign policy achievements: "Presidents have to be oriented toward the future in the use of their resources. They serve a fixed term in office, and they cannot automatically count on support from the populace, Congress, or the administrative apparatus. They have to be careful, therefore, to husband their resources for pressing future needs. But because the consequences of events in foreign affairs are potentially more grave, faster to manifest themselves, and less easily reversible than in domestic affairs, presidents are more willing to use up their resources" (Wildavsky 1966, 25).

Nixon's presidency provided ample proof for Wildavsky's thesis. As the Vietnam War waged without end, Nixon easily thwarted numerous congressional attempts to stop funding the unpopular conflict. Nixon maintained that without funds U.S. soldiers would be stranded in the Southeast Asian rice paddies without a bullet. In 1972, after Nixon briskly told congressional leaders of "a decision I have had to make" concerning the mining of North Vietnamese harbors, veteran Republican legislator Leslie Arends lamented, "There's no change in the pattern. I've yet to sit in on one of these conferences and hear the president say: 'What do you think we ought to do?'" (Hughes 1973, 258). Congress made a feeble attempt to put limits on the foreign policy president by reversing Nixon's veto of the 1973 War Powers Resolution, which every president since—including Bush—has ignored.

Bush's presidency has seen the return of Wildavsky's "two presidency" thesis. Amid misgivings, Congress voted in October of 2002 to give Bush the authority to attack Saddam Hussein's Iraq at a time of his choosing. The only proviso contained in the congressional resolution required Bush to report to Congress on the war's progress at sixty-day intervals—something Bush happily accepted, since "major combat operations" proved to be short, even though the U.S. later risked becoming bogged down in another Vietnam-like guerilla conflict. Despite this blank check, the resolution won strong bipartisan support—including votes from prominent Democrats such as Tom Daschle, Dick Gephardt, John Kerry, John Edwards, Joseph Lieberman, and Hillary Rodham Clinton.[3]

On the other hand, Wildavsky's domestic president often had to yield to an array of special interests and local considerations that stymied administration initiatives. The exceptions were rare and include the following:

- Woodrow Wilson's command of an unusual Democratic congressional majority after his 1912 victory.
- Franklin D. Roosevelt's first hundred days following his landslide win over Republican Herbert Hoover in the midst of the Great Depression.
- The aftermath of John F. Kennedy's 1963 assassination and Lyndon Johnson's breathtaking defeat of Republican Barry Goldwater in 1964.
- The brief honeymoon that Ronald Reagan enjoyed in 1981 following an unsuccessful assassination attempt.
- The national unity George W. Bush achieved in the days following the terrorist attacks of September 11, 2001.

Only in such unique circumstances were presidents briefly able to suspend the laws of gravity that normally brought their domestic agendas crashing to earth. The failures of Franklin Roosevelt's court-packing plan, John F. Kennedy's civil rights programs, Jimmy Carter's energy initiative, and Bill and Hillary Clinton's health-care reform plans illustrate how hard it is for presidents to engineer major changes in domestic policy. Indeed, the domestic president has but one great power: saying "No!" by vetoing whatever odious legislation may arrive on the president's desk.

The terrorist attacks of September 11 signaled a return to Wildavsky's "two presidency" model. On matters that had a foreign policy emphasis, Bush won broad congressional support. Soon after the tragedy, Congress approved the U.S.A. Patriot Act, which gave the federal government broad powers to detain noncitizens, wiretap cell phones, intercept e-mails, and monitor Internet usage.[4] Congress also approved the creation of the Transportation Security Agency, which would screen airline passengers, replacing the private security agencies the airlines had previously used to perform this task. Bush initially opposed the legislation but quickly got onboard after the public demanded that the federal government assume this responsibility. Finally, Bush won approval for the creation of the Department of Homeland Security, the largest reorganization of a president's cabinet since the Defense Department was created in 1947. Democrats complained that transferring federal employees into the new department was unfair, since their existing union protections would be lost. Bush made the Democratic objections a campaign issue. Georgia Democrat Max Cleland, for one, got caught in the crossfire. Cleland, a highly decorated veteran who lost three limbs in Vietnam, lost his Senate seat to Republican Saxby Chambliss due to this issue. Soon thereafter, Congress bowed to Bush and approved the creation of a Homeland Security Department.

These were impressive victories. But on the domestic front, popular support for Bush lagged considerably. While Americans gave Bush high marks for his handling of terrorism, they also believed that his domestic priorities were skewed toward the rich and powerful. According to a survey in January 2003, 52 percent said that Bush's national priorities were not the same as theirs (*CBS News/New York Times* poll, January 19–23, 2003). Bush's domestic vulnerability was underscored following the invasion of Iraq: 43 percent said he deserved to be reelected, whereas 49 percent wanted someone new in the White House. In a match-up against a hypothetical Democrat, 41 percent supported Bush (the same figure he received in 2000); 41 percent backed the unnamed Democrat (Zogby International poll, November 3–5, 2003). A political rule of thumb has it that anytime the number of voters who want to reelect the president falls below the magic 50 percent mark—that president is in a heap of political trouble.

Certainly, the soaring federal budget deficits further crimped Bush's ability to be an innovative domestic president. Prior to the invasion of Iraq, the federal deficit for the month of February 2003 was a stunning $96.3 *billion.* These numbers pointed to a worsening fiscal picture. During the first five months of the 2003 budget year (which began the previous October), the budget shortfall amounted to $193.9 *billion* (Aversa 2003). Later estimates put the deficit for fiscal year 2003 at a stunning $455 billion and rising the following year to a budget-busting $475 billion. The previous record was the $290 billion deficit recorded at the end of the first Bush administration in 1992 (Rosenbaum 2003). Future forecasts are equally dire: the Office of Management and Budget has projected the new federal debt to total *$1.9 trillion* between 2003 and 2008 (Weisman 2003c).

Bush cited the war on terror and a stagnant economy as primary reasons for the huge deficits, but Democrats countered that Bush's tax cuts were to blame. Presidential candidate Howard Dean spoke for many in his party: "This is the most fiscally irresponsible president since Herbert Hoover. Republicans don't balance budgets anymore. Democrats do" (Nagourney 2003b). Some polls found the Democrats gaining traction on this issue. According to a March 2003 poll, for example, 65 percent of respondents supported reducing Bush's tax cut (*ABC News/Washington Post* poll, March 27, 2003). At the same time the Republican-controlled Senate was trimming the second Bush tax cut, it also blocked the president's plan to drill for oil and gas in the Arctic National Wildlife Refuge. These Senate defeats occurred in the early phases of the war in Iraq and came despite Bush's elevated job-approval ratings.

As the two major parties resumed their squabbling, state and local government officials faced massive deficits and the prospect of either cutting popular programs or increasing taxes. Most opted to do some of both, and many were angry that monies promised by the Bush administration to help "first responders" (that is, police and fire departments) to meet the terrorist threats at home were not readily forthcoming. Moreover, the ongoing controversy surrounding the war in Iraq (including the failure to find weapons of mass destruction), coupled with bad economic news, transformed the picture of Bush from the symbol of national unity he became after September 11, 2001, back to the partisan president he had been the day before. In a November 2003 poll, just 48 percent approved of Bush's job performance and 52 percent disapproved (Zogby International poll, November 3–5, 2003). These figures were nearly identical to Bush's ratings prior to September 11.

The Fifty-Something President

Third years of presidential terms are often difficult. In late 1963, Kennedy's approval rating dipped to 58 percent due to his support for civil rights legislation (Gallup poll, November 8–13, 1963). Kennedy's stance was especially unpopular in the South and he traveled to Dallas, Texas, on that fateful November day to shore up his sagging public support. Compounding Kennedy's troubles was an October poll done by his pollster Louis Harris that showed him losing to former vice president Nixon 39 percent to 54 percent (Louis Harris poll, October 1963).

Lyndon B. Johnson also suffered from third-year blues. Following his victory against Republican Barry Goldwater in 1964, Johnson presciently forecast his political future: "I was just elected by the biggest popular margin in the history of the country, fifteen million votes. Just by the natural way people think and because Barry Goldwater scared the hell out of them, I have already lost two of these fifteen and am probably getting down to thirteen. If I get into any fight with Congress, I have already lost another couple of million, and if I have to send any more boys into Vietnam, I may be down to eight million by the end of the summer" (Evans and Novak 1968, 514–15). By 1967, Johnson's prophesy came to pass—and then some—as the stalemate in Vietnam tried the public's patience and alienated many Democrats. Only 46 percent of LBJ's fellow Americans approved of his performance, and he was receiving just 40 percent of the vote in a prospective race against Nixon (Gallup poll, December 7–12, 1967).

Nixon, too, suffered from the third-year doldrums. By 1971, Johnson's war in Vietnam had become Nixon's war. The economy was also plagued by an unusual phenomena economists termed "stagflation"—a persistently high unemployment *and* inflation rate. At the end of 1971, Nixon's job rating stood at just 50 percent (Gallup poll, December 10–13, 1971). And in a hypothetical three-way race with Democrat Edmund S. Muskie and independent George C. Wallace, Nixon received 42 percent; Muskie, 42 percent; and Wallace, 11 percent (Louis Harris and Associates poll, December 28, 1971–January 4, 1972). Victory was far from certain, compelling Nixon and his reelection team to engage in the Watergate shenanigans that prematurely ended his presidency in 1974.

Carter likewise had trouble in his third year, as American hostages were seized in Iran, and Carter's so-called misery index—the combination of inflation and unemployment—remained stubbornly high. In November 1979, prior to the hostage taking, only 38 percent liked the way Carter was doing his job. Moreover, in a Carter-Reagan contest, the incumbent received just 50 percent support to Reagan's 40 percent (Gallup poll, November 16–19, 1979). Clearly, Carter was well on his way to becoming a one-term president.

George H. W. Bush also had his third-year woes. Although he led the United States to victory in the Persian Gulf War in early 1991, the recession deepened, and by year's end fellow Republican Patrick J. Buchanan threw his hat into the GOP presidential primaries. Bush's stratospheric 89 percent approval rating early in the year dropped to a perilous 47 percent. Meanwhile, an astounding 75 percent thought the country was on the wrong track (Wirthlin Group poll, December 19–22, 1991). Those Democrats who exited the presidential race early in 1991 thinking that the elder Bush was unbeatable regretted their decisions, and Clinton was poised to seize the opportunity fate placed in his hands.

Clinton, too, had his third-year blues, following the devastating Democratic losses in the 1994 midterm elections. At a famous 1995 press conference, Clinton asserted that he remained "relevant" to the goings-on in Washington, D.C. (Office of the Press Secretary 1995). By year's end, only 51 percent said they approved of Clinton's job performance; 44 percent disapproved (CNN/*USA Today*/Gallup poll, December 15–18, 1995). Though his numbers would improve as the election year wore on, Clinton was held to 49 percent of the vote the following November in his race against Republican Bob Dole.

Only Reagan defied recent history, as his approval ratings rose throughout calendar year 1983. In January, only 38 percent said they liked the way Reagan was doing his job (Gallup poll, January 17–19, 1983). But by year's end an improving economy boosted his rating to 54 percent (Gallup poll, December 9–12, 1983). Reagan was headed to a landslide victory over Democrat Walter F. Mondale.

Like most of his predecessors, Bush has been subject to these rhythms of history. After the fall of Baghdad, only 45 percent of those polled thought the country was headed on the right track, and 48 percent thought otherwise (Zogby International poll, November 3–5, 2003). Meanwhile, Bush remained a polarizing figure: 86 percent of Republicans gave him high marks, whereas 79 percent of Democrats disapproved of his performance. Of some comfort to Bush and his supporters was the 59 percent positive rating he received from independents (see table 4.1).

Bush's third-year woes were compounded by the continued sniping at U.S. and coalition forces in Iraq. The mounting casualties contributed to a growing public uneasiness about continued U.S. involvement in that country. According to a *Washington Post/ABC News* poll, eight in ten respondents were concerned that the United States "will get bogged down in a long and costly peacekeeping mission" in Iraq (Broder 2003b). And a *CBS News* survey found just 45 percent saying that the United States is in control of events there (Broder 2003b). An ongoing controversy about whether Bush knowingly lied to the country when he referred in his 2002 State of the Union address to a British intelligence report claiming Saddam Hussein had attempted to purchase uranium from Niger intensified the political partisanship. Fifty-six percent said the Bush administration hid important elements of what they knew or were lying regarding Iraq's alleged weapons of mass destruction (Broder 2003b).

In many ways, the renewed partisanship following Saddam Hussein's demise mirrored the 2000 election results. The East was less likely to support Bush, while the South remained a bastion of Bush (and GOP) support. The Midwest remained competitive, but out West, despite Democratic governor Gray Davis's recall, Democrats still claimed California as their own. Other electoral divisions associated with the Bush-Gore contest have also begun to reappear. In polls testing Bush against a hypothetical Democrat, whites strongly favor Bush, whereas blacks remain overwhelmingly hostile toward him. Hispanics are a source of serious competition between the two parties, and Bush may be making some important headway with this key constituency. As table 4.1 shows, just 42 percent of Hispanics approve of Bush's job performance; however, in a hypothetical race against an unnamed Democrat, Bush wins 42 percent of the Hispanic vote. This is important because back in 2000, Bush received just 35 percent of the Hispanic vote (Voter News Service exit poll, November 7, 2000). As Bush pollster Matthew Dowd has noted, if Bush were to win the same percentage of Hispanics in 2004 as he did four years earlier, he would fall three million votes short of a majority in the popular vote, rather than the half-million deficit he experienced in 2000 (Kiefer 2001).

Despite some encouraging signs for Bush, other indicators suggest that Bush continues to be seen as a likeable though divisive partisan

TABLE 4.1

George W. Bush's Approval Rating, July 2003

Demographic group	*Job approval rating (%)* *Excellent/ good*	*Fair/ poor*	*Demographic group*	*Job approval rating (%)* *Excellent/ good*	*Fair/ poor*
Republican	86	14	18–24	29	71
Democrat	21	79	25–34	58	42
Independent	59	39	35–54	58	42
White	57	43	55–69	49	51
African American	39	61	70+	53	46
Hispanic	42	57	Less than high school graduate	43	57
Male	56	44	High school graduate	53	47
Female	51	49	Some college	61	38
Married	59	41	College graduate or postgraduate	50	50
Single	46	54	Less than $15,000 yearly income	43	55
Children under age 17 living at home	61	39	$15,000–$25,000	37	63
No children under age 17 living at home	50	49	$25,000–$35,000	59	39
Catholic	52	47	$35,000–$50,000	54	46
Protestant	63	37	$50,000–$75,000	53	47
Born-again	71	29	$75,000 +	54	46
Not born-again	53	46	Consider self to be a member of the investor class	61	38
Attend church weekly	63	37	Do not consider oneself to be a member of the investor class	50	50
Never attend church	30	70	Country is headed in the right direction	88	12
Liberal	21	78	Country is on the wrong track	13	86
Moderate	49	51			
Conservative	83	17			
East	51	49			
South	60	39			
Central Great Lakes	52	47			
West	48	52			

Source: Zogby International poll, July 16–17, 2003.

figure. One reason for this is his inability to overcome lifestyle differences among Americans that have contributed to a growing values divide (White 2002). For example, those families with children under the age of seventeen living at home are strongly pro-Bush, whereas those without children living at home are considerably less supportive. This is important because for the first time in U.S. history, according to the 2000 census, the number of Americans living alone surpassed those who were married with children (Cohn 2001). Likewise, there are strong differences of opinion between people who are married and people who are not: those who are married tend to like Bush and give him high job-approval ratings, whereas those who are single give him much lower marks. Religion, too, divides the country: two-thirds of those who participate in weekly church services strongly support Bush, but less than one-third of those who never attend back him (see table 4.1).

Some years ago, Richard Scammon and Ben Wattenberg described the "real majority" in American politics as being "un-young, un-poor, and un-black." (Scammon and Wattenberg 1970, 45–58). Today, Bush is performing well with Scammon and Wattenberg's real majority. The problem is that this once-formidable real majority is now an electoral *minority*. Meanwhile, Bush's partisanship both at home and abroad has intensified the Democratic antipathy toward him. California senator Dianne Feinstein captured the feelings of her Democratic colleagues: "There is a kind of noblesse oblige, a sense that he knows best and we should all just fall into line. I do not believe he takes the United States Senate seriously at all" (Dewar 2003a). Louisiana's Mary Landrieu agrees: "For Democrats who were trying to work with the president on national security issues and support a more hawkish stand than might seem natural for a Democrat, this president discounts it, ignores it, and acts as if it's not relevant," adding, "Unfortunately, the president has earned this polarization. It hasn't just happened. He pushed it to happen" (Dionne 2003). Rhode Island Republican Lincoln Chafee notes that Bush's partisan approach has made life in the Senate difficult: "On so many issues, they [the Bush administration] just pound the wedge in" (Bai 2003, 32). But Chafee hardly spoke for his party, as most rank-and-file Republicans elevated Bush to the equivalent of political sainthood. According to surveys conducted by the *Los Angeles Times*, Bush's extraordinary high approval ratings among Republicans exceed those garnered by Reagan (Brownstein 2003).

As the 2004 contest commenced, Democrats' dislike of the war and their concerns about the economy contributed mightily to their alienation from Bush and made for what can best be described as a "Goldwater moment." Back in 1964, Barry M. Goldwater sought to distance himself from "me-too Republicans," who often uttered their support for Democratic programs, by offering himself as "A Choice, Not an Echo." Today, Democrats seem hell-bent on finding a presidential candidate who will draw a sharp contrast with the partisan Bush. When Democrats are asked, for example, whether they prefer hypothetical candidate *A*—"who opposes the president's tax cut plan because it favors the rich and says that under Bush this country is facing a class struggle between the superrich, who are favored by this administration, and regular, hardworking Americans"—or candidate *B*—"who also dislikes the president's tax cut and would like to remove some of the provisions, like elimination of taxes on stock dividends, but generally avoids talk about a class struggle"—candidate *A* wins decisively, 57 percent to 35 percent (Zogby International poll, March 5–7, 2003). Former Vermont governor Howard Dean has taken advantage of this Goldwater moment. In his stump speeches before large crowds of interested voters, Dean woos the party faithful by making the following case for his nomination: "The only hope Democrats have left to beat this president is to behave like Democrats and stand up for what we believe!" (Nieves 2003).

This intense partisan bickering has made Bush a "fifty-something" president—someone who is often able to win 50 percent support—but little more—in a polarized country. Given the heightened partisanship in Washington, D.C.—a partisanship that reflects the deep issue and cultural lifestyle differences between the two major parties—Bush remains politically vulnerable. Not surprisingly, when a poll conducted in March 2003 paired Bush against specific Democratic opponents, his numbers hovered at the 50 percent mark (table 4.2). With the exceptions of Joseph Lieberman and Dick Gephardt, the votes received by the Democratic contenders have little significance since they remain largely unknown.

TABLE 4.2

George W. Bush versus the Democratic Candidates, 2004

George W. Bush 52%	Howard Dean 31%	George W. Bush 49%	John Kerry 36%
George W. Bush 51%	John Edwards 32%	George W. Bush 50%	Joseph Lieberman 38%
George W. Bush 50%	Richard Gephardt 38%	George W. Bush 58%	Al Sharpton 25%
George W. Bush 50%	Bob Graham 32%	George W. Bush 52%	Dennis Kucinich 26%

Source: Zogby International poll, March 14–15, 2003.

The final resolution of the war in Iraq and the course of the nation's economy remain uncharted. What is clear is that, unlike his predecessors who won bitterly contested elections after losing the popular vote, George W. Bush will not be remembered as having merely occupied the White House. Rather, historians are likely to conclude that his policies shaped the political debate for many years. Certainly, the war against terrorism will be an important part of the American experience for the rest of this decade, even as the effectiveness of our response remains in doubt. So, too, will the lingering effects of the Bush economic plan be felt for years to come. History will judge this administration's successes and failures. But an important interim critique will occur on November 2, 2004, when Americans will once more go to the polls and answer the question, Who will be our next president?

5 GEORGE W. BUSH AND WILLIAM J. CLINTON
The Hedgehog and the Fox

John F. Harris

George W. Bush rarely mentioned the incumbent president's name on the 2000 campaign trail, nor did he need to. With one oft-repeated phrase—a pledge to "restore honor and dignity to the White House"—he defined himself preeminently by who he was not, a message that was unmistakable to voters without his uttering the name *Bill Clinton.* After eight years of remorseless battle in the nation's capital over Clinton's programs, style, and personal conduct, even many voters who happened to like Clinton nodded appreciatively at Bush's promise to "change the tone in Washington."

The Republican nominee's low regard for Clinton, it should be noted, was reciprocated from Clinton's side with a certain casual disdain. Though Clinton likewise rarely mentioned the other fellow by name, presidential aides and confidants in 2000 quite freely shared his view of Bush as the quintessential coaster—an incurious man who did not work hard and who seemed to regard the White House as a kind of inheritance from the Republican Party generally and from his family specifically. Yet Clinton's scant regard for Bush the person did not preclude a healthy respect for Bush the politician. Do not underestimate this man, Clinton was telling fellow Democrats as early as 1999. Far from a dullard, Bush was a shrewd man, Clinton believed, with a message that could resonate. That message, as Clinton heard it, was to take conservative Republican ideology and dress it up in centrist language to make it sound like something Clinton might say. High praise indeed in Clinton's book.

And so Clinton was among the first to grasp an intriguing irony at the heart of the relationship between the nation's forty-second president and its forty-third. Two leaders who did not much like each other find themselves inextricably linked in popular discourse—each man taking definition in the public mind through contrast with the other. Their reputations often rise and fall in inverse proportion. In the aftermath of September 11, 2001, when Bush won praise for his purposeful response to the terrorist attacks against the United States, there was a wave of critical inquiries into how Clinton handled the rising terrorist threat. Later, as Bush's march to war against Iraq fanned anti-Americanism in Europe and elsewhere, critics of the incumbent president compared this to the extraordinary popularity that Clinton engendered abroad in the later years of his presidency.

The two leaders share some important similarities. They are the same age, both were educated in the Ivy League, and both managed, with a certain amount of artful maneuver, to avoid service in Vietnam. They are both buoyant, optimistic people, both religiously observant, with a keen understanding of the role of faith in the public square. And both are consummately political men who face the same essential challenge: How to lead political parties dominated by ideological activists while still presenting themselves as sensible, problem-solving pragmatists to the growing mass of independent and largely apolitical voters on whom presidential elections swing?

Still, it is the differences between the two men that pack more political energy. Bush is a scion of a political dynasty; Clinton grew up in family barely clinging to the middle class. Clinton was plotting his path to the presidency from the time he was a teenager; Bush entered electoral politics in 1994, when he was 48, after a booze-soaked extended adolescence that showed scant promise for leadership. In many ways, the two men are a kind of political Rorschach test: Voters who admired Clinton's cosmopolitanism, his intellectuality, and his smooth Southern cadences find Bush's moralizing and his often astonishing inarticulateness a constant affront. Voters who found Clinton slick and equivocating find reassurance in Bush's guttural certitudes.

The comparisons between Clinton and Bush are irresistible not only to voters but to any student of the modern presidency. The Bush leadership model, however, remains blurred in journalistic and academic commentary alike. One popular view of Bush, which held sway especially in the opening phases of his presidency, portrays him as "more Clintonesque than Clinton"—presiding over a White House that voraciously consumes polling data and willingly trades its ostensible principles when there is political advantage to be gained (Harris 2001b). By 2003, another view of Bush, quite at odds with the first, began to gain in currency. Politically, said Bill Keller in an influential *New York Times* profile, this son of a president is "not Daddy's Boy, he's Reagan Jr." That is, he is fixated not just on personal success but is determined to remake the nation's ideological landscape. Like Reagan, Bush is dismissed by Washington elites as a genial but dim man even as he moves steadfastly toward purposes far more ambitious than his opponents ever supposed (Keller 2003a). Steven E. Schier offers a more academic statement of this same thesis in this volume's introduction. Bush's methodical pursuit of a clarifying showdown with Saddam Hussein's regime in Iraq—following several years in which Clinton preferred to live with the ambiguity of containment—reinforced a picture of a leader motivated by inner certitude and drawn to bold actions.

How to reconcile these competing notions of Bush—the president of cynical calculation versus the president of righteous conviction? Though in tension, these interpretations are not necessarily mutually exclusive. Bush does indeed use Clintonesque political tactics to pursue Reaganesque goals. The mystery, still unsolved after his third year in office, is what informs his decisions about when to strike boldly and when to find compromise. Is there a clear method, or simply artful improvisation? Yet the outlines of an answer, however tentative, are coming into view. They suggest if not an explicit method at least some recognizable signatures of how Bush balances his desire to advance a bold and ideologically charged agenda with his desire for political survival and success with a largely nonideological electorate.

The Bush enigma can be illuminated by comparing him with the man who came just before. Among the most salient questions:

– To what extent does Bush borrow, as Clinton believes, from his predecessor's political techniques? There are notable points of overlap in the Clinton and Bush political operations, suggesting Clinton fundamentally altered the way modern presidencies operate, particularly in their use of polling data to coordinate politics and policy.

– Clinton's presidency was marked by investigations and a steady barrage of reporting and commentary on a multitude of ethical and policy controversies; Bush has largely avoided similar uproars. What explains this? The American Left, for the moment, does not have the single-minded zeal, nor the organization, nor the ability to use the investigative apparatus of independent counsels and congressional committees to harass and distract Bush in the fashion that the Right pursued Clinton.
– Clinton's first two years were marked by a huge policy failure with the demise of comprehensive health-care reform, followed swiftly by a historical electoral repudiation with the Republican takeover of Congress in the 1994 midterm elections. Bush's first two years were marked by passage of the leading items on his domestic agenda, a tax cut and an education reform bill, and culminated in historically significant gains for his party in Congress. Why did Clinton, an experienced and articulate politician, stumble, while Bush, who came into office facing doubts about his legitimacy and his personal depth, soared? This president moved with greater discipline and sure-footedness than Clinton and faced a more favorable political climate for his objectives both in Washington and the country at large.
– What are the differences in their assumptions and decision-making styles in foreign policy? The terrorist attacks against the United States on September 11, 2001, helped prompt the most dramatic reorientation of American foreign policy since the end of World War II. But the attacks were not the sole cause of these stark shifts in style and priorities. The conflict in Iraq displays the differing worldviews in sharp relief. Both Clinton and Bush used similar language to describe the threat posed by Saddam Hussein's weapons of mass destruction. But as both contemplated the reality of widespread international opposition abroad to confronting Iraq, Clinton's mind gravitated instinctively to the risks of a frayed international consensus, while Bush's mind gravitated instinctively to the risks of not meeting a threat with force.

The contrasts between the two men summon the analogy that philosopher Isaiah Berlin first invoked in a famous 1953 essay, "The Hedgehog and the Fox." Borrowing from the Greek poet Archilochus's observation that "The fox knows many things but the hedgehog knows one big thing," Berlin said writers, thinkers, and above all political leaders seem to divide into these categories. "There exists a great chasm," Berlin wrote, between people "who relate everything to a single central vision," and those whose casts of mind allow them to "pursue many ends, often unrelated and even contradictory—connected, if at all, only in some de facto way" (Berlin 1993, 3). Clinton, in politics and in life, was a classic fox: always pursuing multiple ends, reacting to diverse pressures, his agenda a loosely bound bundle of good intentions. Bush, even before September 11, 2001, had the mind of a hedgehog. Like Reagan, he believed that successful people need not necessarily work frenetically hard but that they set large goals and delegate their implementation broadly. After al Qaeda struck the nation, Bush's agenda became even more organized around a "single central vision."

A word is in order on my own vantage point. As a White House reporter for six of Clinton's eight years in office and a historian of his presidency, I can say with due modesty that I am as familiar with the mechanics of his political operation as it is possible for an outside observer to be. I have not been a White House reporter in the Bush years, though I did a series of stories for the *Washington Post* on Bush's first year in office that brought me into contact with most of his senior advisers. So I regard myself—with far more modesty due—as an informed observer but far from an expert on Bush's political operation. I have seen at close hand the ways that Washington's political and journalistic culture changed in the Bush administration, partly as a result of post-September 11 governance but also the result of the distinct style and values of this president.

The Clinton Model of Presidential Leadership

All modern presidents, since the emergence of public opinion surveys in the days of Franklin D. Roosevelt, have followed polls. None has followed them with the same intensity—or with the same restless imagination about how they might be used to navigate the challenges of the presidency—as Clinton. For the forty-second president, polls fulfilled a powerful psychic need. Political consultant Dick Morris once wrote of his client: "In a room he will instinctively, as if by canine sense of smell, find anyone who shows reserve toward him, and he will work full time on winning his approval and affection. . . . America is the ultimate room for Clinton. For him a poll helps him sense who doesn't like him and why they don't. In the reflected numbers he sees his shortcomings and his potential, his successes and failures" (Morris 1999, 11). Morris's mortal enemy in the Clinton operation, Harold Ickes, endorsed this view as he described the weekly meetings in 1995 and 1996 when Morris presented his polling data. "I have never seen such a role reversal," Ickes said. "Bill Clinton dominates every other conversation I have witnessed, including with other heads of state. But with Morris it was almost as if he had some supernatural hold on him. He would sit for thirty minutes, not saying a word" (Harris 2000a).

Polls were also the lifeblood for the particular brand of defensive, survival-based politics that Clinton practiced after Republicans routed Democrats and put his back to the wall after the historic midterm elections of 1994. Never again, Clinton resolved, would he allow his policies—and how those policies were perceived by the public—to become so estranged from the political center. He summoned Morris, who had been with him at the start of his career in Arkansas but had in recent years been outside his circle, back to the fold. The essence of the refashioned presidency that emerged from the Clinton-Morris collaboration was the comprehensive merger of White House policy, political, and communications operations. With nearly nonstop polling, Clinton would constantly monitor the public mood and calibrate his administration's actions. A conventional political operation under previous administrations would poll the president's approval rating or public reaction to a major speech. Morris insisted on surveying all policies before they were even up for presidential consideration, as well as the specific language that might be used to sell such policies. At the most absurd level, Morris surveyed public opinion about where Clinton might most profitably spend his summer vacation. More substantively, though, the political model that Clinton and Morris used in 1995 and 1996 was a terrific success. The electorate might have been hostile to government in the abstract, but Clinton found specific programs—large ones, supporting education and environmental protection, and small ones like tougher federal laws against fathers who do not pay child support—that were highly popular and used those to decisively win the larger argument that Newt Gingrich and his would-be conservative revolutionaries provoked about the proper role of the government in American life. Independent voters, at least, may have been suspicious about government in the abstract but found it quite useful in the particular. Clinton also used polls to find policies and rhetorical stances that connected with the cultural values of the so-called swing voters. From this research sprang such initiatives as Clinton's endorsement of V-chips to help parents filter out offensive television programming, his promotion of school uniforms, and a major initiative against the tobacco industry (Morris 1999, 207–34).

The Morris model continued long after Morris himself left the Clinton fold in a sex scandal in August 1996. Pollster Mark Penn filled the new role, becoming not only Clinton's most important political adviser but essentially one of his top domestic policy advisers. If Domestic Policy Advisor Bruce Reed or National Economic Adviser Gene Sperling had an idea, Penn's polling operation was the first stop in getting the proposal on Clinton's agenda. The process worked in reverse, too. When Penn's polling showed that voter concerns about privacy in the computer age were scoring off the charts in his weekly polls, he pressed policy officials to come up with initiatives that would respond to public demand. In league with Sperling and Reed, Penn arrived at the successful rhetorical formulation, "save social security first," which Clinton employed late in his presidency to counter Republican demands that government surpluses be returned in tax cuts, arguing instead that the money be used to pay down government debt (which ostensibly would put Social Security on sounder footing) (Harris 2000b).

By no means did Clinton always do what the polls told him was the most popular course. He pursued a peace settlement enforced by U.S. troops in Bosnia in 1995, despite polling showing clear political risks. So too did he defy polls earlier that year when launching a politically unpopular, but financially successful, intervention in a Mexican currency crisis. Still it was Clinton's shrewd use of polls as a tool of political positioning that allowed him to capture and hold the political center for the balance of his presidency. These tactics, one must emphatically add, worked only when combined with policies that were producing (or, even in the most skeptical light, coinciding with) all manner of favorable trends in economic growth and social stability. One of the echoing what-ifs of his presidency is whether he might have turned the defensive, survival-based style of politics into something more affirmative, setting the agenda on his own terms instead of reacting to circumstances and the excesses of Republicans. It was not to be. The eruption of the Monica Lewinsky scandal in January 1998 ensured that Clinton would remain on a defensive footing. But his secure hold on the political center and the loyalty of swing voters helped him survive this too. Despite widespread doubts about his personal character—just 20 percent of voters in the last *Washington Post/ABC News* poll of his presidency thought Clinton possessed "high personal moral and ethical standards"—some 65 percent of Americans approved of the way he handled his job as president, among the highest approval ratings for any departing president of recent decades.

The public plainly liked Clinton's centrist policies. But they did not necessarily like how he arrived at them. The notion of a president relying so heavily on polls offended many voters' idealistic notions of leadership. One of Bush's best applause lines on the 2000 campaign trail was to promise leadership "based on principle, and not polls and focus groups."

Bush has his own psychic relationship to polls. The idea of obsessively monitoring public opinion seems to offend his self-image as a decisive and principled man and to be a reminder of one thing Bush found personally distasteful about Clinton. He sometimes cuts people short when they mention polling data in his presence. And aides take pains to insist that he always decides policies first and uses polling data only to decide how to present ideas to the public (Green 2002). Just as real men don't eat quiche, real leaders don't take polls. Or so Bush seems to believe.

So there was inevitably an element of "gotcha!" when it became clear, starting early in Bush's term, that he had a political operation that bore striking resemblance in certain respects to Clinton's (Harris 2001a; Green 2002). Clinton's political team met weekly (with the president in attendance) to review polling data and discuss strategies for merging policy and politics. Bush's White House has a group, under the auspices of senior adviser Karl Rove and his puckishly named Department of Strategery (the name poking fun at Bush's penchant for malapropisms), that performs nearly the identical function. Like Clinton's team, Bush's political group meets weekly (though without the president's attendance). Like Clinton's team, Bush's team reviews the weekly polling data and discusses how to merge politics and policy in the coming weeks. Just as Clinton's group methodically tested specific language, so does Bush's team use polls to gauge reaction to certain key phrases, which find their way into presidential rhetoric. The unveiling of Bush's controversial energy program featured ceaseless use of such words as *balanced* and *comprehensive* and *modern,* after survey research found these helped put skeptical voters at ease (Green 2002).

Moreover, a number of Bush policy decisions display a transparently political dimension. Bush closed a Navy bombing range in Puerto Rico largely because of what administration officials said was concern about the reaction of Hispanic voters in presidential swing states. After initially resisting imposing new laws to combat corporate fraud, Bush in 2002 retreated and endorsed such legislation after its popularity became evident during a spate of accounting scandals. He had done something similar earlier in signing an overhaul of campaign finance rules into law. And he did it again when, after first opposing creation of a separate cabinet agency in charge of "homeland security," he then switched sides and embraced the idea as his own. Clinton had a reputation for expediency, but in six years of covering his administration, I can think of no action he took that so directly contradicted his ostensible principles as flagrantly as the decision by supposed free-trader Bush to impose protectionist tariffs against foreign steel, an obvious bid to curry electoral favor in the industrial Midwest. (Trading partners abroad reacted with understandable outrage, and the administration negotiators later withdrew many of the most objectionable provisions.)

It is clear the Clinton political model survives heavily intact even with a new president in the White House. There are even some notable similarities between Rove and Morris. Both are hyperkinetic men, both are drawn to sweeping historical analogies, both have reputations as specialists in negative campaigning, and both have displayed a willingness to roll over dissenters in campaigns and White House political deliberations. Most important, both are possessed of a conviction—an odd if admirable streak of idealism, to my mind, in men of such cynical reputations—that politics at the end of the day is driven above all by policy (Cannon and Simendinger 2002). Political reporters, many consultants, and anyone who tends to follow politics as sport tend to focus on politics as an exercise in image manipulation. This is part of the story—but the larger part is that politics is about responding to voter needs and grievances through substantive remedies.

As one notes the similarities between Clinton's political operation and Bush's, a pause is in order to emphasize important differences. The Clinton model, authored by Morris, involved positioning the president as an independent force between liberal Democrats and conservative Republicans in Congress—"triangulation," in Morris's portentous phrase. The consultant (who previously worked for such Republicans as Trent Lott and Jesse Helms) was loathed by Democrats in Congress, and his boss was not always in such great standing either. Bush and Rove worry much more about cultivating and placating the Republican base. In addition to worrying about Bush's standing with swing voters, Rove serves as all-purpose ambassador to the Right—a role in which he is by all accounts personally and ideologically comfortable (Edsall and Milbank 2003). An even more consequential difference is in the two presidents' sense of timing about the inevitable compromises in politics. Clinton, after 1994, tried to transcend Republican opposition by being more popular. Therefore, he was wary of any position that might prove unpopular with swing voters. In essence, the compromises were built into his agenda even before he publicly unveiled it. Bush, by contrast, is not at all averse to making public proposals that are more ambitious than moderate voters would prefer. He has done this twice, once in 2001 and again in 2003, with expensive tax-cut proposals. The theory seems to be that Bush will make bold proposals, and in so doing he will move the political center of gravity toward him. If at the end of the day political reality forces him to compromise, so be it—but only at the end of the day. "We aren't going to negotiate with ourselves," Bush admonishes aides he believes are too quick to compromise (Harris and Balz 2001). This model is akin to the one Clinton followed (with poor results) in 1993 while pursuing health-care reform, but it is in signal contrast to the model he followed from 1995 onward.

A Vast Conspiracy?

Any reporter who covered the Clinton administration can in the Bush era expect to receive calls regularly from old sources asking the same question: Why are you letting them get away with this? As Rahm Emanuel, a former senior adviser in the Clinton White House and now a Democratic Congressman from Chicago, put it: "The Washington press corps have become like little puppy dogs. You scratch them on the tummy and they roll right over" (Harris 2001a). These complaints can be whiny, self-absorbed, and unbecoming of a proud opposition. They also very often happen to be accurate. President Bush and his administration get away with all manner of things that would have been huge uproars in the Clinton years. Or so it seems to one who kept up a busy trade writing about Clinton and his uproars. The difference—Emanuel's complaints to the contrary—has very little to do with the attitudes of establishment reporters toward Bush, or their willingness to report aggressively on him. Instead, Bush's comparatively soft treatment—not only from the press but from Congress and the political opposition writ large—derives from a constellation of historical and contemporary factors that have aligned to make Washington a much more favorable political and governing climate for Bush than it was for Clinton.

This did not come about by accident. There are three important factors. One is the success—so far—of a deliberate political strategy executed by Bush's White House. Another is that Bush's Democratic opposition is not nearly so methodical or zealous in its pursuit of a president than was the conservative opposition that Clinton faced. Finally, there is the natural tendency for power to flow to the executive during times of national security crisis. All three factors bear some discussion.

It is clear that when Bush promised to "change the tone" in Washington, an important part of what he meant was that he would not allow himself or his administration to be harried by political adversaries, legal investigations, or news media critics in the ways that beset most of his recent predecessors. The Bush administration has set about a purposeful campaign to bring permanent Washington's hostile institutional forces to heel. When the General Accounting Office, the investigative arm of Congress, wanted documents from the energy task force chaired by Vice President Cheney, the White House steadfastly said no—and successfully expanded the circle of executive privilege claims after an appellate court ruled in favor of the White House.

So, too, has a measure of defiance worked with the Washington news media. This White House, paradoxically, gets better press by seeming to worry about it less. Bush is far less prone to commenting on the Washington story-of-the-day than Clinton was. Newsworthy events that Clinton gravitated toward—such as natural disasters or the homecoming of captured U.S. airmen after their plane was forced down in China—Bush often ignores. Before the September 11 catastrophe, Ron Brownstein of the *Los Angeles Times* dubbed Bush the "A4 President," since articles on his repetitious pronouncements often appeared deep inside the papers. But on the whole, Bush has been well served by a willingness not to dominate every news cycle. White House beat reporters, for their part, live in chronic frustration at how little White House aides help them in their routine work of understanding presidential decisions and putting them in context. It is not true, however, that Bush denies all access. He and his senior aides have given extraordinary access to senior Washington journalists like Bob Woodward and Dan Balz of the *Washington Post.* Largely favorable portraits of a president who is more commanding in private than he often seems in public were the result. The Bush lesson is not to ignore the news media but to be selective and poised in deciding when to cooperate. Bush himself, in a private session late in 2001 with former White House press secretaries of both parties, boasted of how, as one participant in the session later described it to me, his administration did not let itself be "pushed around" by the Washington press corps.

While his strategy may have been shrewd, it likely would not have worked so well but for a much larger factor: The comparative impotence of the Democratic opposition. In the Clinton years, an aggrieved and methodical corps of conservative activists woke each morning thinking of ways in which to make the president's life more difficult. Plenty of Democrats generate plenty of bile over Bush, but there simply is no comparable corps on the liberal side.

Hillary Rodham Clinton complained famously of a "vast right-wing conspiracy." She had her adjectives right but got the noun wrong. Far from a conspiracy, its members operate essentially in plain view, and its attacks on Clinton—while often mean-spirited and sometimes flatly false—were (with some exceptions) not beyond the pale of legitimate political discourse. The modern Right in Washington can be properly thought of as a loose network. The network's activities are not necessarily coordinated in an explicit sense—though this is sometimes indeed the case through a variety of informal associations—but there was a great tendency for the Right's efforts against Clinton to reinforce one another. The Whitewater controversy was fanned by the editorial page of the conservative *Wall Street Journal,* whose fulminations helped produce pressure in Congress for legislative inquiries as well for appointment of an outside prosecutor. The hearings and legal proceedings that resulted from these inquiries were in turn vastly amplified and made more politically potent by conservative commentators like radio host Rush Limbaugh, who at his peak was heard by nearly 20 million people. This symbiosis—between expressly conservative opinion forums and the investigative apparatus of Congress and various independent counsels—was able to make what would ordinarily be small and perishable controversies, such as the firing of eight employees at the White House travel office, into large episodes that echoed for years.

These echoes bounce far beyond conservative precincts. Establishment news media do not take their cues from right-wing organs, but it is inescapable that reporters do gravitate toward controversy, and conservative opponents labored prodigiously to ensure that Clinton's actions were viewed in the most controversial light. When Clinton early in 1993 deferred to criticism from Western senators and dropped a proposal to increase grazing fees on federal land—a minor part of his agenda—this was widely reported in ways to reinforce an existing perception of Clinton as weak and vacillating. Bush in his first year retreated on items that were far more central to his agenda—agreeing not to push his plan for educational vouchers, for instance—with little commentary from either side of the ideological divide. Likewise, he was able to appoint an openly gay person to his White House staff with little controversy. Clinton's selection of gay nominees generated considerable uproars.

The obvious question is why is there not a liberal, anti-Bush equivalent of the conservative, anti-Clinton network. The principal reason is that the conservative network sprang from particular historical circumstances. A generation earlier, many conservatives concluded that they would never catch a fair break from an elite news media and academy that they believed were irretrievably liberal in values and outlook. Spiro Agnew was this movement's most colorful voice, attacking liberal universities, and calling the establishment press "an effete corps of impudent snobs." Fired by these grievances, conservatives set about creating and cultivating their own forums—magazines like *National Review* and the *American Spectator*, radio shows like Limbaugh's, think tanks like the Heritage Foundation. Grievances, moreover, tend to unite those who share them and create a sense of movement. There are liberal-leaning columnists like E. J. Dionne and Michael Kinsley, just as there are liberal-tilting think tanks like the Brookings Institution. But there is little in the work of such columnists or the typical Brookings fellow like Michael O'Hanlon to suggest they think of themselves as part of a movement or that their work is a weapon devoted to a larger ideological mission. The editorial page of the *Wall Street Journal*, by contrast, or even the columns of a veteran journalist like Robert Novak, are avowedly voices of a movement. In some cases, the traditional line between journalist and activist is not merely blurred, it is obliterated. The *American Spectator*'s reportage on Clinton's alleged sexual escapades was famously funded by the reclusive right-wing millionaire Richard Mellon

Scaife, who sponsored an "Arkansas Project" with the aim of unearthing embarrassing material about the then-president. Days before the Monica S. Lewinsky scandal broke into the open, the lawyer for scandal provocateur Linda Tripp was delightedly playing copies of Tripp's notorious surreptitious recordings of Lewinsky for the listening pleasure of conservative commentator Ann Coulter, in Coulter's apartment (Toobin 1999, 214). Hillary Clinton was right to suspect a nexus of conservative commentators and conservative legal activists was out to undermine her husband, even if she did not at first acknowledge the excellent raw material her husband had provided their enemies.

Nothing in politics stands still, and in due course liberals may indeed try to match the conservative achievement in creating their own combative policy and communications platforms. Indeed, such veterans of the Clinton administration as Senator Hillary Clinton and former chief-of-staff John D. Podesta are doing so now (VandeHei 2003b). Former vice president Gore has discussed the possibility of starting a progressively oriented radio or cable television network (Tumulty 2003). For the moment, it remains unclear whether there is sufficient demand on the Left for such an avowedly activist, grievance-based media platform. In any event, at the outset of Bush's term, such an apparatus did not exist, and his presidency has been easier because of it. In addition, Bush was aided immeasurably by the expiration of the independent counsel law. The Watergate-era institution was allowed to die by bipartisan consent, amid complaints that the law gave excessive rein to prosecutors to operate without due sense of proportion or public accountability. When ethical controversies arise about Bush—such as whether he acted properly in his dealings with Harken Energy Co. and has answered questions truthfully about it—there is no clamor for a time-consuming and expensive investigation of the sort that bedeviled the Clintons over Whitewater.

Finally, no factor has been greater in expanding Bush's presidential power, and reducing the intensity of opposition he faces in Congress, than the September 11 attacks and their aftermath. Power has flowed to this presidency as it has to nearly all presidencies at the outset of war. It is worth recalling that war expands presidential power in the early stages, but exhausts it—as happened to Lyndon B. Johnson in Vietnam—in the later stages if war policy is seen to be failing. By early 2003, however, it was clear that war had vastly enhanced Bush's governing influence. Despite widespread doubts among civil libertarians, the Bush administration successfully asserted the right to indefinitely detain suspected terrorists and to expand the secrecy claims on official presidential papers. Despite widespread doubts among Democrats, generally about the course of his Iraq policy, Bush easily won a resolution supporting his decision to go to war against Saddam Hussein's regime. Despite the Constitution's provision requiring that Congress pass declarations of war, Bush like other presidents since World War II essentially rendered this provision moot. (Congress itself is largely to blame for this constitutional erosion; on the whole, legislators seem not to want the power, and accountability that comes with it, for approving military ventures.)

It is worth pondering, even if the answer is unknowable, whether Clinton or Gore would have received similar deference from the opposition if either of them had been president on September 11. It is worth pondering further still the lasting consequences of this deference. In 1973, in the midst of Watergate, historian Arthur Schlesinger Jr. wrote *The Imperial Presidency* (Schlesinger 1973). Schlesinger's concern was not with a strong presidency—something liberals of his generation supported—but with an unaccountable one. Schlesinger's imperial presidency rested on three pillars: expansion of the presidential war-making power at the expense of Congress; expansion of executive branch secrecy; and use of powers expanded to meet a foreign adversary against domestic citizenry. The first two of these circumstances have indeed come to flower under Bush, and at least some critics believe the third has, too. Against radical Islam and terrorism, Bush indeed is facing a foreign crisis different in character than ones the nation has known previously, but the aggrandizement of presidential power in the midst of such crises is a story with many precedents.

The Hedgehog and the Fox, at Large in the World

Foreign policy is the most fertile ground for exploring the differences between Clinton and Bush, nowhere more so than on the question of Iraq. The difference here is not principally over how the two men perceived the threat of Saddam Hussein and his suspected pursuit of weapons of mass destruction. Rather, the difference lies in how they perceived the costs of confronting this danger.

Here was President Clinton, in February 1998, after Hussein had thrown out the United Nations weapons inspectors that were mandated in the terms of surrender in the 1991 Persian Gulf War: "What if he fails to comply, and we fail to act, or we take some ambiguous third route which gives him yet more opportunities to develop this program of weapons of mass destruction? Well, he will conclude that the international community has lost its will. He will then conclude that he can go right on and do more to rebuild an arsenal of devastating destruction. And some day, some way, I guarantee you, he'll use the arsenal."

After a year of frustrating diplomacy, during which the administration could not persuade France, Russia, and other nations to support multilateral action against Iraq, Clinton authorized four days of missile strikes against Iraq. Then, the problem retreated from the front pages and from a prominent place on his presidential agenda. In other words, Clinton responded precisely with an ambiguous third route that did not force inspectors back in the country and gave the Hussein regime more time and more freedom. Bush—even after September 11 and the vulnerabilities to civilized society that atrocity exposed—faced roughly the same international opposition to an Iraq confrontation that Clinton did. Yet, even so, he methodically pursued a policy to dislodge Hussein. In so doing, he strained relations with many longtime U.S. allies very nearly to the breaking point, risked a dangerous backlash in the Arab world, and put his own presidency on the line. Why did Bush choose to ignore the same risks that led Clinton to choose a more cautious path?

The answer, I believe, can be found in two places. One is the different assumptions that essentially conservative leaders like Bush and essentially liberal ones like Clinton bring to basic issues such as the use of force and the role of world opinion. The other is more personalized to the two men—a difference in their casts of mind and the nature of their decisions.

It is sometimes said that terms like *liberalism* and *conservatism* are too broad to have useful meaning. Certainly it is true that some leaders and policies defy neat categorization. Yet there remains a lasting fault line in American politics that does break largely along ideological lines. At bottom is a question about human motivation, as it is translated in international relations: Does the world operate more by fear or by affinity? In other words, is it better to have other nations respect American military might, even if they loathe America's larger purposes? Or is it more important to persuade other nations to share, or at least understand, American interests? Is the world driven more by raw power or by enlightened cooperation? By force or by diplomacy? Of course, as a practical matter, everyone believes that force and diplomacy ideally should work in concert. But all manner of foreign diplomacy debates —Iraq chief among them—turn on the question of which is more important.

Bush and his team quite evidently believe that at the end of the day force matters most. After diplomacy failed to produce a United Nations resolution supporting a war against Hussein's regime, the administration went ahead anyway. The calculation was that opposition in the Middle East and Europe alike would matter little once Iraq and the world saw a convincing display of American power. This is the world of force in which Bush and most conservatives believe.

Democrats, including Clinton, saw this course as incurring grievous costs. According to the liberal critique, Bush had damaged the United Nations by spurning its judgments and relevance. He had damaged American moral authority by turning large populations of common folk around the world against the United States. He had damaged American strategic interests in the Middle East, by pursuing an optional war first instead of diplomatic priorities, such as trying to negotiate a peace settlement between Israeli and the Palestinian Authority. Bush, in other words, had badly stumbled in the world of affinity in which Clinton and most foreign-policy liberals believe.

In this battle between these different conceptions of human motivation and theories of international relations, both sides have arguments to make. Believers in a world of force can point to a case like Libya. Little has been heard from this international bad actor, after the punishing air strikes in the Reagan era showed there was a price for supporting terrorism. Believers in a world of affinity can point to the blossoming societies of Eastern Europe: In the end, it was not American military might that liberated Eastern Europe (however valuable containment was in protecting Western Europe during the Cold War.) Instead, brave leaders like Vaclav Havel in the Czech Republic were sustained during their years of dissent by the illuminating power of American culture, free markets, and free ideas. In Tiananmen Square in 1989, likewise, protesters carried miniature Statues of Liberty and copies of the Declaration of Independence. And though that rebellion was brutally crushed, in the end one must believe (and devoutly hope) that China's tyrannical regime will be loosened by American ideals of free markets and free ideas rather than by American arms. Bush's Iraq campaign will eventually be judged by its results—too early to do at this writing. My point is not to endorse either a foreign policy of force or of affinity but to underscore the continuing relevance of this basic ideological divide.

Another divide is in the intellectual instincts of both minds. It is in foreign affairs where Isaiah Berlin's insight—that political leaders divide between hedgehogs and foxes—echoes most consequentially. Clinton, the man of fox-like calculation, was a relativist. That is, he believed that most important values in governance are ultimately in tension with one another—as in Iraq, where the imperative of containing weapons of mass destruction competed with the imperative of maintaining international consensus. Clinton's mind gravitated toward complexity. This is a president who in a less exalted context said, "It depends on what the meaning of 'is' is," but this statement aptly captured his approach in many matters. To a relativist, improvisation is the supreme virtue. And in foreign policy, the natural fluidity of Clinton's mind and language—his ability to see things from multiple sides and find rhetorical formulations to bridge differences, his skill at improvisation—could at times be a great asset. He was a welcome presence in peace negotiations in Northern Ireland and the Middle East precisely because of these qualities. But Clinton's mind also tended naturally to fix on the risks of absolute solutions, and prefer instead contingent ones. If Clinton were defending his Iraq policy with full candor, one suspects he would say something like: "I may not have solved the problem of Saddam Hussein for all time, but I solved it for my time. He was contained on my watch, and let Bush deal with the problem on his watch."

Bush, whose hedgehog-like mind clears away contradiction and nuance like so much underbrush on his Texas ranch, has the instincts of an absolutist. He believes in a hierarchy of values and gravitates naturally to simplicity—what's right is right and what's wrong is wrong. To the absolutist, adherence to principle is the supreme virtue. In the Iraq context, this led him—with little evident self-doubt or agonizing—on a path of confrontation with Saddam Hussein within weeks of the September 11 attacks, even though no direct linkage has been established between al Qaeda and the Baghdad regime. In Bush's mind, the risks of bold action were less than the risk of inaction.

Presidential Comparison and Its Limits

Where do these comparisons lead us? President Bush and President Clinton have similar political operations and face similar political challenges. In foreign affairs, they share similar assessments, at least rhetorically, about the menace of a man like Saddam Hussein. Yet they have not only starkly different policies but also starkly different styles by which they arrive at these policies. In domestic affairs, Bush occasionally borrows from Clinton's techniques in service of an agenda that reverses Clinton's fiscal policies. This irony is surpassed by another: Bush, vastly less experienced as a politician, proved in his first two years vastly more surefooted in advancing his substantive agenda and building popular support for it than the supposed political master he succeeded had managed in his first two years. Clinton presided over a rout of historic proportions for his party in 1994; Bush presided over a triumph of lesser but still remarkable proportion in 2002.

Bush, if he is wise, will celebrate his early victories with a measure of restraint. After all, two years after Clinton's 1994 humiliation came a reelection campaign in which his victory was scarcely ever in doubt. Life is full of surprises. There are good breaks, like the one Clinton found in 1995 with a Republican Congress chronically prone to political overreach. There are bad breaks, like the one that beset George H. W. Bush in 1991, when economic recovery began but not quickly enough to show results by the time he needed them. There are also, as if anyone needs a reminder, violent lurches of history in our unsettled age. The post–Cold War prophecy of an "end of history"—no more titanic clashes of systems and values now that Western free markets and free ideas had emerged supreme—proved a bit premature. What would Bush's presidency be like now if it had continued on the trajectory it was following on September 10, 2001? The point is that circumstances will always find new ways to frustrate prophets and political handlers alike. As John Maynard Keynes said, "The inevitable never happens; it is the unexpected always."

Students of the presidency, if we are wise, will likewise render our early judgments on Bush's presidential style with a measure of restraint. The Clinton-Bush comparison holds a lesson about the relevance of the kind of things political scientists study—and the limits of such inquiries. Political science tends to be interested in institutions and their systems. The similarities between Bush's political operation and the one that preceded it with Clinton suggest that the presidency is a cumulative institution. A successful innovator like Clinton, who wielded presidential power in new and distinctive ways, is apt to influence his successors. John F. Kennedy created a television presidency—using a new medium that his predecessors had not mastered in the previous decade—one that even less telegenic men like Johnson and Nixon felt obliged to continue. Reagan set standards for how to use important ceremonial occasions like State of the Union addresses or D-Day commemorations that Clinton borrowed from explicitly. Presidential experience is cumulative in negative ways, too. Bush is by all accounts fixated on how to avoid the political failures of his father, just as Clinton was fixated on how to avoid the failures of his Democratic predecessor, Jimmy Carter.

But political models in the end matter less than individual character. Bush no doubt would like to do something like Clinton did—retain the loyalty of his party base while reaching out to independents, win a second term, win continuing popular support for his policies. Yet Bush could never emulate, nor would he ever care to do so, the basic character of Clinton's agenda or the style of presidency that supported that agenda. Ideology, instinct, values—these are what matter most. Bush and Clinton will remain linked in popular and scholarly conversation—but with their names invoked as opposites rather than for some passing similarities in their styles.

6 GEORGE W. BUSH AND RELIGIOUS POLITICS

James L. Guth

Few of George W. Bush's Yale fraternity brothers would have predicted his rise to the presidency, despite his distinguished political heritage. Even fewer would have expected *Newsweek* to dub his administration the "most resolutely 'faith-based' in modern times" (Fineman 2003). In fact, it was for good reasons that the first "insider" book on Bush's tenure opened with an anecdote about religious life in the White House and closed with a Biblical story (Frum 2003b).

Religion has influenced the Bush administration in several ways. To begin with, faith has played a crucial role in Bush's personal life, moving him away from a life of frivolity and giving him a sense of calling that pervaded his drive for the presidency and his behavior in office. Friends view this as a source of strength, but critics see Bush's religiosity leading to a host of dangers. Religion has also supplied a vital context for his electoral strategies and policy agenda. The religious configuration of the electorate was never far from Bush's calculations (or those of adviser Karl Rove), and his policies often envisioned new roles for religious institutions. Key personnel in his administration, as well as their decisions, often reflect the GOP's dominant religious forces.

Religious Groups in American Electoral Politics

Any assessment of contemporary American religious politics must consider two competing interpretations of religious alignments. The first is the *ethnocultural* theory that emphasizes the role of the historic European religious traditions and denominations that migrated to America and often multiplied on reaching her shores. Nineteenth-century party politics in the United States consisted largely of efforts to assemble winning coalitions of these contending ethnoreligious groups (Kleppner 1979). And well into the twentieth century the GOP represented the historically dominant mainline Protestant churches, such as Episcopalians, Presbyterians, and Methodists, whereas the Democrats were the party of religious minorities, including Catholics, Jews, and Evangelical Protestants (especially in the South). By the 1980s, these configurations had shifted, as mainline Protestants dwindled in number and influence, Evangelicals moved toward the GOP, the ancient Catholic-Democratic alliance began to fray, and African American Protestants became an important Democratic bloc. Growing religious diversity added new elements, as Muslims, Hindus, Buddhists, and others entered politics, usually on the Democratic side. Thus, even today, many analysts still think in ethnocultural terms, referring to the "Evangelical," "Catholic," "Jewish," or "Muslim" vote.

An alternative perspective is the *culture war* theory. Perhaps the first time many Americans heard about this idea was in Pat Buchanan's prime-time speech to the 1992 Republican convention (Heineman 1998, 201). Although journalists were puzzled by the notion, Buchanan merely echoed an academic debate triggered by sociologist James Davison Hunter's *Culture Wars: The Struggle to Define America* (1991). Instead of the old ethnocultural struggles, pitting Democratic Catholics, Jews, and Evangelicals against mainline Republicans, Hunter saw bitter divisions *within* each tradition, based largely on theological understandings. The "orthodox" are committed to "an external, definable, and transcendent authority," and adhere firmly to the traditional doctrines of their faiths, whereas "progressives" resymbolize historic faiths "according to the prevailing assumptions of contemporary life," replacing old religious tenets with beliefs based on personal experience or scientific rationality (Hunter 1991, 44). The progressives were joined by growing numbers of secular Americans, who had rejected religion entirely and tended to see morality in the same way. These divisions quickly congealed around hot-button issues such as abortion, feminism, gay rights, and the role of religion in public life but soon showed evidence of affecting a broader range of political attitudes.

Although Hunter's thesis captivated some scholars, most analysts concluded that his dualist model was too simplistic, that moral battle lines shifted from issue to issue, and that most citizens were noncombatants in the war (Williams 1997). Some scholars have confirmed, in part, the political cleavages Hunter envisioned (Layman 2001; Leege et al. 2002), but the old markers of religious tradition and ethnicity retain much electoral influence. Thus, a full analysis of religious politics in the Bush era requires a combination of ethnocultural and "culture war" perspectives to delineate the complex coalitions supporting and opposing his administration.

Bush's Religious Strategy

Although as a youth George W. Bush had joined in his family's dutiful mainline Presbyterian/Episcopalian observance, he experienced a dramatic religious rebirth as an adult. As his oil business foundered in the mid-1980s and his drinking became a problem, he fell into a period of introspection. After conversing with old family friends such as the Rev. Billy Graham about spiritual concerns, he renewed his religious faith in 1986, joined a Bible study group, and reassessed his life's direction—experiencing one of those "moments that set you on a different course." From this point on, Bush read the Bible and prayed regularly, spoke often of his faith, and gave generously to religious causes (Carnes 2000). He eventually joined his wife Laura's Methodist church but clearly inhabited the evangelical wing of that mainline Protestant denomination. Indeed, at one point his newfound religious zeal even elicited a reproof from Billy Graham, who urged him to hold his faith with more humility (Fineman 2003).

His new religious interests quickly proved useful politically. During his father's 1988 presidential campaign, Bush acted as an informal liaison to Evangelical leaders, especially in the large Southern Baptist and Pentecostal communities, revealing an uncanny ability to communicate with this constituency (Rosin 2000). Later, as governor of Texas, Bush experimented with the strategies and policies that eventually shaped his national religious appeal. He cultivated religious conservatives, especially among the state's dominant Southern Baptists and in the burgeoning suburban megachurches, but also wooed noted African American pastors such as T. D. Jakes, Tony Evans, and Kirbyjon Caldwell, who were attracted by his evident personal faith and sympathy for their vision of a broader social role for religious institutions. As governor, Bush experimented with such "faith-based" policies, allowing religious groups to provide public services such as drug rehabilitation, adoption and child welfare, and even operation of prisons. His thinking about these issues was increasingly shaped by Evangelical theorist Marvin Olasky, a journalism professor at the University of Texas (Westbrook 2000; Ivins and DuBose 2002). But Bush's relationships with the militant Christian Right activists who were busy capturing the Texas GOP were only diplomatically "correct." This pattern eventually defined his relationship with Christian conservatives: Bush's appeal to ordinary clergy and church goers always exceeded his rapport with movement leaders, who doubted his commitment to their priorities.

Bush has testified that his call to run for the presidency came through a sermon at his second inaugural as governor (Goodstein 2000). In any case, his campaign strategy, shaped by Rove, focused on the GOP's two key resources: business money and religious votes. Bush's faith gave him unique advantages in his pursuit of the latter: he was by upbringing and affiliation a "mainline" Protestant; his Episcopalian, Presbyterian, and Methodist roots put him squarely at the center of the "old" GOP religious clientele. But by experience, belief, and sensibility he was an "Evangelical," speaking fluently the religious language of the "new" party constituencies. (This perhaps explains why the 2000 National Election Study shows far more Evangelicals identifying Bush incorrectly as a *Baptist* than correctly as a Methodist!) He often bypassed the most visible (and often unpopular) Christian Right figures, such as Pat Robertson, James Dobson, and Jerry Falwell, relying instead on former Christian Coalition director Ralph Reed, evangelist James Robison, and several Southern Baptist leaders. These enthusiasts assured Evangelical clergy that Bush was one of them, aided by the candidate's famous declaration that Jesus was his "favorite political philosopher." Although Bush faced other Republicans close to religious conservatives, such as Christian Right leader Gary Bauer and anti-abortion activist Alan Keyes, this appeal was effective. Bush not only was the overwhelming favorite among Evangelical ministers from the start, but he also carried almost three-quarters of their primary votes and benefited from considerable pastoral activism (Guth 2003). Exit polls show that he did almost as well among their parishioners, who gave him a boost in the crucial South Carolina and "Super Tuesday" GOP primaries (Berggren and Levine-Berggren 2000).

This "Evangelical strategy" complicated pursuit of another group targeted by Rove, traditionalist Catholics, a large voting bloc crucial to Bush's campaign (DuBose, Reid, and Cannon, 2003, 150–55). Bush's speech at fundamentalist Bob Jones University during the South Carolina primary allowed John McCain to tar him with the university's historic anti-Catholicism. Although McCain's ploy swayed some Catholic primary voters in Michigan and New York, Bush countered with a public apology to Cardinal John O'Connor, an old family friend, and ensured that Catholics—preferably with clerical collars—were highly visible during the rest of the campaign. Thereafter Bush consulted frequently with conservative Catholic activists, addressed issues vital to traditionalist Catholics (such as the Vatican's observer status at the United Nations), visited Catholic churches, criticized the Clinton FDA's approval of the abortion drug RU-486, and larded his speeches with quotations from Pope John Paul II.

Once his nomination was secure, Bush moved again to broaden his religious base, reassuring mainline Protestants that he was not a prisoner of the Christian Right. Although he rejected softening the GOP's strict anti-abortion plank, he insisted that pro-choice Republicans were welcome in the party. He avoided anti-gay pronouncements and signaled that there would be gay appointees in his administration. In touting faith-based programs for solving social problems, he talked more about the poor than is typical of GOP nominees. This was designed to attract religious minorities, such as African American Protestants, and Catholic traditionalists, who find the staunch economic individualism of Evangelical Republicans out of tune with Catholic social teachings. The GOP convention itself was replete with highly visible roles for African American Protestant and Catholic clergy. During the fall campaign, Bush stressed broad ethical themes, asserted that America would benefit from spiritual renewal, and repeatedly featured the benefits of faith-based social programs (Bruni 2000).

The Bush Religious Coalition

Did Bush's religious strategy work? Obviously, it did not provide him with a comfortable popular vote majority but, together with the religious counter-campaign by the Gore-Lieberman ticket (Seegers 2002), it probably did enhance the impact of religious forces on the outcome. Many careful observers have argued that the 2000 presidential vote was defined by cultural rather than economic divisions. News magazines printed red and blue electoral maps, vividly depicting Bush's dominance of the cultural "heartland," versus Gore's majorities on the "postmodern" coasts. "So what is it that divides the two nations?" asked political analyst Michael Barone. "The answer is religion" (Barone 2001, 27).

These divisions were not new; indeed, the Bush coalition mimicked the "normal" religious makeup of the contemporary GOP. To delineate that coalition, we use the third National Study of Religion and Politics, conducted in the spring and fall of 2000. The religious categories in tables 6.1, 6.2, and 6.3 incorporate the old religious traditions, such as Evangelical Protestants, mainline Protestants, white Catholics, African American Protestants, and Jews (along with several smaller groups) but also recognize the culture war divisions within major traditions. (Rather than using Hunter's dichotomous division between "orthodox" and "progressives," we divide the three large white Christian traditions into theological "traditionalists," "centrists," and "modernists.")[1] As table 6.1 shows, Bush scored best among Evangelical Protestants, less well among mainline Protestants, and barely carried white Catholics. Furthermore, in looking at the "culture war" divisions, we see that Bush prospered among traditionalists, did less well among centrists, and lost by solid margins among modernists, especially in the mainline and Catholic traditions. Except for a virtual sweep of Latter-day Saints (Mormons), Bush lost by landslides among religious minorities, from African American Protestants to Jews, and carried only a third of the seculars. The totals for the U.S. House of Representatives and party identification follow the same pattern, although GOP House candidates actually did better than Bush among mainline and Catholic modernists and among Hispanic Protestants.

Of course, voters responded not only to Bush but also to Democratic candidates, past and present. A political commonplace holds that the incumbent's popularity influences the fortunes of his party's nominee. Although Clinton retired with decent job ratings, these were not uniform across religious groups (Guth 2000). Latter-day Saints and Evangelicals were most critical, followed by mainline Protestants and then Catholics. Within each major community, traditionalists saw Clinton's performance as "fair" at best, while centrists were more posi-

Table 6.1
Religion and Selected Electoral Measures, Voters Only (percentages)

	Bush vote (two-party)	*GOP, U.S. House vote*	*GOP party ID or lean*	*Clinton job fair or poor*	*Difference in ratings of Bush and Gore*	*Share of total Bush Coalition*
Evangelical	74	73	65	69	1.28	38.5
Traditionalist	80	80	70	78	1.60	33.6
Centrist	49	47	46	58	0.03	3.7
Modernist	46	42	37	41	–0.22	1.4
Latter-day Saints	91	99	96	81	1.81	2.3
Mainline	61	65	59	58	0.50	22.2
Traditionalist	82	77	73	71	1.42	8.8
Centrist	71	74	67	63	1.02	10.0
Modernist	29	44	36	41	–0.91	3.4
Catholic	56	56	48	51	0.18	18.2
Traditionalist	70	70	62	70	0.91	9.7
Centrist	56	54	46	42	0.15	5.1
Modernist	35	41	28	34	–0.82	3.4
Hispanic Catholic	26	28	18	40	–0.55	1.0
Hispanic Protestant	34	50	32	48	0.03	1.0
African American Catholic	23	0	0	23	–1.40	0.7
African American Protestant	4	8	4	12	–2.19	.8
Jewish	29	28	27	34	–1.26	1.4
Other religions	22	26	26	8	–1.36	1.8
Secular	35	31	25	37	–0.76	12.1
Total sample	49	51	44	49	0.01	100%

Source: Third National Study of Religion and Politics (University of Akron, Akron, OH, 2000).

tive, and modernists gave him good grades. Religious minorities—especially African American Protestants and Catholics—awarded Clinton high marks, as did secular voters.

Another way of depicting the candidates' religious constituencies is to compare how close voters felt to the nominees. Using a scale ranging from 1 ("very close") to 5 ("very far"), we subtracted each person's rating of Bush from that for Gore to produce a net assessment. Evangelicals were most positive toward Bush, followed at a distance by mainline

Protestants and Catholics, but there were enormous theological differences *within* each tradition. Evangelical traditionalists averaged over one-and-a-half points closer to Bush, shadowed by mainline traditionalists, and at a distance, by their Catholic counterparts. Although many Catholic traditionalists *voted* for Bush, they did not *feel* much closer to him than to Gore, despite his ardent wooing. Bush's biggest deficit appeared among African American Protestants, with solid gaps among other religious minorities and secular voters. Only among Hispanic Protestants did Bush have an edge over Gore—but that did not carry over into voting. Although many Hispanic Protestants *liked* Bush, they did not usually vote for him. The study also shows that from the time of the spring to the fall surveys, Bush's fortunes changed. He gained among traditionalists, especially Evangelicals, but lost traction among modernists and most religious minorities, especially African American Protestants and Hispanic Catholics, where he started with much better relative ratings than he finished with (data not shown).

To sum up Bush's electoral base (and the religious context within which his administration would work), table 6.1 reports the proportion of the *total* Bush vote drawn from each religious constituency. The most dramatic finding is that *one-third* of his votes came from Evangelical traditionalists, reflecting their large numbers, strong GOP preferences, and high turnout. Indeed, the entire Evangelical community (about 25 percent of the public) supplied almost 40 percent of Bush's votes. Add mainline and Catholic traditionalists, throw in the Mormons, and the total for theological conservatives rises to 60 percent. (And Bush got a few more traditionalist votes from minorities, such as Hispanic Pentecostals, Orthodox Jews, and some Muslims.) Much of the rest of his total came from mainline and Catholic centrists. While theological modernists, religious minorities, and secular voters formed only a tiny part of the "Bush coalition," they dominated the Democratic vote, both for Al Gore and for the Democratic legislators Bush would confront in Washington.

Religious Groups and Issues

Many issues that Bush stressed in 2000 were directed at solidifying the GOP's core religious constituencies, drawing potential swing voters such as traditionalist Catholics and Hispanic Protestants, or reducing the massive Democratic margin among African American Protestants.

TABLE 6.2
Religion and Moral Issues in the 2000 Electorate (percentages)

	Religious group activity good	*Protect religious values*	*Moral issues most vital*	*Restrict abortion*	*Oppose gay rights*	*Favor school vouchers*	*Favor charitable choice*
Evangelical	78	60	41	68	43	49	37
Traditionalist	82	67	45	76	47	53	36
Centrist	66	32	28	45	33	41	40
Modernist	51	26	16	24	11	11	43
Latter-day Saints	64	54	64	83	54	47	25
Mainline	59	39	23	39	28	34	29
Traditionalist	77	55	36	63	34	40	28
Centrist	51	38	21	34	35	35	33
Modernist	53	27	13	25	15	28	26
Catholic	56	34	17	59	21	44	36
Traditionalist	72	45	23	77	24	56	39
Centrist	47	27	13	53	25	36	37
Modernist	42	26	13	38	14	34	30
Hispanic Catholic	66	52	24	43	31	55	65
Hispanic Protestant	84	27	29	34	8	20	53
African American Catholic	53	52	44	26	21	35	76
African American Protestant	84	66	10	47	26	51	64
Jewish	30	10	7	18	10	26	28
Other Religions	42	24	12	26	24	24	34
Secular	36	17	12	16	12	34	30
Total Sample	60	41	23	45	27	41	37

Source: Third National Study of Religion and Politics (University of Akron, Akron, OH, 2000).

Not all these appeals bore fruit in 2000, especially given the Democrats' religious counterattack, but some might attract potential new Republican voters in the future. How did voters react to Bush's issue appeals?

First, table 6.2 shows that at the end of campaign marked by religious rhetoric and appeals by both camps, a majority of Americans thought that religious activity in the political arena was basically positive. That sentiment was most marked among two polar groups on the partisan divide, Evangelical traditionalists and African American Protestants, joined by the smaller contingent of Hispanic Protestants. Only among Catholic modernists, Jews, religious minorities, and seculars did majorities reject religious involvement. Fewer voters, however, saw religious group activity as legitimately directed at the protection of America's "religious heritage." The culture war divisions surface here, with a couple of crucial modifications. Traditionalists—but especially Evangelicals—were most likely to want government to protect religious heritage and practices, while centrists, modernists, seculars, and Jews rejected such policies. On the other hand, Black Protestants and minority Catholics were more inclined to accept a governmental role, deserting the separatist coalition. Thus, although most religious groups approved the participation of religious interests in political life, philosophical divisions remained over what, if anything, government should do to protect or foster religion.

Culture war theories claim that religious politics focuses on "moral" or "cultural" questions such as abortion, gay rights, and religion in schools. To begin with, religious groups differ sharply over the priority of these issues. Asked to name the "most important problem facing the government of the United States," two-thirds of Mormons and almost half the Evangelical traditionalists listed a moral issue, as did a third of mainline traditionalists and a quarter of Catholic traditionalists, Hispanic Catholics, and Hispanic Protestants. (The small community of African American Catholics almost matched the Evangelical traditionalists.) Few centrist, modernist, secular, or Jewish voters named such issues. Clearly, there is a major religious cleavage on national priorities. Turning to specific issues, we see that the pro-life coalition comprises Evangelical, mainline, and Catholic traditionalists, with their Mormon allies, abetted by Evangelical and Catholic centrists and substantial numbers of African American Protestants and Hispanic Catholics. Once again, religious modernists, Jews, and secular voters constitute the opposition. Much the same pattern appears on gay rights, with less support for restrictions on gays than on abortion, suggesting more public backing for pro-life action than for contesting equal rights for gays.

Other social issues exhibit different patterns. School vouchers, promoted gingerly by candidate Bush, evoked culture war differences among white Christians, with Evangelical and Catholic traditionalists most supportive, but also drew strong backing from African American Protestants and Hispanic Catholics. Jewish and secular voters, on the other side, tended to oppose the idea. Bush's conception of faith-based social programs, or "charitable choice," was greeted with considerable skepticism, even among some groups he expected to be supportive. Many traditionalists obviously had reservations about this idea, and the strongest backing actually appeared among African American and Hispanic Protestants and Catholics—most of them Gore voters. These patterns presented an obstacle to Bush's legislative plans in the short run but an opportunity to expand his religious coalition over the long haul.

Contrary to conventional wisdom, religion also seems to influence some important domestic policy questions (table 6.3). To begin with, in the major white Christian traditions, centrists and modernists were often more likely than traditionalists to name economic and social welfare problems as "most important." Jews were strikingly more prone to focus on such issues, but other religious minorities tended to hug the sample average. Still, the religious differences here are certainly less visible than those over the priority of moral issues are. Religious groups diverged more sharply over expansion of social welfare policies. Evangelical, mainline, and Mormon traditionalists were the loudest voices for a smaller government providing fewer services, joined by substantial minorities of Catholic traditionalists and centrists. Arrayed on the other side are modernists, as well as religious minorities and secular voters. The same pattern appears on specific policies, whether on spending to alleviate hunger in the United States, to protect the environment (even if that entails substantial costs in jobs), or to fund a universal national health-care system. The pattern on moral and social issues is basically replicated here, although with some variation on particular issues. Thus, religious alignments on public welfare are not all that different from those on abortion or gay rights; support for conservative presidential policies in most policy arenas may come from members of the same traditionalist coalition, who simply tend to put more emphasis on social issues.

Religious alignments may even shape foreign policy and defense attitudes. During the campaign, Bush pledged to minimize American involvement in "nation-building" and foreign ventures generally, whereas Al Gore supported a strong U.S. presence abroad. As table 6.3 shows, Americans were as divided as their leaders about international involvement. Religious groups, moreover, exhibited few distinct differences, although African American Protestants and Hispanics favored less foreign intervention. At the same time, two-thirds of all voters wanted to maintain or increase defense spending, but the strongest demand came from

TABLE 6.3

Religion and Policy Issues in the 2000 Electorate (percentages)

	Economic problem most vital	*Cut govern-ment services*	*Spend more on hunger*	*Spend more on environ-ment*	*Favor national health care*	*Reduce foreign activity*	*Maintain or add defense spending*	*Support Israel over Arabs*
Evangelical	22	53	36	41	30	40	72	52
Traditionalist	18	59	35	37	27	41	73	56
Centrist	39	30	33	55	39	44	73	39
Modernist	31	25	61	63	38	17	61	22
Latter-day Saints	15	56	29	47	14	37	91	37
Mainline	31	44	42	56	32	37	64	30
Traditionalist	26	58	32	44	17	35	75	39
Centrist	32	40	41	56	32	42	61	27
Modernist	34	36	52	67	44	31	56	24
Catholic	38	37	51	56	42	36	69	25
Traditionalist	35	42	45	45	31	37	72	26
Centrist	35	42	39	48	40	44	68	22
Modernist	44	26	71	77	59	26	66	27
Hispanic Catholic	16	37	52	62	62	48	55	33
Hispanic Protestant	33	24	56	51	51	39	38	50
African American Catholic	34	22	43	30	60	48	65	47
African American Protestant	28	27	66	47	51	44	53	21
Jewish	61	25	72	69	58	30	44	70
Other Religions	30	27	60	74	62	35	50	28
Secular	34	31	53	67	48	38	52	27
Total Sample	30	39	48	54	40	39	62	35

Source: Third National Study of Religion and Politics (University of Akron, Akron, OH, 2000).

religious traditionalists, with more restrained approval from religious minorities, Jews, and seculars. Most voters wanted "even-handed" treatment of Israel and the Arabs in the Middle East, but over a third thought the United States should favor Israel. This posture was supported by Jews, heavily Democratic, but also by the strongly Republican Evangelical traditionalists, who were also quite hostile to Muslims (data not shown). These divisions had special relevance to religious politics after the events of September 11.

The Bush Administration: Personnel and Policy

From the very beginning of his administration, Bush continued the religious themes that had permeated his campaign. Although inaugurations are often accompanied by ritual expressions of "civil religion," the Bush ceremonies struck many observers as more revealing of both the man and his religious coalition. The pre-inaugural prayer meeting, attended by clergy and laity from many faiths, was held at St. John's Episcopal Church, near the White House. The prayers at the inauguration itself were offered by Franklin Graham, heir apparent to his father Billy Graham's evangelistic organization, and by Kirbyjon Caldwell, an African American Methodist friend of the president. Bush's inaugural address was full of religious symbolism, and one of his first acts after taking the oath of office was to issue a proclamation designating his first Sunday in office as a "national day of prayer." All these efforts elicited considerable criticism from liberals for their conservative Christian tone but won warm praise from many religious conservatives.

Both in personal and political actions the new president sought to solidify his base while reaching out to other religious groups. The president maintained his regimen of daily prayer and Bible reading, as well as regular Sunday worship in various settings, and during his first months in office met frequently with clergy, concentrating on those religious sectors important to his electoral and policy concerns. Evangelical leaders were not only critical links to that vital constituency but would also prove crucial to action on several administration proposals. African American Protestant clergy, who had a special interest in the faith-based initiative, were frequent White House visitors, as were Roman Catholic priests and bishops, continuing Bush's wooing of that important constituency. Indeed, in just one month the president awarded a posthumous congressional Gold Medal to the late Cardinal John O'Connor, ate dinner with the archbishop of the District of Columbia, inaugurated the John Paul II Cultural Center in Washington, and met with forty-five Catholic clergy (Lopez 2001).

The religious appeal went beyond rhetoric and symbolism. Bush's personnel choices represented the GOP religious coalition more fully than did the earlier Reagan-Bush administrations. Although no systematic data exists on the religious traits of presidential appointees, any close examination reveals the distinctive religious coloration of both the White House and cabinet. Religious traditionalists were generally pleased by

Bush's selections. Many of his White House staff were quite observant religiously, albeit from different traditions. Speechwriter David Frum, himself a Canadian Jew of secular leanings, noted the Evangelical flavor of the Bush White House, "where attendance at Bible study was, if not compulsory, not quite *uncompulsory*, either" (Frum 2003b, 3–4). Chief speechwriter Michael Gerson, a devout Evangelical, would be responsible for many of the president's most memorable lines over the next two years, often drawing on religious expression. Chief-of-staff Andrew Card's wife was a Methodist minister, presidential counselor Karen Hughes was a Presbyterian elder, National Security adviser Condoleeza Rice was the daughter of a Presbyterian pastor and a devout Christian, and the list goes on. Even staff from minority traditions, such as Jews, tended to be devout (Milbank 2002b).

Bush liked to start Cabinet meetings with prayer and preferred executives who could offer them without discomfort. Although the cabinet ran the gamut of American Christian communities, it also favored the faithful. From Secretary of State Colin Powell, an active Episcopalian, to Education Secretary Rod Paige, a Baptist Sunday school teacher, deacon, and usher, to Commerce Secretary Don Evans, a devout Methodist and old Bible study partner of the president, many had strong religious credentials. Some appointees, moreover, attracted attention for just this reason. John Ashcroft's nomination as attorney general aroused enormous controversy, as secular and religious liberals doubted whether a devout Pentecostal could enforce federal laws such as the Access to Clinics Act, while Evangelicals saw his confirmation as a test of Bush's moral commitment. Later, Ashcroft's prayer groups at the Justice Department were criticized as violations of the Constitution's Establishment Clause, and he remained a lightening rod for liberals while not always moving fast enough on issues such as pornography for many social conservatives (Toobin 2002).

Bush also appointed traditionalist Catholics to cabinet posts at Housing and Urban Development, Health and Human Services, and Veterans Affairs. HUD Secretary-designate Mel Martinez occasioned a stir in conservative circles when his extensive religious reflections upon accepting Bush's nomination were "censored" from transcripts in many national papers. HHS Secretary Tommy Thompson, the pro-life former Wisconsin governor, had not always followed Catholic teaching in political decisions, but his feuds were usually with Catholic liberals, such as Rembert Weakland, the Archbishop of Milwaukee. Catholic traditionalists were especially numerous at second- and third-tier posts, joining many Evangelicals. Bush also appointed one prominent pro-choice Catholic, Tom Ridge, as Secretary of Homeland Security, after passing him over as a vice presidential possibility during the 2000 campaign.

Although the cabinet also featured some mainline Protestants and one or two members with no detectable religious connections, its composition heralded a reversal in fortunes for top religious lobbies. Evangelical leaders and Catholic bishops now had access, while the liberal mainline Protestant leadership, epitomized by the National Council of Churches (NCC), lost the preference they enjoyed under Clinton. As Bush's policy priorities became clear, ranging from tax cuts to education reform, the NCC members voiced increasingly strong opposition, reaching a crescendo during the Iraq crisis of 2002–2003. And although the administration was notable for the absence of Jews from the cabinet, Jewish groups enjoyed a surprising degree of access to the Bush White House, in part because of the receptiveness of Evangelical staffers there (Edsall 2002a; Frum 2003b, 246–60).

During the first two years of his administration, Bush sought to make public policy align with his own values and those of his religious coalition. He pushed for marriage incentives in welfare reform legislation, allowed federal funds to be used to restore historic houses of worship, challenged state medical marijuana laws, and responded to Evangelical concerns about the persecution of Christians abroad, to name only a few. In these instances, the GOP traditionalist coalition united in support of administration policies. On some key issues, however, critical divisions within that constituency created strategic problems for the White House. Three issues illustrate these variations: abortion and stem-cell research; the faith-based initiative and educational vouchers; and the Iraq crisis and Middle East peace initiative.

For many religious groups, the classic litmus test for the president was his performance on the abortion issue. Although Bush clearly had pro-life sympathies, he had always moved cautiously. He had chosen a pro-life running mate, Dick Cheney, but refused to exile pro-choice Republicans from his entourage or, later, from his administration. The First Lady was on record as opposing the overturning of *Roe v. Wade,* and Bush himself doubted that public opinion was ready for that change, arguing that he wanted first to create a "culture of life" among Americans (Toner 2000). Nevertheless, he moved to implement pro-life policies within the existing limits of opinion. Although he disappointed some anti-abortion activists by not reversing the Clinton FDA decision approving RU-486, he quickly reinstated Reagan's "Mexico City" policy, which prohibited U.S. government agencies from funding international organizations that promote abortions, and he promised to veto any congressional action reversing this decision. He also supported other controversial pro-life initiatives, such as the Unborn Victims of Violence Act, and advocated medical coverage for unborn children under the Children's Health Insurance Program (Burger 2002). Finally, the president consistently promoted legislation banning "partial birth abortion," which finally passed both houses of Congress and was signed into law by Bush on November 5, 2003.

Bush's chief contribution to the pro-life cause may not have been in legislative or administrative form but in his federal court nominations, which included many pro-life jurists, often traditionalist Catholics or Evangelicals, such as noted church-state law expert Michael McConnell (Glaberson 2001). Although most cleared the Senate, a few vocal pro-life nominees were bitterly resisted by Democrats on the Senate Judiciary Committee, including Texas supreme court justice Priscilla Owen, former Clinton Justice Department official Miguel Estrada, and Alabama attorney general William H. Pryor Jr. The hearings for Pryor, a devout Catholic, eventually erupted into full-scale partisan warfare when Republican senators charged Democrats with anti-Catholic bias, eliciting angry responses (N. Lewis 2003). Meanwhile, both pro-choice and pro-life groups mobilized over these candidates, prepping for a future Armageddon over a Bush Supreme Court nomination.

While partial-birth abortion and judicial nominations united pro-life forces behind Bush, his prolonged deliberation over stem-cell research divided them. Although many scientists saw such research leading to useful treatments for many dread diseases, most pro-life groups, as well as the Catholic bishops, wanted an absolute ban on federal funding for such research, which involves destroying human embryos to acquire the cells. Indeed, the pope himself lobbied Bush for a ban. But other conservative religious groups were not as adamant, sensing perhaps growing public support for such research, even among Evangelicals and Catholics. Bush had endorsed a ban during the campaign, but HHS Secretary Thompson pushed to keep the issue open, and as some conservative political and religious leaders reconsidered their position, so did Bush. After elaborate and well-publicized consultations with scientists, clergy, and ethicists, he rendered a Solomonic decision allowing research funding for "existing lines" of stem cells but not for those produced by future destruction of embryos. The president's decision disappointed fervent pro-lifers but met with surprisingly positive responses from most Evangelical leaders and even from some Catholic traditionalists (although the Bishops' Conference complained). In the end, Bush avoided a serious rupture with the pro-life community while partially accommodating researchers' demands (Goodstein 2001; Frum 2003b, 106–10). Moreover, Bush continued to fight for a total legislative ban on human cloning, and by the time of the 2002 election most pro-life groups were once more firmly aligned behind the White House.

The faith-based initiative and educational voucher issue presented even more complicated constituency problems for Bush. To some extent, these questions divided religious leaders along culture war fractures, with traditionalists leaning toward the president and modernists and seculars opposing him. But the battle lines were not quite that simple. The Catholic Church, with long experience in providing social services, was generally supportive. The leaders of some religious minorities, such as African American Protestants, also favored allowing religious institutions to deliver public services, whether drug treatment or education, but were often suspicious of an "illegitimate" Republican president offering such policies. Evangelicals were deeply split: some groups supported the faith-based idea enthusiastically, but others feared such programs would compromise their religious mission or result in unacceptable regulation of religious institutions.

Despite these crosscurrents, Bush plunged in. On January 29, 2001, he announced a major initiative to foster cooperation between religious groups and federal agencies, created the White House Office of Faith-Based and Community Initiatives and satellite offices in five cabinet departments, issued executive orders removing some barriers to religious participation, and proposed legislation to lower other legal obstacles. The legislative issues proved too difficult to resolve quickly, however. John DiIulio, the Catholic scholar who headed the initiative's White House office, found the tides of religious politics too strong to negotiate agreement behind the president's plan (Frum 2003b, 100–103). After a public feud with Evangelical leaders, the irascible DiIulio resigned, to be replaced by another Catholic, Jim Towey, who related better to Evangelicals (Mercer 2002). Although Bush's proposal cleared the House, it foundered in the Senate over the critical issue of whether religious groups providing public services could restrict hiring to those sharing their faith. Such provisions were demanded by most Evangelical and Catholic traditionalists but were rejected by religious liberals and church-state separationists, fearing discrimination on the basis of race, gender, or sexual preference. Eventually Bush settled (temporarily) for legislation encouraging charitable contributions but continued to fight for religious groups' right to hire within the faith, even when using public funds (Allen and Cooperman 2003). Meanwhile, the administration issued new regulations paving the way for religious groups to qualify under existing law (Conn 2003). Eventually seven cabinet agencies created offices on faith-based services, funded pilot projects with religious charities, and conducted outreach to encourage participation by religious institutions.

Bush's wary campaign commitment to educational vouchers was quickly overshadowed in 2001 by his proposals for stricter testing and accountability for public schools, as he worked with Senator Ted Kennedy to produce the "No Child Left Behind" Act. Nevertheless, the administration was emboldened to renew its advocacy of vouchers by the Supreme Court's decision in *Zelman v. Simmon-Harris,* in June 2002, upholding a program in Cleveland that included religious schools (Leaming 2003). Opponents criticized what they perceived as the "real" educational objective of his voucher plan—to aid religious institutions—and jumped on Secretary Rod Paige's praise of Christian schools in 2003 as proof (Cooperman 2003). Their suspicions were also fueled by guidelines issued by Paige in early 2003 that seemed to expand the scope for religious activities in public schools. Despite the opposition, Bush continued to push for pilot programs including religious schools, most notably in Washington, D.C.

In normal times, one might expect that Bush's interactions with religious groups would center on abortion, charitable choice, and other social policies. Ironically, however, the issues that subjected Bush's religion to intense media and academic scrutiny were not domestic but national security questions. The attacks of September 11, 2001, Bush's policies on Iraq, and renewed engagement with the Israeli-Palestinian conflict brought the president's own personal faith and the handling of religious issues into sharp relief (Rosenberg 2003; Keller 2003b).

The attacks on the World Trade Center and the Pentagon evoked even more religious rhetoric from Bush than is typical of presidential civil religion during national traumas. In the days after the disaster, whether in memorial services, speeches to Congress, or public statements, the president drew on religious themes, with the aid of speechwriter Mike Gerson, drawing broader meanings from the events. Although the language was often Christian in origin, Bush was usually careful to express religious themes in the most ecumenical vein possible, especially after an incautious reference to a "crusade" against evildoers angered Muslims. Nevertheless, a host of religious and secular critics saw his rhetoric drawing too strongly from Christian dualism, painting international conflicts as a simple struggle between good and evil.

Although the immediate effect of September 11 was to unite the American religious community behind the president in classic "rally 'round the flag" fashion, events did raise the problem of dealing with Islam, especially in the form of the American Muslim community. Here the president got high marks from most observers, as he forcefully reminded Americans that the "war on terror" was not directed at that faith or its adherents. Bush invited Muslim clerics to participate in the national memorial services for September 11 victims, visited a Washington mosque, met Muslim leaders in the White House, and hosted an Id al-Fitr event there on November 19. In these highly publicized events, the president repeatedly emphasized interreligious religious harmony, despite criticism from some conservative Christian supporters. And although his antiterrorism policies eventually strained relations with many American Muslims, the president certainly helped minimize anti-Muslim reaction by the public.

The united religious front created by September 11 soon broke down, however, as the administration instigated hostilities abroad. Afghanistan began the erosion, as liberal Catholic and mainline Protestant organizations worried about the scope of the military campaign and the prospect of civilian casualties. Evangelical groups, as well as leading Catholic traditionalists, quietly supported the administration. As Bush moved against Iraq, however, a full-blown religious war erupted, as mainline denominations, both individually and through the NCC, protested vigorously. Indeed, few events of the past two decades have evoked such an outpouring from the mainline leadership—including that of Bush's own denomination, the United Methodist Church. Although the press portrayed a united Protestant front against the president's policies, Bush still drew strong backing from many Evangelicals, including officials from the Southern Baptist Convention and Assemblies of God. The leadership of most Jewish organizations was divided over the war and for the most part stood apart from the national religious debate (Goodstein 2002, 2003).

Perhaps the most visible struggle over Iraq occurred within the American Catholic community, always of strategic concern to Bush. As Pope John Paul II warned against military action the American bishops followed suit, arguing that Bush had not satisfied the criteria for a "just war." Catholic traditionalists were torn between their affection for the president and their respect for religious authority. Some traditionalist leaders such as Deal Hudson and Michael Novak argued that the just war criteria were in fact met and that, in any event, such prudential judgments were reserved for political, not religious leaders. Novak even visited the Vatican to press Bush's case with church officials, without apparent effect (Allen 2003).

The impact of all this "elite" religious agitation on public opinion was unclear. The press reported extensive discussions among conflicted American Catholics on whether to follow the president or the pope and bishops, and observed some heated debates in mainline Protestant churches (Bernstein and Daspin 2003). Polls showed that churchgoers did hear a good bit about Iraq from the pulpit, and when they did, it usually followed the dominant position of their tradition: Evangelical clergy favored the war, Catholic, mainline and African American Protestant pastors opposed it (Pew Center 2003). But religious critics of the war were soon lamenting their lack of impact, as the people in the pews rallied behind the president as military action began.

As the administration turned west toward the Israeli-Palestinian conflict in the spring of 2003, the lines of religious division shifted again. Evangelicals have joined American Jews as fervent supporters of Israel, and their increasing prominence in the GOP has bolstered the Israeli position, especially in Congress, where Evangelicals dominate House leadership posts. Mainline Protestant and Catholic churches, for various reasons, have been more sympathetic toward the plight of the Palestinians. During Bush's first two years, the pro-Israel coalition was generally pleased with his apparent "tilt" toward Israel, although it mobilized effectively when Bush showed signs of wavering. Later, when Bush announced his "road map" for Middle East peace, his supporting coalitions were temporarily reversed, as the initiative was praised by mainliners and Catholics but criticized by many Evangelical and Jewish leaders. Indeed, the press soon claimed that Bush's subsequent "vacillations" were due to adverse reaction by Evangelical lobbies and legislators, such as Southern Baptist Tom DeLay, the House majority leader (Wagner 2003). This perception loosed a torrent of op-ed pieces blasting the influence of Christian conservatives over the White House, often hinting that Bush shared the apocalyptic vision supposedly informing Evangelical support for Israel. Whatever the validity of these perceptions, by the summer of 2003 Bush was carefully threading his way among the domestic religious constituencies increasingly mobilized around Middle East policy.

The Bush Impact: Presidential Evaluations, 2000 and 2002

All of the policy debates we have sampled here show the president working within the confines of his religious constituency, although conflicts within that coalition often complicated his task. Of course, religious concerns were only one aspect of these presidential deliberations; we certainly do not contend that they provide a full explanation of any decision.

In the end, how did the Bush administration "play" among religious voters? We can offer a preliminary assessment from the 2000 and 2002 National Election Studies, focusing on panel respondents interviewed in both years. Given the limited number of panel respondents on whom we have full religious information (*N* = 1,069), in table 6.4 we consider only the larger religious communities. The 2002 NES is limited in another way, as it asked only a few issue questions, mostly on foreign and economic policies. Still, we can draw some inferences about reaction to Bush's social policies from the changes in his ratings among respondents who reported traditionalist locations or took conservative stances on these issues in 2000.

During the 2002 congressional elections, the president was riding high in the polls, but his evaluations still varied markedly among religious groups, in much the same fashion as they had in 2000. Evangelical traditionalists were still warmest toward Bush, with seculars, Jews, and African American Protestants least approving. Note, however, that Bush had strong job-approval ratings among Catholics, most notably among traditionalists and, more surprisingly, modernists. Bush's "thermometer ratings" (how "warmly" voters felt toward him) followed an almost identical pattern (data not shown). In the same vein, an index of four variables tapping approval of Bush's international policies showed similar results.[2] More surprisingly, public approval of his economic man-

TABLE 6.4

Bush Evaluations, Religious Groups, and Outcomes in the 2002 Election (percentages)

	Bush job approval in 2002	*Approve Bush foreign policies*	*Approve Bush economic job*	*Approve Bush 2001 tax cut*	*GOP U.S. house vote*	*Reported 2002 turnout*	*Average number campaign acts*	*Average move toward GOP*
Evangelical	76	76	68	48	68	59	0.48	0.17
Traditionalist	87	81	78	56	79	73	0.56	0.27
Centrist	69	73	60	40	56	50	0.53	0.20
Modernist	64	68	58	39	50	44	0.21	-0.12
Mainline	71	71	53	46	60	71	0.44	0.14
Traditionalist	78	78	67	61	76	80	0.64	0.15
Centrist	75	74	59	50	59	64	0.42	0.12
Modernist	61	62	37	31	50	71	0.33	0.16
Catholic	78	77	60	47	61	65	0.51	0.22
Traditionalist	84	80	70	56	63	85	0.70	0.30
Centrist	72	76	51	46	67	68	0.47	0.11
Modernist	82	78	66	43	49	52	0.45	0.32
All Other Religions	69	66	44	42	30	49	0.32	0.13
Secular	54	64	41	35	31	61	0.35	0.00
Jewish	48	65	28	35	19	89	0.71	0.17
Black Protestant	45	48	27	36	25	48	0.60	-0.18
Total Sample	69	70	53	44	53	61	0.46	0.12

Source: National Election Study 2002. Panel respondents 2000–2002 (N = 1069)

agement and of the 2001 tax cut also conformed to the very same pattern, although at somewhat lower levels in all religious groups (due largely to the number of "undecided" respondents). Thus, the same basic religious coalition undergirded most Bush administration policies across the arenas of foreign and economic policy.

What about social issues? Unfortunately the 2002 NES contains no items on abortion, vouchers, or faith-based initiatives, so we are handicapped in assessing how religious groups reacted to Bush's actions here. Still, we can make some strong inferences. Given the effects of international events, Bush's ratings went up most dramatically among those religious groups that opposed his election and disagreed with most of his campaign commitments. In the same vein, Bush's thermometer scores rose most from 2000 to 2002 among voters who are pro-choice, rather than those who are pro-life, who strongly supported him throughout. On an NES social traditionalism scale,[3] Bush's temperature rose four degrees among strong traditionalists, eight among moderate traditionalists, eleven among moderate libertarians, and almost thirteen among the most libertarian voters. A multivariate analysis shows that the conventional explanation for Bush's popularity in 2002 was correct: foreign crises elicited a rally phenomenon with the greatest influence on those who were initially critical of Bush.

Finally, table 6.4 shows several ways that the GOP's success in 2002 congressional elections may have been shaped by religious group behavior. The 2002 House vote followed the 2000 religious template, but with some modifications (see, for example, Green 2003). Religious traditionalists voted Republican in large numbers, reported high turnout rates, and were more likely to be active in the campaign than their centrist and modernist counterparts. (They were also most likely to report mobilizing contacts from GOP organizations, religious lobbies, and similar sources.) The only Democratic-leaning groups reporting high activism were Jews and African American Protestants, and the latter had relatively low voter turnout. Furthermore, the entire panel reported a small movement toward Republican Party identification over the course of Bush's first two years. The largest such movements were among traditionalist and centrist Evangelicals—and, more portentously, among traditionalist and modernist Catholics, perhaps rewarding Bush's assiduous attention to their faith over the previous three years.

Religion and Bush's Future

Like Bill Clinton, George W. Bush had to negotiate the shoals of cultural and religious conflict in the United States. And like Clinton, Bush had an almost intuitive understanding of parts of the American religious community and was a quick learner about others. And even more than the case with Clinton, Bush's private behavior, public rhetoric, and policy proposals were infused by religion. The president's electoral base was rooted in a coalition of theological conservatives from the three major white Christian traditions, especially Evangelicals. His campaign promises and policy initiatives were designed, in part, to solidify his base, while extending the GOP's appeal to Catholics, as well as Hispanic and African American Protestants. In office, Bush exhibited a deft touch dealing with issues crucial to his traditionalist constituency, such as abortion, satisfying many of their expectations without alienating other religious groups. In the short term, however, he was unable to execute his "expansionary" policies, such as the faith-based initiative and educational vouchers. Solid Democratic resistance in Congress, divisions among his traditionalist supporters, and skepticism on the part of religious leaders in the targeted minority religious communities stymied his efforts.

Bush's religious strategy was, of course, affected by events unforeseen when he took office. Just as Clinton benefited from economic prosperity that kept his ratings high even in the midst of impeachment battles, Bush's popularity was sustained by the international conflicts dominating the national agenda after September 11. That popularity largely overrode the normal Democratic propensities of several religious constituencies, at least as long as terrorism and the war in Iraq headed the national agenda. That popularity provided a boost for Republican congressional candidates in 2002, but the Bush religious coalition did not guarantee a national majority for Republican presidential candidates, as the 2000 election had demonstrated. This was especially true if a stagnant economy replaced the war on terror as the main focus of attention. In that event, even the traditionalist coalition backing Bush's economic policies would be attenuated and his support among religious minorities and secular voters would plummet. Should an economic recovery occur by 2004, the president would still have to go beyond his religious base and pursue an expansionist religious policy, focusing on the very same religious groups targeted in 2000. He would seek to extend his modest success among white Catholics to Hispanic Catholics and Protestants and, perhaps, to still-suspicious African American Protestants. The president and his adviser Rove gave every indication of following that strategy as they planned Bush's legislative agenda for the fall of 2003 and his presidential campaign in 2004 (Lemann 2003).

The best-laid campaign plans are often upset by unexpected events. The Supreme Court's 2003 decision striking down state sodomy laws and the subsequent decision of the Massachusetts Supreme Court striking down restrictions on same-sex marriage evoked a massive reaction among religious conservatives that threatened to raise these questions to the forefront of the public agenda. Such issues, which Bush had always soft-pedaled, seem tailor-made for dividing traditionalists and centrists within the GOP and potentially reducing the party's appeal to independent voters. If traditionalist forces mobilize to protect traditional understandings of marriage, whether through statute or constitutional amendment, the Bush administration faces the inevitability of either disappointing core supporters or forfeiting the middle ground. An unexpected vacancy on the Supreme Court would raise similar problems. In any event, whether the election 2004 brings a focus on economic issues or foreign policy or a revival of hot-button social issues, the Bush administration's actions will be shaped in part by religious forces.

III

Washington Politics

7 ONE PRESIDENT, TWO PRESIDENCIES
George W. Bush in Peace and War

Peri E. Arnold

George W. Bush has enjoyed an unprecedented pattern of popular approval over the course of his first term. Beginning with dubious legitimacy and no mandate, he has centralized the executive branch, launched substantial changes in economic and domestic policy, and refashioned U.S. foreign policy. Bush's success in office is related to the Republican Party's resurgent strength, its unity, and the president's harmonious relationship with its conservative base. The Republican Party, despite an evenly divided electorate, has the advantage of strong ideological consensus, control (albeit narrow) of both houses of Congress, and a structural advantage in the Electoral College due to the overrepresentation of small-population states. However, to fully understand Bush's leadership we must examine his use of the presidency's institutional resources and possibilities.

Bush has in effect occupied two different presidencies. In his conventional, constitutional presidency, in which he is constrained by checks and balances, Bush held a questionable legitimacy, lacked the ability to claim an obvious mandate, and depended heavily on his partisan advantages. In his war presidency he is armed with great unilateral powers, possesses a high degree of legitimacy, claiming what John

Pitney elsewhere in this volume calls a "khaki mandate," and demands bipartisan support.[1]

Incumbent, Institution, and Context

The president is an incumbent within an institution wrapped in a political context. Bush brings to the office his style, skills, partisanship, and ambition. He is constrained by the possibilities available to him within the office. The office contains authority, organization, symbolic meaning, and potential for power. The political scientist Hugh Heclo says of the presidency that it shapes what incumbents do in office: "In terms of its *deep structure* . . . the office is largely a given. . . . The total effect is to program the modern president" (Heclo 1999, 24–25). Additionally, we must see that the issue and political contexts in which the president works affect presidential authority and capacity. Thus, presidents shape their leadership—their use of the presidency's capacities—responding to the challenges of their contexts.

The presidency's deep structure contains dual sources of authority. Domestic issues engage presidential capacities differently than do foreign threats. For reasons both of constitutional authority and precedents, the presidency's national-security role exhibits broader and more unilateral authority than the institution's domestic leadership role. Thus, George W. Bush has been president in two very different contexts, each triggering different kinds of presidential authority. This chapter conceptualizes these two kinds of authority as two different presidencies. The first is the conventional, domestic presidency. The second presidency emerged on September 11.

Before September 11: Bush's Conventional Presidency

On January 20, 2001, Bush entered the conventional, constitutional presidency. The presidency's prominence and authority expanded during the twentieth century (Lowi 1985), yet the office remains constrained by constitutional design and limited by the intensity of American interest group politics. Politics as usual constrain a new president's freedom to turn campaign promises into public policy (Skocpol 1997). These constraints have driven incumbents to increased public rhetoric and highly personal leadership, going directly to the people to finesse the conventional office's constraints (Kernell 1993). Indeed, rhetorical assertion was a crucial means for Bush's legitimacy claim to the presidency after the Supreme Court's decision in his favor. One of his advisors described the president-elect's challenge as "making the case that he has a legitimate claim to the presidency, without ever really acknowledging that there is any real question of legitimacy" (Sanger 2000, A1). President-elect Bush quickly stated that his status was that of an elected and not a chosen president. He announced, "I was not elected to serve one party, but to serve the country" (Sanger 2000, A18). Bush's solution to his legitimacy problem was to act and speak as a president with unquestioned legitimacy, and partisanship made the strategy work. Republican control of Congress, along with fervent Republican support for Bush, mitigated possibilities that his legitimacy would be effectively questioned.

Assembling a Republican Administration

The post-election struggle cost Bush a month of the brief time that he had to prepare his transition into office (Pfiffner 1996). Nominees had to be identified for cabinet and subcabinet positions and the White House staff selected. Policy priorities had to be developed, and the new administration had to tweak the executive budget for fiscal-year 2002, prepared by the last administration and due in Congress in February 2001. While he was inexperienced with national government, President-elect Bush relied on an experienced Republican government-in-waiting. His choice of Richard Cheney as the vice-presidential candidate signaled Bush's ties to veterans of the Ford, Reagan, and the first Bush administrations.

Cheney directed the transition. He had been President Ford's chief of staff, the first President Bush's defense secretary, and he had worked on four presidential transitions. The 2000–2001 transition used twenty-two planning committees, twenty of which were chaired by former federal officials (White 2000, A31). The breadth of government experience available in the 2000–2001 transition gave it a marked efficiency compared with the Clinton administration's 1992–1993 transition to office (Burke 2002). Political scientist Paul Light said that the Bush transition accomplished in its first two weeks more than the Clinton transition had done after seven weeks (Bennet 2001, 26).

With two exceptions, Bush's fourteen cabinet nominees received quick Senate approval. The nomination of Senator John Ashcroft, a hero of Christian conservatives, for attorney general, survived a strong attack.

Linda Chavez, a veteran conservative of the Reagan and first Bush administrations, failed to receive approval for secretary of labor following news that she had employed an undocumented worker. In this case Bush revealed a crisp efficiency, contrasted with President Clinton's nomination problems. Clinton had allowed Zoe Baird's nomination as attorney general to dangle for nine days after it was revealed she had not paid payroll tax for a household worker. Bush had Chavez withdraw her name fifty-five hours after negative news broke (Allen 2001, A1). For all of the experience it mobilized, the Bush transition did suffer a disadvantage from its delayed start. Bush was slow in filling positions below cabinet rank. Four-fifths of these remained unfilled as of June 2001, a pace that fell significantly behind Clinton's (Hines 2001, A20).

Eight Months in the Conventional Presidency

A transition prepares a new administration to govern. In his inaugural address, Bush stated his goals, reiterating the policy themes he had stressed in his campaign as a "compassionate conservative." He promised to "reclaim America's schools," reduce taxes "to recover the momentum of our economy and reward the effort . . . of working Americans." And he declared that compassion for those in need was more than the work of government; it is the purpose of religious bodies. "Church and charity, synagogue and mosque, lend our communities their humanity, and they will have an honored place in our plans and our laws" (Bush 2001a, 13). Implying that the outside world could be kept at arm's length, Bush devoted just two of the speech's twenty-nine paragraphs to foreign affairs.

The new administration entered office with another, unstated, priority. At the end of his term, President Clinton had used presidential authority in a number of areas Republicans considered controversial. Large tracts of public domain were given additional protection against economic use. Federal agencies issued rules and guidelines on workplace safety, on national forests, energy efficiency standards, and stricter meat inspection, among other matters. Bush embraced his executive authority to order, where possible, that these rules and orders not be implemented until reviewed by his appointees (Rosenbaum 2001a, 4:16).

Tax cuts and education reform were Bush's highest legislative priorities. His arguments for the tax cut were twofold. He cited the latest official projections of more than $5.6 trillion in federal revenue surpluses over the next decade (Pianin 2001, 8). Repeatedly Bush pronounced that the surplus was not government's money but belonged to the hard-working taxpayer and that free-spending government would waste it. He argued that tax reductions would have the additional benefit of stimulating a slowing economy. Was there a contradiction between the claim that the economy was slowing and that there would be huge revenue surpluses as far out as the eye could see? If so, it did not appear to trouble the president or the electorate.

The politics of the tax bill exhibited Bush's tactical use of the crafted message. If one assumes that the public begins with little knowledge about a particular policy issue, then what people think will echo what they hear. And the most prominent politician can fill that knowledge vacuum with a well-crafted message (Jacobs and Shapiro 2000). Bush used the presidency's bully pulpit to articulate punchy, simple reasons why the country needed the tax cut. His message fit either scenario, a large budget surplus *or* a sinking economy. In the first instance, the surplus was the "people's money"; in the second, the tax cut was a "jobs and growth" policy.

On June 7 Bush signed the "Economic Growth and Tax Relief Reconciliation Act of 2001," passing his tax proposals into law. The new law would reduce government's revenue by a projected $1.35 trillion over the next ten years. Bush said, "Tax relief is an achievement for middle class families squeezed by high energy prices and credit card debt." He claimed also that the bill's passage was a sign of a new bipartisanship he had brought to Washington because it had drawn a number of Democratic votes. "Tax relief is the first achievement produced by the new tone in Washington, and it was produced in record time" (Bush 2001a).

In fact, the president's crafted message ignored the reality of the law's distributional effects. True, it reduced marginal rates for the lowest income tax payers, and as a compromise with congressional Democrats, the law backdated to 2000 the reduction in the lowest tax rate and issued refunds to reflect the new rate. But, as Ray Tatalovich explains elsewhere in this volume, the largest effect of the law was to substantially reduce the tax burden of the highest income Americans. It was estimated that the top 1 percent of income earners would receive a total of 38 percent of the law's benefits once the estate tax was phased out (Kessler and Eilperin 2001, A1).

Bush's education bill went to Congress just after the inauguration, although it was not signed into law until January 8, 2002. Compared to the tax cut, it was a model of bipartisanship. Bush accommodated Democrats, dropping from the bill his campaign promise for school vouchers. He agreed to Democrat's demands for increased school funding (although his later budgets did not incorporate that promised funding). When signing his "No Child Left Behind Act," the president praised the leading Democrats on education policy, Massachusetts senator Ted Kennedy and California representative George Miller.

President Bush's moderation in education policy was anathema to his most conservative supporters. Columnist Robert D. Novak, for example, wrote, "A loyal Republican congressman, heartsick that George W. Bush had capitulated to Ted Kennedy and George Miller on education . . . asked a House GOP leader to explain. How could the party leadership support this unholy alliance that so betrayed Republican principles?" (Novak 2001). But in the conventional presidency, Bush could not rely only on core conservatives if he wanted to have a successful 2004 campaign. But five months into his presidency public opinion polls suggested that the president's effort to present himself as a moderate were failing. A *New York Times/CBS News* poll reported that only 39 percent of respondents approved of Bush's handling of the environment and 33 percent approved of his energy policy. In the same poll, 57 percent thought his policies favored "the rich." Furthermore, 64 percent thought it preferable that federal dollars be used for Social Security and Medicare rather than a tax cut (*New York Times* 2001, A1).

Consequently, the White House sought to soften the president's image by reshaping his policy messages. As Frank Bruni reported, "The administration also intends to keep having Mr. Bush promote his energy plan as an environmentally sensitive one. Today, he posed with giant sequoias in California; next week, he is to be in the Everglades in Florida" (Bruni 2001a, A24). The president visited the Everglades, appearing in public with the state's two Democratic senators and with a Democratic congressperson and avoided appearing with Republican legislators (Berke 2001, A1).

During the summer of 2001, events conspired to additionally embarrass the administration. The president's judgment in rejecting the Kyoto Protocol on global warming was questioned in a June 6 report prepared by a panel of experts from the National Academy of Sciences. The report affirmed "the mainstream scientific view that the earth's atmosphere was getting warmer and that human activity was largely responsible (Seelye 2001, A1). Then Senator Jeffords of Vermont abandoned the Republicans, explaining that the party's extremism caused his departure. Later that summer, the Congressional Budget Office forecast a sharp drop in the budget surpluses that were expected for the current fiscal year, undermining one of Bush's reasons for the tax cut. A March 2001 report projected a surplus of $122 billion for the current fiscal year. In August, that surplus had shrunk to a trivial $600 million (neither estimate includes Social Security revenues) (Stevenson 2001, A1). After his quick legislative success with tax cuts, Bush seemed to have lost a sense of how he would use the presidency. He seemed adrift, without an agenda. And his public rhetoric seemed less energetic and purposeful. In midsummer 2001 Republican political strategists questioned the administration's political skills, suggesting, "that the White House political compass has often seemed askew (Berke and Bruni 2001, A11). All through August of 2001 Bush vacationed at his ranch in Crawford, Texas, contributing to a sense that the administration had run out of energy and ideas (Bruni 2001b, 1:1).

As if characterizing a diminished presidency, the *New York Times* reported on September 9, 2001, that Bush would flip a coin in the White House Rose Garden to open the National Football League's season, determining which team would get the ball in ten different stadiums. The *Times* wrote that the coin toss by the nation's "First Fan" demonstrated that "the man adores sports. He installed a T-ball diamond on the South Lawn of the White House. And he prefers chatting about balls and strikes to the fuzzy math of the federal budget" (Van Natta Jr. 2001, 4:3).

Post–September 11: Bush's War Presidency

September 11 made the First Fan into a warrior president. Those observing him reported they saw a dramatic personal transformation. Former Democratic governor of Colorado, Richard Lamm, said of Bush's speech to the nation nine days after the attacks: "It was just what the country needed. I think he's grown years in the last days" (Schrader and Soragher 2001, A16). Bush's political intimates saw his performance after September 11 as something they "knew" he had in him. His longtime aide, Karen Hughes, said, "I don't see him as a different person. From my perspective, he is the same President Bush that I saw going through different issues in Texas" (Kornblut 2001, A1).

Like most journalists, and many political scientists, Lamb and Hughes assumed that Bush's character explained his performance. But this perspective captures only *one* dimension of presidential leadership and overlooks the institution and its context. For Bush to invoke his national-security role in response to terrorist attacks was to call on a strain of authority unavailable to the conventional presidency while solidifying his legitimacy and expanding his ability for action. Thus, the changes in Bush's leadership after September 11 were more than an expression of personal character; they reflected the emergence of a different presidency within a threatening new context.

The War Presidency's Authority

National-security crises trigger new authority and mitigate separation of powers. Such crises also heighten citizens' acceptance of unilateral presidential powers. Finally, national-security crises expand the president's possibilities for effecting long-term institutional and policy changes. War is associated with great changes in American government and its policies (Eisner 2000). Observing war's impacts on government and society, the political scientist Bartholomew Sparrow writes, "States make wars; wars make states" (Sparrow 1996, 3). In wartime America, the presidency is an engine of change.

Presidential war powers have been shaped more by usage and precedent than by the Constitution's text. The Constitution grants to Congress the power to declare war, while it grants to the president both the commander-in-chief's responsibility and the leading role in the nation's foreign affairs. In Federalist Number 69, Alexander Hamilton explains that the president's constitutional power regarding war is nothing more than "the supreme command and direction of the military," while it was Congress that would have the authority of "declaring" war and "raising and regulating" military forces (Hamilton, Jay, Madison n.d., 448). This neat separation of authority, however, collapses when the question becomes, Is it the president or Congress that has the power to act in international affairs regarding the national interest? In the great debate following President Washington's 1793 neutrality proclamation, Hamilton argued that the president needed neither an act of Congress or a specific constitutional provision to legitimize his proclamation of America's neutrality in the war between Britain and France. This was, in Hamilton's argument, a proper exercise of executive discretion (Hamilton and Madison 1976).

Over the course of American history, the reality of unilateral presidential prerogative powers in the national-security arena grew alongside the Constitution's formal separation of powers (Pious 1996, 81–107). Crisis demanded a decisiveness that the Constitution's checks and balances could not quite accommodate. Abraham Lincoln presumed it was a presidential responsibility to launch a war to save the Union, only consulting Congress months after the fact. During the Cold War, presidents exercised a de facto war power, initiating foreign military interventions in Korea, the Dominican Republic, Vietnam, Granada, Panama, and Iraq without congressional declarations of war. Thus, at the beginning of the twenty-first century there was widespread acceptance of a unilateral presidential war power in fact, if not in name (Koh 1990). The constitutional scholar Louis Fisher wrote, "there appeared to be no limit on what a president could do in committing the nation to war" (Fisher 2000).

In addition to expanding the president's unilateral powers, national-security crises and war make the president the focus of undivided public attention. War highlights the office as the center of national responses to threats as well as a focal point for reassurance and interpretation of events (Geertz 1983; Hinckley 1990). Consequently, after September 11, Bush entered a new presidential role. And that role expanded Bush's unilateral executive possibilities while dramatically expanding the public's approval of his presidency.

As of this writing, Bush has occupied the war presidency for about two years. In that time he has made war, extended government's surveillance of private individuals, and, not least, reorganized and centralized the executive branch. In some instances he has expressed unilateral powers under the rubric of national security. At other times he has demanded unfettered delegation of power from Congress, relying on his national-security leverage as well as the partisan advantage of Republican majorities.

A Warrior President: Afghanistan

Amidst the chaos of September 11, Bush understood the presidency's symbolic importance. In south Florida that morning, he sought security in a series of air bases rather than returning to Washington, DC. Later that day, Bush overrode security concerns, asserting, "The American people want to know where their president is" (Balz and Woodward 2002, A1). That night he spoke on television from the White House, declaring war on terrorism: "The search is underway for those who are behind these evil acts. We will make no distinction between the terrorists who committed these acts and those who harbor them" (Bush 2001c). The first targets would be al Qaeda and Afghanistan's Taliban regime that sheltered it.

In a memorial service at the National Cathedral on September 14, Bush again addressed the nation as a war president. "This conflict has begun on the timing and terms of others. It will end in a way, and at an hour, of our choosing" (Bush 2001d). As Bush interpreted America's new crisis, it was as if he was entering the presidency anew. The journalist R. W. Apple Jr. wrote afterward that Bush eased "the doubts about his capacity for the job and the legitimacy of his election that have clung stubbornly to him during his eight difficult months in the Oval Office" (Apple 2001, A1).

Once launched, the war in Afghanistan quickly toppled the Taliban and wreaked havoc on al Qaeda's organization and camps. However, al Qaeda's top leadership slipped out from under the American forces and their Afghan allies, and with them Taliban leadership and fighters disappeared into the tribal areas between Afghanistan and Pakistan. Osama Bin Laden himself would become an elusive and charismatic figure, appearing occasionally through videotape on Arab television.

What would be the next battlefront in the war against terror? Evidence appeared of al Qaeda cooperation with indigenous radical Islamist movements in Muslim Asia; terrorism in Pakistan, Indonesia, and the Philippines demonstrated that link. The United States entered into the delicate diplomatic task of attempting to provide military and intelligence support to those countries while maintaining a low profile. Additionally, European countries and Canada mobilized their internal security services to monitor radical Islamist groups within their countries. Conservative foreign-policy intellectuals close to the administration proposed a number of countries as potential targets for the war on terrorism, including several in the Middle East. However, in his 2002 State of the Union address, Bush settled this debate for the time being by declaring three states as an "axis of evil": Iran, Iraq, and North Korea. Those three had notably nasty regimes. They were committed to developing weapons of mass destruction. And all three were promiscuous distributors of weapons to bad actors. The Bush administration was particularly fixated on Iraq. The Iraqi regime had been left in power by the first Bush administration after the 1991 Persian Gulf War. Officials from the first Bush administration, returning to power with the second, now had a chance to undo their earlier error (Bumiller and Schmitt 2002, A20).

While the administration developed its plans for a new Iraq war, events in Afghanistan might have given it some second thoughts about its optimistic promises for a postwar Iraq. What were the prospects for the United States to establish political stability and economic recovery in Afghanistan? Arguably, Afghanistan posed a less challenging case for postwar stabilization and development than that posed by a postwar Iraq. If the United States could not generate commitment sufficient to meet Afghanistan's needs, what was the prospect that it could take on restoration and democratization in a far larger and more complex country? The United States' ability to encourage democratic development in these societies might be the West's strongest weapon against Islamist terrorism (Ignatieff 2003). However, continuing difficulties in stabilizing Afghanistan, two years after the defeat of the Taliban, signal the challenges posed in attempting reconstruction of a society from the ambivalent stances of uncertain occupier and hesitant benefactor (Gall 2003, A1)

Homeland Security and Executive Power

Bush's war presidency had strong implications for the justice system and the conduct of the executive branch more generally. The September 11 terrorists had lived and trained in the United States. Greatly tightened domestic security measures seemed justified. Under conventional circumstances, due process guarantees protect citizens and legal residents from government action, but war diminishes those protections. Lincoln unilaterally suspended the Constitution's habeas corpus guarantees in the Civil War. During World War I, Woodrow Wilson restricted freedom of press and speech, and in World War II, Franklin D. Roosevelt relocated innocent Japanese Americans to isolated internment camps. Under threat, governments seek greater control over their societies and more information about their populations (Scott 1998).

After September 11, the administration proposed legislation substantially increasing its powers in domestic security. The U.S.A. Patriot Act (H.R. 3162) became law just five weeks after the attacks. It expanded the powers of federal agencies in domestic surveillance and internal security actions. It expanded the capacities of those agencies to gain information about individuals' choices and communications from libraries, Internet service providers, and retail merchants. And it expanded the activities that could be covered by the legal definition of terrorism and gave U.S. foreign intelligence agencies freedom to conduct domestic intelligence activities. Insisting on the importance of a delegation of unqualified authority for the executive branch, Attorney General John Ashcroft "implied that anyone who wanted to do anything different [than the proposed legislation] was jeopardizing the security of the United States" (Toobin 2002, 61).

Simultaneously, the immigration and naturalization service increased scrutiny of residents and visitors from Middle Eastern and Muslim countries. This practice included the incarceration without court hearing of nearly a thousand individuals in the period after September 11. Additionally, members of American Muslim communities became continuing targets in domestic antiterrorism activities. Young Muslim men were required to register their locations in the United States, and citizens and legal residents of Arab ethnicity were subjected to interviews by federal law enforcement agencies. The Bush administration resisted efforts by immigration and civil liberties groups to gain legal due process for people caught up in the new security system after September 11, or for those captured in Afghanistan and detained at the U.S. military base at Guantánamo Bay, Cuba. Even some U.S. citizens in government custody were denied due process rights after being declared enemy combatants by the president. Yet, after September 11, few voices dared criticize the Bush administration for its very aggressive domestic security activities. As public opinion polls suggested, most Americans felt safer because of the president's expanded powers in domestic security.

Also, under the rubric of domestic security, Bush initiated the largest reorganization of the executive branch since the Defense Department was established early in the Cold War. He proposed the creation of the Department of Homeland Security, relocating twenty-two federal agencies and about 170,000 employees from other cabinet departments to the new department (Dewar 2003b, A1). Its creation demonstrated the president's dominance of the national security arena, as well as his political agility. During early 2002, congressional Democrats promoted the idea of a domestic security department and criticized as inadequate Bush's White House office of homeland security, headed by former governor Tom Ridge (Becker 2002, A16). Bush vehemently opposed the idea for an additional cabinet department. The Democrat's criticism of the White House office was twofold. First, they saw it as too small to meet the daunting challenges of protecting the country from terrorism. Second, they opposed centering security policy in a White House office that would maximize presidential control over information related to homeland security.

In a nimble political move, Bush announced on June 7, 2002, his own plan for a new department (Oliphant 2002, E7). It may have been other than coincidence that the president's announcement occurred on the first day of congressional testimony by FBI whistle blower Colleen Rowley describing her agency's failure to respond to pre–September 11 warnings about potential terrorists in the United States. Through a political alchemy enabled by his wartime presidency, Bush used the proposal for a new department that he originally opposed to shield his administration from criticism of its pre–September 11 conduct in domestic security. In a further political inversion, during the 2002 congressional campaigns, Bush attacked Democrats for holding up legislative creation of the Department of Homeland Security by resisting his demand for broad executive discretion in the new department's personnel policy, organization, and budget.

The demand Bush brought to legislation creating the new department was that it should delegate to the president maximum flexibility over work rules, personnel policy, and budget. The department would incorporate agencies transferred from other departments, such as the Coast Guard from Treasury and Immigration and Naturalization from Justice. The president insisted that existing work rules and protections could no longer apply in those agencies and that normal civil service protections would be lifted from employees within the new department. Furthermore, the legislation specified that collective-bargaining rights would be denied to the new department's employees. Senate Democrats fought those provisions during the fall of 2002, and Bush charged that they consequently endangered American security. After the Republican victory in the 2002 election, a lame duck session of the Senate passed the homeland security reorganization, including the managerial discretion the president demanded (Lee and Barr 2002, A31).

Centralizing the Executive Branch

The centralized power that Bush gained in the Department of Homeland Security was one instance of the administration's larger effort to control executive branch agencies and their agendas. The administration aimed at reducing bureaucracy and opening them to market competition, along the way reducing civil service protections and weakening public service unions (Office of Management and Budget 2001). A central goal of Bush's management reform was reducing the federal civilian workforce through "competitive outsourcing" of federal jobs. As the "President's Management Agenda," released in August 2001 stated, "nearly half of all federal employees perform tasks that are readily available in the commercial marketplace" (Office of Management and Budget 2001, 17). Subsequently, the White House mandated all federal agencies to review their workforces to determine the feasibility of eliminating jobs through substitution of services or products obtained from the private sector. Agencies were ordered in 2002 to review 5 percent of their jobs for potential outsourcing and 10 percent during 2003 (Barr 2002, B2). The administration labeled its administrative reform goals as "freedom to manage," but critics saw that initiative as a thinly veiled drive to weaken established protections for government employees while offering patronage to private business. They point out that the federal agencies lack the means to assess the actual cost of government work to compare it to the cost of work outsourced to the commercial market (Barr 2001, B2).

Another signal of Bush's intense control within the executive branch is his administration's penchant for secrecy. Claiming to reenergize the presidency's place in the constitutional system after a period of decline beginning in the 1970s, Bush has resisted congressional demands for information. When Tom Ridge served as the White House assistant for homeland security, the administration denied congressional committee requests for testimony from Ridge, despite the obvious appropriateness of Congress' concern with domestic security. The president's claim was that presidential assistants are not required to testify before Congress. In response, members of both parties in Congress argued that because Ridge was given operating responsibilities, he was subject to congressional oversight (Milbank 2002a, A33). The Ridge controversy disappeared when he was appointed to head the Homeland Security Department, clearly making him an officer who was subject to congressional oversight. However, other controversies over secrecy remained unresolved.

In another high-profile case of executive secrecy having no relationship to security, members of Congress sought information from Vice President Cheney's office about the interest groups and individuals consulted during 2001 by his task force as it framed an administration energy policy. Cheney had claimed executive privilege and refused to share that information with Congress. Eventually, the General Accounting Office (GAO), an investigative and auditing arm of Congress, initiated its first-ever lawsuit against the executive branch, demanding release of the information. Instead of compromising, the administration fought the suit. After a federal district judge dismissed the case in early 2003, the GAO decided against an appeal that would demand "significant time and resources over several years" (Victor 2003).

The administration's penchant for secrecy extends beyond White House operations to many of government's policy areas. For example, Bush's Department of Justice has notably withheld information requests by Congress, often by simply ignoring them. The department has been resistant to inquiries about the implementation of the Patriot Act and its actions against potential terrorists. The Republican chair of the House Judiciary Committee said that the Justice Department under Attorney General Ashcroft was the least cooperative of any he had dealt with in his twenty-four years in the House (Victor 2003). As well, the administration has stonewalled requests from Congress and the press regarding information ranging from environmental policy to military procurement and the space program. A reporter covering Congress observed, "by delaying the release of information that could be used as ammunition to its critics, the Bush administration has sidestepped political confrontations and kept the country focused on the president's agenda" (Bolton 2002, 1).

Without the crisis of September 11, Bush's partisan commitments alone might have fueled his ambition to revive presidential power over the executive branch agencies and against Congress. But the status of the war presidency has expanded Bush's ability to justify unilateral power and fend off Congress. And September 11 radically changed the public's perceptions of him. Additionally, as illustrated in his unilateral initiation of war in Afghanistan, his realm for operation apart from Congress had expanded greatly. We can see in the pace of executive orders Bush issued in his first two years a marked increased after September 11, implying an expansion of his unilateral powers.

Executive orders are the means whereby a president directs agents and organizations of the executive branch, and it is the tool affording him the most unilateral control over executive branch organization and policy and, ultimately, over the citizenry outside government (Mayer

2001). For example, it is through executive orders soon after his inauguration that Bush quickly put into place his faith-based initiative. Between his inauguration and September 11, the president issued twenty-four executive orders. But in the nine months following the terrorist attacks he issued forty-three such orders, twelve of which were directly concerned with the war on terrorism (U.S. National Archives n.d.). While there is no specific probability of executive orders occurring in the first year of a presidency, it is likely that presidents will need numerous executive orders after entering office to fit the institutional presidency to their own purposes (Moe 1999). Thus, the pattern of executive orders after September 11 was against the grain of a normal expectation for the distribution of executive orders (Mayer 2001, 88–89).

A Warrior President: Iraq

The lead up to the war in Iraq indicated Bush's tight control over executive branch agencies and information. In the weeks before the fall 2002 congressional election, he focused publicly on the threat Iraq posed to America's security. The president, and his advisors, described Iraq as collaborating with terrorism and producing weapons of mass destruction. While making the public case for the war, the White House was exerting strong pressure on the national security and intelligence agencies to produce supporting analyses for an Iraq war. Just as the administration had learned the political effect of a disciplined and unified message in building popular support for its tax policy, it crafted a message about Iraq that described its evils unambiguously and, in doing so, ignored conflicting information (Ackerman and Judis 2003). That pressure would later be revealed as questions arose about the reliability of the administration's factual claims while building its case for war.

While the president spoke of Iraq's danger to the United States, Republicans were aware of the domestic political implications of focusing on Iraq's threats to America prior to the 2002 congressional elections. In January 2002, Karl Rove advised the Republican Party's winter assembly that the party must use the war presidency for its potential domestic political advantage (Berke and Sanger 2002, A1). Illustrating the tangling of domestic policy and national-security issues, the president's chief of staff, Andrew Card, said the president would publicly turn attention to Iraq in September 2002 because "from a marketing point of view, you don't introduce new products in August" (Milbank 2002c, A1). As if to push national security issues to the top of voters' concerns in the upcoming congressional election, in September 2002 the president demanded that Congress pass a resolution that would support his use of force against Iraq. Consequently, national security dominated the 2002 congressional campaigns, marginalizing the domestic issues on which Democrats might have had an advantage.

Bush, within the war presidency, was victorious on the congressional campaign battlefield. The 2002 election was the first off-year race since 1934 in which an incumbent president's party increased its seats. Republicans gained in the House, and the Senate returned to Republican control. Although Republican majorities were small in both houses, the outcome seemed to be a strong vote of approval for the Bush administration, offering the electoral warrant that the president had missed getting in 2000. The election also gave the administration a political license for the war in Iraq. Bush had sought through the fall and winter of 2002–2003 to gain the UN Security Council's support for war. He succeeded in reviving the UN weapons inspections in Iraq, but the administration could not convince the Security Council to adopt a specific timetable for possible military action against Iraq. Then claiming support from some smaller countries, "a coalition of the willing," on March 17, 2003, Bush announced initiation of war on Iraq. Britain was the only country providing substantial military assistance to that effort.

A month after starting the war, Bush staged a dramatic—and televised—event, landing in a war plane on the deck of an aircraft carrier and declaring that hostilities were over. In fact, the war had seen few major confrontations of large-scale troop formations. Coalition forces met scattered resistance from irregular fighters, but there had been virtually no confrontation with Iraq's regular military forces. These, including the vaunted Republican Guard divisions, seemed to melt away even before the heat of battle. Now the more difficult phase of the Iraq war began: regime replacement. The task was to fashion a stable social order and representative government in a place that had never experienced representative government or stability without repression.

As the United States worked to stabilize and rebuild Iraq, issues arose that made replacing the regime more difficult than removing it. The war had been less intense than was expected, but the peace was anything but peaceful. The administration had predicted that the coalition forces would be welcomed as liberators. Yet Americans discovered their forces caught in continuing low-level warfare amidst a chaotic, postwar Iraq. It also became clear that the cost of the American occupation force in Iraq would be far greater than the administration had expected, and American troops would be in the country far longer than the administration had suggested. In short, the postwar reality clashed sharply with both the administration's rationale for going to war and its conception of the postwar situation. Four months after the war began, no weapons of mass destruction had been uncovered while American lives and wealth were being spent in Iraq. Under increasing political pressure about the administration's justification for war, in July 2003 the White House admitted that dubious information about an Iraqi nuclear program had been included in the president's 2003 State of the Union address (Sanger 2003, A1). But, simultaneously, the president continued to insist on the soundness of his policy toward Iraq.

Whether controversy over his justification for the war weakens Bush or not, consequences of his war presidency will remain after he has left the scene. Wars, and their presidents, fade away, but each leaves its impact on federal organization and public policy (Eisner 2000; Sparrow 1996). The Department of Homeland Security will remain a continuing monument to Bush's war presidency, and it is virtually certain that the Bush administration's expanded surveillance powers for domestic security will remain, no matter who enters the presidency in January 2005.

National Security, Domestic Politics, and the 2004 Election

Bush has strong political incentives for attempting to sustain his authority as a war president. He discovered the constraints of the conventional presidency during his first eight months in office. By contrast, the occasion to claim a war presidency assured legitimacy, produced towering popular approval, and gave him a mandate. Additionally, the 2002 election demonstrated the war presidency's potency in domestic politics.

Going forward, the challenge for Bush was to adapt his war presidency to promote his domestic policy agenda and to position himself for reelection in 2004. In his 2003 State of the Union address, Bush revealed an agenda of fundamental changes in national public policy. He proposed a new wave of tax cuts, amounting to a revenue loss of nearly $1 trillion over ten years. These cuts would significantly reduce taxation on income from investments and greatly increase already large projected budget deficits. They would also represent the first time in U.S. history that the nation reduced taxes while fighting a war. Bush also proposed a Medicare reform that would privatize the program, forcing the elderly to choose private health plans to receive prescription drug coverage. He reiterated his support for private accounts in Social Security and proposed limits on awards in medical malpractice litigation. He called again on Congress to pass his energy plan featuring drilling for oil in the Arctic National Wildlife Refuge. Finally, he revisited his argument for faith-based solutions to social problems, a kind of semi-privatization of welfare state services (Bush 2003b).

Bush's public approval ratings after the U.S. invasion of Iraq, along with Republicans' control of Congress, would seem to ease the way for his domestic agenda. However, there are indications of some limits to the president's capacities to use the war presidency to win domestic policy battles. Congressional Republicans signaled the White House that they would not support linking prescription drug benefits with Medicare privatization. The Senate again rejected drilling for oil in the Arctic National Wildlife Refuge. And while Congress eventually passed legislation that included elements of Bush's proposed tax cut, what emerged was crafted by Congress to appear to have a significantly lower impact on the federal deficit, compared with the president's original proposal. Writing about the reaction of Congress to Bush's proposed tax cut in early 2003, reporter Richard W. Stevenson observed that it was "a lesson in the limits of [Bush's] political power, even at a time when the nation was rallying behind him as commander in chief" (Stevenson 2003a, A19).

More telling of the limits of the war presidency was Congress's refusal in April 2003 to give Bush the discretion he sought over a supplemental appropriation for the war in Iraq. The president asked Congress to appropriate $78.5 billion with minimal restrictions on its specific purposes, leaving him free to allocate expenditures. While approving the appropriation request, Congress required that they be spent as designated by categories in the legislation. A leading Democrat in the House, David Obey (WI) said, "They came up here asking for a blank check, and we gave them checks and balances" (Morgan 2003, A9).

The fate of the Bush presidency, and of George W. Bush's chances in the 2004 election, is suspended between the extraordinary authority he has gained as war president and the possibility of political failure because of a stumbling economy, expanding budget deficits, and postwar conditions in Iraq.

Before the 2004 election campaign began in earnest, Bush offered a preview of how he would mobilize his war presidency in campaign

2004. When he stoked popular support for his 2003 tax cut, Bush cabinet members traveled the country touting the importance of reduced taxes for economic revival and job expansion. The president campaigned, using defense plants and military bases as platforms for promoting economic recovery through tax cuts. And as he raised funds for the 2004 campaign, the president honed his crafted language to a fine, new edge, articulating his commitment to growing the economy while protecting the nation from terrorism.

However, there are moments when the crafted message fails and we're given a glimpse of its tactical mechanics. In the face of the stumbling economy and budget deficits, Bush had crafted a message in late 2001 and 2002 explaining that deficits resulted not from tax cuts but from terrorist attacks and a recession that began on Clinton's watch. He routinely reminded audiences that during campaign 2000 he had pledged in a Chicago speech to protect budget surpluses unless there was a war, a recession, or a national emergency. And then he would hit hard on his punch line, "this administration got all three." However, that message lost its effect when it was revealed that Bush never made that statement "in Chicago, or anywhere else" (Zeleny 2002, 2:3).

Bush's larger crafted message on the economy was that his new wave of proposed tax cuts would expand jobs, and the administration simultaneously minimized the importance of budget deficits. However, the administration provided little objective evidence that the plan would stimulate the economy, and experts overwhelmingly agreed that the tax cuts would add to a rapidly mounting federal deficit. According to official estimates from both the Congressional Budget Office and the Office of Management and Budget, the federal budget may be running annual deficits of $400–500 billion for many years. By that time the baby boom generation will be reaching the age to draw on Social Security and Medicare, requiring that those entitlement programs absorb larger and larger proportions of the federal budget (Weisman 2003b, A1). Alan Schick, a leading expert on the federal budget process, observes that behind the crafted language of job growth to sell the tax cut is a covert strategy for altering the federal government. Schick argues that Bush fully realizes "the short- and long-term . . . implications of the revenue losses he has imposed on the federal government. . . . He wants to strip the government of future revenue" as a way to shrink government and reduce demand for its programs (Schick 2003, 3). Surprisingly, this thesis gains support from an ally of the president's. In an op-ed essay in the

Washington Post, Grover Norquist, a leader of the conservative movement, lauded the tax cuts as covert efforts to radically reform the tax code while severely restraining government. Tying together terrorism and taxes, Norquist observed, "The Bush administration is demonstrating that it can operate successfully on two fronts, fighting the war on terror and . . . embarking on fundamental economic reform" (Norquist 2003, A21; Broder 2003a, A25).

As the 2004 campaign season approached, the administration devised another way to use the advantages of the war presidency. The White House has planned a 2004 Republican National Convention that will associate Bush's renomination with the commemoration of the terrorist attacks of September 11. The 2004 convention, meeting in New York City, will be the latest ever scheduled by the Republican Party. The president plans to give his acceptance speech to the convention on September 2, close enough to September 11 to be able to merge with commemoration of the attack on the World Trade Center. Additionally, the late convention date gives the Bush campaign a spending advantage over the Democrats. Federal law specifies that from the party's convention to the election, candidates accepting federal funding must be limited to those funds. During August 2003, while Democrats have to conserve public funds for the fall campaign, after their late-July convention, the Republicans will be able to purchase a massive media campaign funded by private contributions (Nagourney and Stevenson 2003, A1).

Through the lens of the "two presidencies," two quite different sources of presidential authority come into focus, one conventional and the other related to national security and war. Each "presidency" is a response to specific conditions and entails a different kind of relationship to the public and to other branches of government. So powerful are the effects of the different combinations of context and authority that Bush's leadership has been notably different within each. In a conventional presidential context, Bush appeared distracted in office, communicated clumsily with the public, and lacked a sense of purpose. After September 11, he became a focused leader capable of rallying the nation. The context of war raised the stakes for Bush's leadership; it focused him and demanded his deepest personal resources.

Bush is attempting to leverage domestic policy and politics as a war president. But his success is not guaranteed because the war presidency itself is an unstable role. How he fares politically will depend on Americans' perceptions of his Iraq policy, on their views of the American economy, and, not least, on the awful contingency of terrorism. Bush's war presidency could erode if events do not reinforce it. Should that happen, Bush would be pitched back into the greater political vulnerabilities of the conventional presidency. Thus, though we can examine Bush's enormous institutional and political advantages in the war presidency, we cannot predict with confidence the outcome of the 2004 election. However, we do already know that Bush's term in office provides an extraordinary window into the contextual variability of presidential power and the political implications of that variability.

8 A STAKE IN THE SAND
George W. Bush and Congress

Bertram Johnson

I'm proud of the United States Congress. The Congress is focused on results, and they have delivered tremendous results for the American people: Major tax cuts so the working people can keep more of their own money; education reform; Homeland Security Department to better secure America; trade legislation. No, this Congress, instead of endless bickering and needless partisanship, has focused on . . . doing [what's] right for the American people.

PRESIDENT GEORGE W. BUSH

George W. Bush's praise of Congress is unusual. Most presidents are re membered for their frustration with the institution and not for their approval of it. Jimmy Carter complained of "the inertia of Congress" (Carter 1996), George H. W. Bush criticized "the sticky web of 284 congressional committees and subcommittees" (Bush 1992), and Bill Clinton fought with both Democratic and Republican Congresses over health-care reform, the budget, Medicare, and other matters. Theodore Roosevelt perhaps best expressed the feelings of most presidents when he famously remarked, "Oh, if I could only be president and Congress too for just ten minutes" (Henning 1992, 240).

Given the long history of animosity between presidents and Congresses, what accounts for President Bush's cheerful congratulation of his colleagues at the other end of Pennsylvania Avenue? To be sure, it would be an exaggeration to say that Bush's relationship with Congress has always been cordial. Nevertheless, Bush has had good reason to be satisfied with what Congress has produced. The president's top two legislative priorities—education reform and tax cuts—were taken up quickly and passed within six months of his inauguration. Subsequent presidential initiatives, including the U.S.A. Patriot Act, creation of the Department of Homeland Security, further tax cuts, and Medicare reform, all have met with favorable treatment on Capitol Hill.[1] By one estimate, Bush exceeds all presidents but Nixon in the last fifty years in the amount of major legislation enacted in the first half of a term (C. Jones 2003).

Presidential Leadership

It is tempting to see Bush's success as a triumph of presidential leadership. After all, Bush advertised himself in the 2000 presidential campaign as someone who knew "how to lead" and had "shown the ability to get things done" (Transcript of Debate 2000). Leadership is a complex phenomenon, however. Political scientists have long been skeptical about whether presidents have unilateral command (Neustadt 1990). Presidents are constrained by a number of factors largely beyond their control, including public opinion, the political parties, and the makeup of Congress. Each president must face an electorate that may be fickle, parties that have their own goals and concerns, and a maze of congressional committees, each of which may have jurisdiction over critical policy areas. In negotiating this thicket, presidents do make meaningful choices, but "the range of maneuvering on these choices is often quite limited" (Peterson 1990, 266). As George Edwards has argued, presidential leadership operates "at the margins" of an existing political environment (Edwards 1989).

This is not to say, however, that presidential leadership is irrelevant. In politics, often a "marginal" push in one direction can make the difference between success and failure of a policy proposal. This analysis does, however, illuminate what effective presidential leaders do: they recognize the constraints inherent in their environment and make the best of them. As Richard Neustadt argues, "a President's own prospects for effective influence are regulated (insofar as he controls them) by his choices of objectives, and of timing, and of instruments, and by his choice of choices to avoid" (Neustadt 1990, 90).

Congress

If presidents must operate under the constraints of particular political environments, it is important to characterize the environment George W. Bush faced in the first several years of his presidency. As research on presidential leadership implies, broad trends began forming before Bush entered the White House. Three aspects of this context are of particular importance: recent increases in party polarization in Congress, the greater agreement within the Republican Party on economic issues than on social issues, and Republican control of the House of Representatives.

Recent Party Polarization

Parties in Congress are more united today than in decades past. One way to see this is to note that members of the same party in Congress vote together more often than not. The *Congressional Quarterly* defines a vote as a "party-unity vote" if a majority of one party votes against a majority of the other party. Party-unity votes have been increasing since about 1970, when about a third of House and Senate votes were party-unity votes. Now, despite a slight decrease since the mid-1990s, party-unity votes make up around 45 percent of all votes (Stanley and Niemi 2000, 254–55; *Congressional_Quarterly* 2001–2002). There has been a recent dip in partisan voting, therefore, but party votes still occur more often now than they did in the 1970s. Furthermore, the percentage of party members voting with the party on party-unity votes has continued to increase. This suggests that the downturn in party-unity votes may not reflect a decrease in overall partisanship.

Most political scientists explain this recent increase in united partisan voting by pointing out that an electoral realignment in the South caused the number of southern Democrats to shrink, as these conservative Democrats were replaced by Republicans. As a result, the Democratic Party became more liberal overall, and the Republican Party became more conservative. The parties became more homogenous in their preferences and therefore became more likely to vote together. Others have added that polarization may also be due to increased ideological consistency in the voting public—non-South as well as South (Jacobson 2000).

While it seems clear that the preferences of members of Congress have become more homogenous within the two parties, it is a matter of some dispute whether this preference homogeneity has also led to a more powerful party leadership. John Aldrich and David Rohde have argued that when preferences align *within* parties, and differ substantially *across* parties, party members will delegate substantial powers to their leaders. In the 104th Congress, for instance, the new Republican majority in the House granted Speaker Newt Gingrich substantial new powers (Aldrich and Rohde 1997; Aldrich and Rohde 2000). According to this point of view, increases in party unity reflect both agreement among party members and party discipline by a powerful leadership.

Keith Krehbiel, on the other hand, argues that legislative outcomes are determined by legislative majorities or, in the case of the Senate (in which filibusters must be broken by a vote of sixty of the one hundred senators), supermajorities. The content of legislation will reflect the preferences of those legislators who are best positioned to make the critical difference between success and failure (Krehbiel 1998). According to Krehbiel, recent high levels of partisan voting simply reflect the fact that members of both parties are more likely to agree with their fellow partisans now than they were in the past (Krehbiel 2000). Party discipline lacks the power to force members of Congress to approve of policies they do not prefer in the first place. When faced with an issue on which party members disagree, Krehbiel would argue, the party leadership will be unable to compel conformity to a particular alternative.

Social Issues versus Economic Issues

One way to evaluate the theories proposed by Krehbiel and by Aldrich and Rohde is to identify policy areas in which party members are likely to agree, and to distinguish these from policy areas over which members are likely to disagree. If the leadership can compel solidarity on issues with which members are not naturally inclined to agree, we can conclude that party leadership is endowed with real power. If, on the other hand, party coalitions dissolve when these issues come to a vote, then party leaders can be said to have less real power.

These two possible sets of circumstances suggest different strategic courses of action for a president seeking to advance a policy agenda. If party leaders are powerful, the president need only negotiate with congressional party leadership, no matter what the policy issue. Party leaders might then be expected to use their authority to bring the rest of the president's party into line. But if leaders can command stable coalitions only when most members of the party agree, the president would be wise to engage in more hands-on coalition building with nonleadership members of Congress, especially on policy issues that divide the party.

Circumstantial evidence suggests that economic policy issues unite the Republican Party more readily than social policy issues. First, an analysis of the views of Republican Party activists in the electorate shows that there is significantly more variability of opinion on such topics as Christian fundamentalists and the poor than there is on the subject of "big business."[2] Since elected officials are likely to be similar to party activists in their convictions, this suggests that Republican members of Congress, too, might be more united on economic policy. Second, a comparison of interest group ratings of Republican members of the House of Representatives reveals a similar pattern. Many interest groups rate each member of Congress on a scale from one to a hundred, based on their votes on issues of concern to that interest group. Two such groups are the National Taxpayers Union (NTU), which concerns itself with economic policy, and the Christian Coalition, which focuses on social policies.[3] The NTU's ratings of Republican members of the House in 2000 cluster together more than the Christian Coalition's ratings. Most Republicans receive mildly favorable ratings from the NTU, but Christian Coalition's ratings are spread out in a lopsided way, with a large number of Republicans scoring very positively but a significant minority scoring around 50 or below.[4]

The above evidence, though not definitive, suggests that if disagreement among substantial groups of congressional Republicans is to occur, it would likely be over social issues. If Aldrich and Rohde are correct, party leadership should have the power to surmount these short-term disagreements over social policy because of long-term agreement over the public agenda as a whole. If Krehbiel is correct, Republican coalitions will split over social issues. I argue that Krehbiel's theory more accurately reflects reality, at least in the first years of the Bush administration. While the Republican Party marched in effective unity on economic policy such as tax reductions, it repeatedly split over social issues, such as education reform. This difference in internal Republican Party dynamics led to different presidential tactics when dealing with social policy and economic policy.

Control of the House

Although any president would rather have a united party behind him than a disunited party, party unity is less useful when the president's party is not in control of Congress. Furthermore, in circumstances in which parties are unified, it is much more advantageous to control the House of Representatives than to control the Senate. This is because the rigid, less flexible rules of the House serve to magnify the power of the chamber's leadership, while the less organized, less hierarchical Senate rules serve to magnify the importance of individual, independent senators. The percentage of Republican members of Congress voting with the party on party votes has historically been similar in both the House and Senate, and remains similar today (Stanley and Niemi 2000, 254–55; *Congressional Quarterly* 2001–2002). In the House, however, the leadership has the power to structure the rules of debate in such a way as to minimize the impact of individual dissenters within the party.[5] The House Rules Committee can write restrictive rules for floor debate; the leadership can withhold committee assignments from recalcitrant partisans, and so on. In the Senate, however, so much of what the chamber does rests on unanimous consent agreements that one stubborn member can often slow down or stop Senate business (Binder and Smith 1997).

Blessed with a united party, therefore, a president's strongest flank is in the House of Representatives. This is likely to be true whether or not party unity leads to increased leadership authority (as Aldrich and Rohde argue) or whether parties are less important (as Krehbiel argues). The rules of the House give the leadership relatively constant powers of agenda control and organization that the Senate leadership does not possess. One or two recalcitrant members of the House are unlikely to be able to delay the progress of a bill; one or two Senators, however, are well positioned to do just that.

The Bush Strategy

Bush's domestic policy team, headed by Karl Rove, pursued a strategy during the first several years of the Bush presidency that did its best to recognize the relevant features of the political landscape and make the most of them. Rove appears to have been in charge of setting a clear policy agenda, which was then shepherded through Congress by White House Congressional Liaison Nicholas Calio, and, after his resignation in January 2003, by his successor David Hobbs. Calio, a diminutive Ohioan who held the same White House post in the George H. W. Bush administration, is a seasoned veteran of Washington who spent the years between the two Bush presidencies as an influential lobbyist (Eilperin 2001). Hobbs, who until taking over in 2003 was Calio's chief deputy, had significant experience working on Capitol Hill for several Republican members of Congress. By most accounts, Rove's judgments about policy direction in 2001 and 2002 were based on issues' appeal to particular sections of the American electorate at large. Calio's and Hobbs' knowledge of politics inside the Beltway therefore provided a much-needed complement to Rove's expertise on nation-spanning electoral constituencies.

Apparently cognizant of the broad trends described above, Bush, Rove, and Calio devised a strategy that recognized the limitations of the presidency and made an effort to maximize the president's potential for successful leadership. First, they sought to discipline themselves by advancing a small number of ambitious proposals, to avoid the confusion and overreaching that can occur when presidents try to do too much. As Calio later pointed out in an interview, "The notion that we have this big broad agenda that we can force through Congress is a fallacy" (Auster 2002). In fact, Bush took the fewest number of positions on House roll call votes in his first two years in office (eighty-three) of any president in recent memory. The only other president who comes close to this figure, Gerald Ford, has an artificially low number because he took office halfway through his "first year," due to Richard Nixon's resignation. The Bush number is also the lowest among recent presidents if one measures it as a percentage of total roll call votes (Ragsdale 1996, 378–79, 383–84; *Congressional Quarterly* 2002, 136–47, 3275–88).

Although Bush took an inordinately low number of positions on House roll-call votes, he took an average number of positions on Senate votes. This is the result of a combination of two factors. First, the Senate "positions" include presidential nominations to executive and judicial offices, a factor that remains more or less constant for presidents. Second, and more importantly, much of Bush's lobbying of Congress focused on the Senate, since he was less assured of support in that body.

It is important to stress that the White House sought to make its proposals small in number but sweeping in impact. Rove told *The New Yorker*'s Nicholas Lemann that this was his formula for winning elec-

Table 8.1

Roll Call Votes in House and Senate on which George W. Bush Took a Position, 2001–2002

Topic	*No. of roll call votes*	*Topic*	*No. of roll call votes*
Nominations	81	Iraq	2
Taxes	20	Class action suits	1
Trade	18	Crime	1
Education	15	Bankruptcy	1
Terrorism/homeland security	14	Liability	1
Appropriations	11	International law	1
Budget	6	Missile defense	1
Farms/agriculture	6	Visas	1
Cuba	4	Medical malpractice	1
Environment	3	Military retirees' benefits	1
Federal employees	2	Family planning	1
Abortion	2	Debt Limit	1
Use of Force	2		

Source: CQ Weekly, January 12, 2002, 13–38; and December 14, 2002, 3275–77.
Note: Positions on nominations concern Senate only; other positions concern both the House and Senate.

tions: "Be bold. People want to hear big, significant changes. They don't want to be fed small micropolicy" (Lemann 2003, 80). Hence, the nearly unprecedented tax proposals, for example.

In table 8.1, I break down the aggregate number of presidential positions taken by the Bush administration by subject area. As the table shows, apart from nominations and trade, both of which concern matters on which the president is required to take a stand, President Bush took positions on taxes and education more often than on any other issues. This reflects the fact that Bush and his aides made taxes and education his top priorities in the campaign and generally followed through on this commitment once in office (Brownstein 2001; Fortier and Ornstein 2003, 10–11). Because the Bush team prioritized taxes and education, the case studies presented here concern these policies.

In addition to restricting themselves to a few top priorities, the administration adopted an aggressive Capitol Hill strategy that relied heavily on the House of Representatives. The strategy may be roughly summarized as follows: first, drive a metaphorical "stake in the sand" by pressing for swift passage of a House bill that is close to the president's ideal proposal; second, place pressure on pivotal senators to tow the administration line; and, third, be willing to compromise if necessary, especially with respect to social policy. As the case studies illustrate, in the realm of tax policy, the president and his advisors strongly pressed for their initial proposals and usually achieved swift passage by a united House. When the bills reached the Senate, the president traveled to the states of individual fence-sitting senators, urging voters to place pressure on them to support the Bush plan. When the Senate versions of the bills were finalized, the president declared victory, even if a bill fell short of his proposal. After all, in both the tax policy cases, his proposals were so large that few would have expected that in the end Bush would have received most of what he asked for.

In the case of social policy, however, a united House was much less assured. This required the president to compromise much earlier, often including Democrats in his coalition, even in the House. In the case of the education bill, some conservative Republicans objected to national testing requirements. To build a winning coalition, therefore, Bush dropped a controversial portion of the bill (vouchers) to secure the votes of moderate Democrats.

In both cases involving taxes, the Bush administration was able to secure significant victories by staking out a clear position, relying on the House to enact most of its plan, and finally bargaining with the more moderate Senate from the position of strength that the House bill established. In the case of the education plan, Bush was forced to moderate his position early in the process because of divisions within his party in the House of Representatives.

Case I—The 2001 Tax Cut

Tax cuts were a centerpiece of Bush's campaign for the presidency. Like Ronald Reagan before him, Bush argued that tax cuts would both help individual Americans and reduce the size of government. In a debate with Vice President Gore in October 2000, Bush said, "I believe in limited government. And by having a limited government and a focused government, we can send some of the money back to the people who pay the bills. I want to have a tax relief for all people who pay the bills in America because I think you can spend your money more wisely than the federal government can" (Federal Document Clearing House 2000).

When the new president appeared before a joint session of Congress to deliver his first budget plan, his message was nearly the same: "Unrestrained government spending is a dangerous road to deficits, so we must take a different path," he said. "The other choice is to let the American people spend their own money to meet their own needs" (Federal News Service 2001). His tax cut plan, which the Office of Management and Budget (OMB) calculated would cost $1.6 trillion over ten years, called for cuts in individual income tax rates, increases in the child tax credit, expanded educational savings accounts (special bank accounts that are not taxed as long as the money is used for education expenses), an end to inheritance and gift taxes, and expanded deductions for charitable contributions (Nitschke 2001a).

Less than forty-eight hours after the president delivered his speech, the House Ways and Means Committee (the committee with principal jurisdiction over tax issues) passed most of the Bush plan on a party-line twenty-three to fifteen vote. There was perfunctory debate on the measure, little or no consultation with Democrats, and no witness testimony (Kessler 2001). "This will put real dollars in the pockets of workers today," said Committee Chairman Bill Thomas (R-CA) (Rosenbaum 2001b). Charles Rangel of New York, the top Democrat on the committee, fumed about the autocratic manner in which Republicans handled the measure, even as he admitted certain defeat. "Not allowing the minority to express itself, even when it's going to lose, is not the climate the president is trying to initiate," said Rangel. "This is a reckless course we are following" (Rosenbaum 2001b).

Within a week, on March 8, the income tax reduction had made it to the floor of the House and passed, with support from every single House Republican, as well as a handful of Democrats. "We can't act too quickly to get tax relief to the American people," House Speaker Dennis Hastert (R-IL) explained (Welch and Keen 2001). Emboldened by the success, some Republicans suggested further cuts. "It is time for us to seriously look at a tax reduction larger than the $1.6 trillion that has been proposed," said Majority Leader Dick Armey (R-TX). "I see no reason for us to be boxed in by that number" (Nitschke 2001b).

The bill was about to hit a series of roadblocks on the Senate side, however, and everyone in Washington knew it. With more power reserved for individual members, the Senate was less amenable to rule by the chamber's leadership. Furthermore, with a fifty-fifty split, even a very united Republican Party would have to secure some Democratic support if Republicans were to have a chance of passing some version of the Bush plan. Charles Grassley (R-IA), chairman of the Senate Finance Committee, admitted that he would need "a great deal of bipartisan cooperation" to get a tax cut bill through the chamber. "You have to work toward that," he added. "That means it's going to take time" (Nitschke 2001a). His counterpart on the committee, Max Baucus (D-MT), agreed: "March madness in the House, but it's not a slam-dunk in the Senate" (Welch and Keen 2001).

As the debate in the Senate heated up, the president himself began a more visible public campaign to press lawmakers into adopting his plan. In a move that one senator criticized as "tacky," Bush traveled to North Dakota, South Dakota, Louisiana, and Florida, stumping for his plan and urging voters to contact their senators, all Democrats, in support of tax cuts (Dewar and Balz 2001). "You're just an e-mail away from making a difference in somebody's attitude," Bush told a crowd in South Dakota, Senate Democratic leader Tom Daschle's home state (Lacy 2001).

Back in Washington, Grassley and Majority Leader Trent Lott (R-MS) carefully began assembling a coalition behind some version of the Bush plan. In early April, the Senate floor debate over the nonbinding budget resolution became a key test of how much strength the Bush plan had in the Senate. On dozens of votes in quick succession, the Senate repeatedly split down the middle on increasing the amount of a tax cut, decreasing it, and adding other smaller proposals to the overall plan. "It's like trying to press a wet noodle," remarked Senator Rick Santorum (R-PA). "It's very hard to do" (Kessler and Milbank 2001). Finally, the Senate agreed to a $1.2 trillion blueprint that trimmed Bush's proposed reductions by over $400 billion in favor of spending on education and debt reduction. Tom Daschle and other Democrats saw this reduction of Bush's initial $1.6 trillion proposal as a significant setback for the administration, but if this was true, Bush and his aides were not admitting it. White House counselor Karen Hughes called the Senate vote "a great victory." "What we've really done," she said, "is pour in concrete the tax cut and set it anywhere between almost 1.3 and 1.6 [billion dollars]" (Kessler and Milbank 2001). Bush himself seemed pleased. "It's going to be a heck of a lot bigger than anybody thought," he told reporters (Kessler and Milbank 2001).

Over a month of negotiations followed concerning the shape of the final legislation, first in the Senate Finance Committee and later in negotiations with the House leadership. The resulting version of the bill, negotiated by Ways and Means chairman Thomas, as well as Senate Finance chairman Grassley, Baucus, and Senator John Breaux (D-LA), cut taxes $1.35 billion over ten years. The core elements of the Bush proposal remained, in addition to an immediate tax rebate of $300 for individual taxpayers, an increased earned income tax credit, increased maximum contributions to 401(k) retirement plans, and other measures (Rosenbaum 2001a). A triumphant President Bush said of the bill on May 26, the day of its passage, "Today, for the first time since the landmark tax relief championed twenty years ago by President Ronald Reagan and forty years by President John F. Kennedy, an American president has the wonderful honor of letting the American people know significant tax relief is on the way" (Kornblut 2001). Senator Edward Kennedy repeated a common Democratic criticism: "[This tax cut] has been pushed through Congress by the Republican leadership in unprecedented haste without adequate debate" (Kornblut 2001).

This Republican victory would have been sweeter, however, had it not come at the same time as a major loss for the party. Near the end of the negotiations over the tax cut, Vermont Senator James Jeffords announced that he would leave the Republican Party, become an independent, and caucus with the Democrats, swinging control of the Senate into Democratic hands. Jeffords had been angered during the tax cut negotiations when the White House failed to support his efforts to set aside $180 million for special education funding (Shepard 2001). Jeffords said he had warned Bush that his failure to reach out to moderates could be his undoing. "I told him very frankly that I think he'll be a one-term president if he doesn't listen to his moderates," he said (Lancaster 2001).

Case II—Leave No Child Behind

In the same speech before Congress in which Bush outlined his tax cut plans, he also proposed major education reforms. Calling education his first priority, he set forth a plan to tie increased funding for education to a new system of national testing. Children in grades three through eight would undergo standardized tests selected by the states. Schools and states in which students did poorly for three years running would be punished by losing some federal grant money, while the best schools and states would be rewarded. Though the core of the proposal was the system of testing, a Bush administration "blueprint" for education reform included a provision offering vouchers to students in poorly performing public schools that could be used to attend private schools (Schlesinger 2001).

Signaling that education was their top priority, too, House and Senate leaders assigned the reauthorization of the 1965 Elementary and Secondary Education Act (ESEA) the coveted bill numbers HR1 and S1. Any new education reforms would be added to the ESEA reauthorization as it moved through Congress. This time, the Senate moved first, passing through the Health, Education, Labor, and Pensions Committee a stripped down version of the Bush plan that avoided the controversial voucher issue entirely. It also dropped a separate administration idea, the so-called charter state or straight A's proposal that would allow states with good schools to spend federal money more flexibly. Explaining the committee's decision to drop the most controversial elements, committee member Chris Dodd (D-CT) said, "There's been an effort here to not make the committee process acrimonious" (Schlesinger 2001).

Two weeks later, House Republicans introduced a plan closer to the Bush plan, including the voucher provision, but signaled their willingness to compromise. "I think there's a lot of common ground on this issue," said John Boehner (R-OH), chair of the House Committee on Education and the Workforce (Mollison 2001). In early May, the committee dropped the voucher provision from the bill and sent it to the floor.

The White House and Republican leaders recognized that the education bill had the potential to divide Republicans. The Christian Coalition, for example, had expressed concern that the state-based testing system could turn into a nationalized testing system, thus undermining local control of education (Nather 2001b). This and other concerns among conservatives threatened to create an alliance between some Republicans and liberal Democrats to defeat the measure. On the House floor, Representatives Peter Hoekstra (R-MI) and Barney Frank (D-MA) cosponsored an amendment to drop the testing provisions. After intense lobbying by White House chief-of-staff Andrew Card and Karl Rove, the amendment went down to defeat on a vote of 173–255 (Nather 2001b). Although the House finally passed the bill on a vote of 384–45, this lopsided margin masked several narrow escapes on amendments.

Despite several compromises, the House swiftly passed a bill that set strict standards for student testing, clear penalties for schools and states that underperformed, included provisions for students to choose to attend another public school if their schools underperformed, and nearly doubled funding for ESEA programs. Freshman representative Michael Honda (D-CA), a former teacher, remarked, "As a neophyte here, I was kind of taken aback at how quickly [the bill] was jammed through" (Nather 2001c). In mid-June, the Senate passed its own version, by a vote of 91–8, which included more lenient (and, some critics said, confusing) standards for schools and states, as well as much less funding for ESEA.

Although it had made its way rapidly through both houses of Congress, the education bill languished at the conference committee stage, with conferees battling over funding levels, funding for special education, and the exact nature of testing standards (Nather 2001a). The terrorist attacks of September 11 further distracted conferees, and they were unable to reach agreement until mid-December. At that time, they arrived at a compromise plan that contained the core elements of Bush's proposal: state-administered tests for students in grades three through eight and penalties for schools and states that failed to meet these standards. "To be honest, Bush is going to get a lot of credit" for the bill, said one National Education Association lobbyist, even as he expressed skepticism that the new testing system would work (McQueen 2001).

Case III—The 2003 Tax Cut

In December 2002, as most of the world's attention focused on diplomatic efforts to determine the fate of Iraq, President Bush's economic advisers worked quietly, preparing a new round of tax cuts as part of an effort to boost the economy, as well as to advance major items on the Republican domestic agenda. Though Bush's economic team was itself in a state of flux, Bush's closest aides felt that they had a unique opportunity to capitalize on Republican successes in the 2002 midterm elections.

As the economic package took shape, the administration leaned toward making a cut in taxes on corporate dividends the centerpiece of the plan. R. Glenn Hubbard, chairman of the Council of Economic Advisers, along with other White House aides and some private business groups, saw such a cut as a way to boost markets and increase incentives for corporate accountability (Hirschfeld-Davis 2002). By Christmas, administration officials told members of the press that the president would likely propose to cut dividend taxes by "about half," as part of an overall economic package that would cost around $300 billion over ten years (Andrews 2002b).

Two weeks later, in a dramatic shift, Bush announced an economic plan that would not just reduce but would entirely eliminate taxes on corporate dividends paid to individuals. In a speech to the Economic Club of Chicago, Bush touted the measure, part of an overall plan that would cost $674 billion over a decade, as a way to generate long-run economic growth. "There's no better way to help our economy grow than to leave more money in the hands of the men and women who earned it," he said (Barshay 2003a). Democrats balked at the cost of the plan, and protested that it unfairly benefited the rich. House Democrats, led by Minority Leader Nancy Pelosi of California, announced an alternative $100 billion proposal, focusing on short-term tax rebates, aid to states, and an extension of unemployment benefits. Montana senator Max Baucus, top Democrat on the Finance Committee, produced a similar $135 billion plan (Barshay 2003a). Moderate senator John Breaux (D-LA) told reporters that Bush's plan would be "replaced, and/or dramatically scaled down" (Barshay and Ota 2003).

By early February 2003, the Bush proposal had grown to a $695 billion package that included not only the dividend tax measure but also an acceleration of tax cuts that had been passed in 2001 and increased deductions for small businesses (Ota 2003b). By March, new estimates pegged the cost of the plan at $726 billion over ten years. Some Republicans saw such large figures as cause for concern. California representative Bill Thomas, chairman of the Ways and Means Committee, expressed reservations. "I'm trying to figure out what it means," he told the *Washington Post*. "My job is not to say, 'Attaboy. Good deal'" (Weisman 2003b). Representative Rob Portman (R-OH), a close ally of Bush, admitted that the proposal presented a "challenge" for Congress (Hook 2003a).

Meanwhile, in the Senate, Bush secured the support of one Democrat, Zell Miller of Georgia, but faced skepticism among moderate Republicans. "I won't take it as it is," Senator Olympia Snowe (R-ME) bluntly told the press (Hook 2003a). "Our government is in deficit and we have large expensive challenges ahead," said Lincoln Chafee (R-RI), announcing his disagreement with the president (Barshay and Ota

2003). Critics of the plan found no unity in opposition, however: Democratic leader Tom Daschle of South Dakota fielded his own plan, in addition to the Baucus plan, the Pelosi proposal, a proposal from Senator and presidential candidate John Edwards (D-NC), and a Democratic Governors Association proposal. "The Democratic Caucus is not united," admitted Senator Mary Landrieu. But in consolation, she added, "Democrats are always disorganized" (Barshay 2003b).

If the Democrats were disorganized, the Republicans—at least in the House—were uniting behind their leadership. Tom DeLay (R-TX), newly-elected House Majority Leader, was a firm proponent of the Bush initiative and pressed for an even larger tax cut than the one Bush had proposed. Asked if he had an upper limit in mind, DeLay mused, "Who knows? . . . A trillion dollars?" (Barshay and Ota 2003).

In mid-April 2003, each house voted on a budget resolution, the first step in determining the size and structure of the budget for the next fiscal year. The House resolution included provisions for a ten-year tax cut of $550 billion. This was lower that the president had proposed, but still substantial. Senate Republicans capped a tax cut at $350 billion, however—a deal made to satisfy the concerns of moderate Republicans Snowe and George Voinovich (R-OH). Outraged House leaders claimed they had not been informed of the agreement to set this lower limit and felt betrayed. At a news conference, DeLay angrily accused Senate Republicans of endangering the two houses' ability to work together. "We will continue to press for tax relief that will stimulate more than some senator's ego," he said (Hook 2003b).

By May, the 2003 Bush tax cut had shrunk to a $350 billion package that included $20 billion in aid to suffering state governments. After the House reluctantly agreed with the Senate's lower cap, Bush signed the measure into law on May 28. Rather than appearing disappointed at this outcome, Bush and his aides declared victory. Calling it "bold legislation," Bush argued that the new law was "adding fuel to an economic recovery" (Stevenson 2003b). The president had good reason to be pleased—after all, the $350 billion, ten-year plan stood about at the level the administration started out with back in December 2002, and was far in excess of what Democrats had wanted. "Many Democrats were saying they would not support anything in excess of about $100 billion, as a temporary one-year tax cut," White House press secretary Ari Fleisher pointed out. "It's going to be significantly more than many of the Democrats supported" (VandeHei 2003d). Although it was substantially less than the amount Bush proposed to Congress in February, the new law nevertheless enacted the third largest tax cut in U.S. history.

The Cases in Perspective

The preceding accounts of Bush administration successes are similar in some senses, different in others. They are by no means the only legislative initiatives in which the Bush administration became involved, nor do they cover all the important issue areas that the Bush team prioritized. Nevertheless, a pattern emerges from these cases that suggests that the Bush team has recognized the importance of the House of Representatives and has taken advantage of the recent polarization of the parties in Congress. Bush has had more difficulty with social policies, such as education, but has quickly moved to shift his strategy on these issues, rather than bog down in intraparty disagreements.

Polarization

The increasing unity of the parties in Congress works to the president's advantage, especially with respect to economic policy. In the tax policy cases, President Bush could count on much more united Republican support than a similar president could have dreamed of in decades past. While Lyndon Johnson, Jimmy Carter, and even Ronald Reagan struggled to keep their partisans in the fold, Bush found this practically unnecessary in the tax cut cases. In the 2001 case, the House voted less than two days after the president announced his plan and granted the president practically everything he asked for. In the 2003 case, the House again moved quickly to provide the president a tax cut blueprint that was more than $200 billion larger than even White House insiders had thought possible a month before.

The unity of the Republican Party helped the president's proposals not only in these tax policy cases but also on such measures as the legislation that created the Homeland Security Department in late 2002, on which there was also near-unanimous within-party agreement. Democrats fought to strip the legislation of measures that would change the civil service status of some Homeland Security Department employees, but a united Republican Party successfully thwarted this effort.

Social Policy

The third case, education reform, illustrates the consequence of a disunited party and provides evidence in favor of Krehbiel's theory of the primacy of preferences, rather than Aldrich and Rohde's theory of party leadership strength. In contrast to the tax cases, Republicans were not united behind the Bush education plan, and party leadership was ineffective in forcing the rank and file into line. Because of suspicions among conservative Republicans about the possibility of national testing, Bush found his job much more difficult. Uncertain support among Republicans forced the president to work with Democrats early in the process, and he had to swiftly discard a key component of his agenda: private school vouchers. The resulting bill was much more moderate than either the 2001 or 2003 economic plans. As Krehbiel would predict, party unity lasted only as long as preferences were also united.

The education policy case has parallels in other Bush efforts to advance social policy, such as the 2003 effort to reform the Medicare system. In that case, Republican ambivalence about whether and how to add a new prescription drug entitlement to the program prompted the president to drop what had been a key component of his proposal: a provision that would have offered such a benefit only to those Medicare recipients who joined private insurance plans. With that measure out of the way, moderate Democrats joined the president's coalition, just as they had in the case of education. When the bill finally passed in November 2003, both parties were divided, with many conservative Republicans and liberal Democrats opposing the bill. As Senator John Breaux (D-LA) put it, "This is a great victory for a coalition built from the center out. People on the far left or the far right were not necessarily part of the team" (Pear 2003).

From the perspective of the White House, then, the difference between social issues and economic issues engendered a difference in the timing of compromise. For social policy, compromise was appropriate from the beginning, since a united Republican Party was much less likely. For economic policy, however, the president was better off not compromising until near the end of the legislative process, exploiting the House "stake in the sand" for all that it was worth. Still, because Bush's aides recognized the limitations of the presidency, compromise was almost always part of the process. The key to the stake-in-the-sand approach lies not its inflexibility but in its establishment of an early and ambitious bargaining position. As presidential scholar Bruce Buchanan points out, "Bush makes a big show about playing hardball and not negotiating until absolutely the very last minute. But when it comes time to fish or cut bait, he usually cuts bait" (Powell 2003).

House of Representatives

When the parties are united, the House of Representatives is more valuable to the president than the Senate, even if both houses are controlled by the president's party. In the cases above, this is clear. In all three cases, the House passed its version of the legislation first, and in most cases it passed something very similar to what the Bush administration preferred. These early House votes set the agenda, pulling the Senate in Bush's direction. In the case of the 2003 tax bill, Senators who initially scoffed at tax cuts of more than $100 billion turned around and supported tax cuts of more than triple that amount in light of an even larger House plan.

When problems arose, they usually concerned individual senators, who have more power than do individual members of the House. James Jeffords shocked the nation by switching parties in frustration over special education funding. George Voinovich and Olympia Snowe, both Republicans, frustrated Bush by refusing to back larger tax cuts in 2003.

The stake-in-the-sand approach is not without its risks, even if the Republicans in the House remain united. The principal dangers lie in the Senate, where the president is already at a disadvantage. Chief among these dangers is the one Jeffords exemplified. If the pressure the president places on individual members of the Senate backfires, other members could defect. It is unlikely that Republicans will desert the party in droves, but they could cause trouble for the president's agenda, given the prerogatives granted to individual members of the Senate under the rules of that chamber. Moderate Democrats, whom the president needs in many cases, may also grow to resent the president's tactics. For these and other reasons, some argue that the president's relationship with Congress is as uncertain and tenuous as ever, despite greater party polarization (Fleisher and Bond 2000).

It is also possible that House Republicans will not be united as frequently on future presidential initiatives. With the passage of a second major tax cut in 2003, Bush's economic policy agenda has been largely accomplished. Future presidential legislative efforts may involve social policies, such as welfare reform reauthorization and Social Security reform, which are likely to sow divisions in the Republican Party, just as education and Medicare policy have.

Regardless of what is in store, in his first two years as president, George W. Bush received more unified support from members of his own party than any president in generations (Stanley and Niemi 2000, 254–55; *Congressional Quarterly* 2001–2002). This was particularly important for the Bush presidency because Congress was closely divided between the parties. Johnson, for example, won many legislative victories in his first two years as president with less unified support from his party, because in 1964 and especially 1965 Democrats enjoyed large majorities in both houses of Congress.

That Republicans controlled the House of Representatives, albeit with a slim margin, was also crucial for the president. Without Republican control of the House, Bush could not realistically have used quick House passage of a bill as a bargaining chip. Reagan, for example, was able to pass a successful tax bill through Congress in 1981 but faced a House controlled by Democrats. His strategy therefore relied not only on Republican unity but also on peeling off enough conservative Democrats to successfully move his legislation through the chamber. Reagan's tax strategy, therefore, more closely resembles Bush's social policy strategy.

By exploiting Republican unity and control of the House of Representatives whenever possible, Bush was able to use his "stake in the sand" strategy to great effect in the first two years of his presidency, especially with respect to tax policy. He and his aides also recognized the inherent limitations of the office and therefore held to a limited legislative agenda over which they were willing to compromise. Presidents usually achieve their greatest successes in their first two years of office, so triumphs such as the 2001 tax cut are unlikely to be equaled. This is no surprise, however. The surprise is how successful Bush has been, given his slim mandate.

IV

Foreign and Economic Policy

9 THE FOREIGN POLICY OF THE GEORGE W. BUSH ADMINISTRATION

James M. McCormick

During the 2000 election campaign, George W. Bush announced that he would pursue a "distinctly American internationalism" in foreign policy (Bush 1999a). Unlike Clinton, Bush wanted the United States to be more "humble" in global affairs and to recognize its limits in changing the international system (Election 2000). Put differently, he sought to have a foreign policy that placed greater emphasis on American national interests than on the global interests of the Clinton years. While the Bush administration initially sought to move U.S. foreign policy in this direction, the events of September 11 changed both the content of its foreign policy and the process by which it was made. As a result, the administration came to pursue a foreign policy that was universal in scope and viewed virtually all actions in the international arena as affecting U.S. interests. The universal nature of its policy came to be summarized by its effort to build a "coalition of the willing" to find and defeat "terrorists and tyrants" on a worldwide scale (*National Security Strategy* 2002).

Foreign Policy Legacies after the Cold War

The foreign policy legacies Bush inherited from the Clinton administration and that of his father, George H. W. Bush, provide a point of departure for understanding his foreign policy. Both of those previous administrations experienced the seismic foreign policy shock that occurred with the end of the Cold War, and each administration sought to put its own stamp on efforts to replace the anti-Soviet and anticommunist principles that had for so long guided U.S. foreign policy. Neither administration was wholly successful in setting the United States on a new course, and both left different kinds of legacies. In addition to dealing with these legacies, Bush also had to respond to a more momentous concern, the tragic events of September 11, 2001. In all, the Bush administration confronted a daunting task in seeking to shape and anchor a consistent foreign policy for the United States at the beginning of the twenty-first century.

The Legacy of the First Bush Administration

George H. W. Bush largely came to office with a commitment to continue the course that Ronald Reagan had pursued during his second term. President Reagan, of course, had entered office in 1981 as a staunch anti-Communist and a foreign policy ideologue, seemingly determined to restore U.S. policies pursued during the height of the Cold War. Yet Reagan altered his approach during his second term, holding more summits with the Soviet leadership than any other U.S. president and pursuing a series of accommodative actions with that superpower (McCormick 1998). Such an approach was attractive to President George H. W. Bush, since he was much less a foreign policy ideologue and much more a political pragmatist than Reagan was. As such, Bush's initial impulse was toward a practical political realism (or what might be called "realism light") in which he sought to manage the relationship with the Soviet Union and to stabilize relations with other great powers, even as he dealt with other foreign policy issues.

This commitment to continuity in foreign policy was quickly undermined by the dramatic event that occurred near the end of his first year in office: the tearing down of the Berlin Wall on November 9, 1989. That event in turn opened up a floodgate of other changes that significantly altered the international political landscape over the next two years: the reunification of Germany in October 1990, the democratization of Eastern Europe over the next several years, the independence for the former republics in the Soviet Union, and the collapse of the Soviet Union itself in December 1991. Within a very short time, the end of the Cold War was a reality, and the "north star" that had guided U.S. foreign policy—

the fifty-year struggle against international communism—no longer existed.

By 1990, the Bush administration began to change U.S. foreign policy from being driven by anticommunist principles and toward addressing the new issues facing the international arena. In all, the new policy response took several different forms: The quick U.S. (and coalition) response to the Iraqi invasion of Kuwait in August 1990 was one kind of reaction. The administration's more cautious (and largely noninvolved) response to the ethnic and communal conflicts in the former Yugoslavia was another. And the administration's limited humanitarian intervention in the tragedy in Somalia was yet a third. While the administration responded under the rubric of creating a "new world order," and defended itself on the grounds of political realism and pragmatism in addressing the "instabilities generated by the Cold War's demise" (Eagleburger 1993), it hardly identified a clear and consistent course for U.S. foreign policy. Indeed, the administration was accused of pursuing an "ad hoc foreign policy," one that generated considerable uncertainty over the direction of policy abroad.

The Legacy of the Clinton Administration

Candidate Bill Clinton seized on the uncertainties of the Bush administration's foreign policy to argue for a "a new vision and the strength to meet a new set of opportunities and threats." "We face," Clinton (1991) noted, "the same challenge today that we faced in 1946—to build a world of security, freedom, democracy, free markets, and growth at a time of great change." The George H. W. Bush administration, in Clinton's (1992) view, was "rudderless, reactive, and erratic," and the United States needed leadership that was "strategic, vigorous, and grounded in America's democratic values." Candidate Clinton thus promised to set the United States on that new direction.

During its two terms in office, the Clinton administration sought to do just that. Its initial impulse was to rely on a commitment to expanding the number of market democracies, since, the administration contended, these kinds of societies offer the best prospect of creating a more pacific international system. This "liberal international" approach, focusing on promoting free markets and free peoples around the world as a way to create international peace and stability, stood in sharp contrast to the realism of the first Bush administration. Yet the Clinton administration had to confront some new realities of the post–Cold War world: new and frequent ethnic and communal conflicts in various parts of the world and the emergence of competing centers of powers from Russia and China. Consequently, by Clinton's second term in office the administration took a decided turn toward political realism and away from liberal internationalism, as witnessed by its action in Kosovo and its efforts to strengthen ties with traditional allies (McCormick 2000).[1] Nonetheless, as the first full-fledged post–Cold War administration, it left an array of foreign policy legacies for the new Bush administration.

In particular, the Clinton administration left three key foreign policy legacies: commitments to global involvement, to liberal internationalism in economic and social affairs, and to what came to be labeled the "Clinton Doctrine" in the political-military arena. Clinton's first—and most important—legacy was a sustained global involvement by the United States (McCormick 2000, 74–77). While some on the political Left and Right called for various forms of isolationism or unilateralism with the end of the Cold War, the Clinton administration never wavered in its commitment to internationalism on the part of the United States. Important economic and politicomilitary actions in the global arena demonstrated this commitment. In the economic area, the passage and implementation of the North American Free Trade Agreement was one important signal of this involvement as was the negotiation and passage of the Uruguay Round of the General Agreement on Tariffs and Trade (which created the World Trade Organization). In the military area, the administration remained committed to maintaining a presence in Europe by continuing to have 100,000 military personnel stationed there, and in Asia by having roughly 100,000 troops stationed in Japan and Korea. Further, the decision to seek the expansion of the North Atlantic Treaty Organization (NATO) and to broaden the mission of the organization was another important signal. Significant U.S. military actions abroad—enforcing the "no-fly zones" over Iraq, negotiating the Dayton Accords, committing U.S. peacekeepers to Bosnia, and initiating and prosecuting the war against Serbia over its policies in Kosovo—were important indicators of politicomilitary commitments as well. In this sense, the array of actions taken by the Clinton administration ensured a sustained global role for the United States and not a return to isolationism.

A second policy legacy was the central role that global economic policy now played in U.S. foreign policy. To be sure, foreign economic policy was always a focus of U.S. foreign policy, but the Clinton administration gave issues in this area a particularly high priority, especially at the beginning of Clinton's term in office. In all, the administration completed almost three hundred bilateral and multilateral trade pacts during its tenure. This legacy, too, was an important component of its "liberal international" agenda.

A third important policy legacy, the so-called Clinton Doctrine that called for U.S. intervention over humanitarian crises that arose in global politics (such as in Bosnia, Somalia, Haiti, and Kosovo), was also an important component of this liberal international agenda. These efforts met with mixed success, but they demonstrated the administration's commitment to transforming the internal conditions around the world and promoting democracy as well. To be sure, the Clinton administration received substantial criticism over its failure to define and rank-order these differing kinds of threats and its failure to outline a strategy (or set of strategies) over when and where not to intervene abroad. Still, Clinton left office with a commitment for the United States to remain more involved in humanitarian crises around the world.

Before September 11

Because the George W. Bush administration was more inclined toward a foreign policy approach closer to that of his father's administration, the Clinton foreign policy legacies were generally not welcomed by the Bush administration. Indeed, those legacies were a target of attack by candidate Bush and his foreign policy advisers since they represented a more universal and multilateral approach (liberal internationalism) than the new Bush administration envisioned. Instead, Bush was more inclined toward a foreign policy that embraced the components of classical realism.

Classical Realism and Bush's Initial Foreign Policy Principles

Classical realism starts with several important assumptions about states and state behavior that had direct implications for U.S. foreign policy actions. First, classical realists assume that states are the principal actors in foreign policy and that actions *between* states would trump any efforts to change behaviors *within* states. In this sense, the quality of relations between states is the major way in which to evaluate a country's foreign policy, and U.S. policy would focus principally on state-to-state relations. Second, for the classical realist, a state's "interests are determined by its power (meaning its material resources) relative to other nations" (Zakaria 1998, 8–9). As a state's relative power increases, it would seek to expand its political influence, but it would not do so in a "mad frenzy." Instead, the state would expand its influence only after a careful cost-benefit analysis. The United States can and should use its power to restrain states that could clearly harm it and its interests, but it should do so carefully and selectively. Third, classical realists focus on managing relations among the major powers, since these states are the ones that are likely to be the major threats in the international system. A guiding principle for realists is that no great power, or coalition of great powers, should dominate or endanger a nation or a group of nations. In this sense, some of the broader agenda items from the Clinton years—such as failed states and transnational issues like drug trafficking and terrorism—would not be high priorities for a classical realist. Instead, the United States should focus on strengthening its alliances and on challenging some states. In all, then, the classical realist approach has the United States aiding global stability from its position of strength, but—and importantly—doing so in a highly prudent and selective manner.

Other foreign policy values and policy positions flowed from Bush's initial commitment to classical political realism. By considering what his administration initially supported and opposed in the foreign policy realm, we can gain a fuller appreciation of how fully classical political realism permeated much of the administration's initial months in office.

What the Bush Administration Initially Supported

First and foremost, Bush came to office as a foreign policy internationalist, although a particular kind of internationalist. He characterized his approach as seeking to develop a "distinctly American internationalism." What that phrase connoted, however, was an approach that was more unilateralist than his predecessor's and even his father's. The phrase, too, implied a much narrower definition of U.S. national interests than his immediate predecessors (Bush 1999a).

Second, candidate Bush made clear that a top priority of his administration would be to refurbish America's alliance structure around the world as a tangible manifestation of managing great power relationships. Europe and Asia—and not other areas of the world—would be the highest foreign policy priorities, since those regions contain long-time allies and potential rivals. In refurbishing these alliances, too, all allied countries must be real partners, not satellites, and they must share burdens and risks with the United States. Europe and Japan, for example, should do more to support their own defense.

Third, Russia and China would be viewed in a more skeptical way than they were during the Clinton administration, and U.S. military capacity would be important for exercising U.S. influence with these nations. China, for example, should be viewed as an emerging power and as "a competitor, not a strategic partner" (Bush 1999a). Candidate Bush went on to say that "we must deal with China without ill will, but without any illusion." Before the 2000 election, future national security advisor Condoleezza Rice suggested the policy approach more fully: "It is important to promote China's internal transition through economic interaction while containing Chinese power and security ambitions. Cooperation should be pursued, but we should never be afraid to confront Beijing when our interests collide" (Rice 2000, 57).

According to the Bush administration, the United States should deal with Russia in a somewhat different way, albeit with more skepticism than in the past. We need to be concerned "less by Russia's strength," Rice noted, and more by its "weakness and incoherence" (Rice 2000, 58). Hence, the focus must be on the security of its nuclear arsenal and the dangers that loose nuclear weapons pose. Furthermore, she argued, we must always be aware that Russia, like China, will continue to have interests at odds with those of the United States.

Fourth, candidate (and President) Bush valued the role of "hard power" over "soft power" for the United States (Bush 1999b). Hard power refers to the utility of military capacity, sanctioning behavior, and threat behavior, among other coercive measures, as ways to influence the behavior of nations. Soft power relies on the appeal of American culture and values to enable the United States to influence the behavior of other states. In Bush's view, hard power is to be preferred, since there are still adversaries in the world who do not like what the United States represents and will take actions to harm it. Moreover, the forces hostile to the United States today only understand traditional hard power; they are unlikely to be dissuaded by soft power.

Fifth, and in line with refurbishing alliances and with the use of hard power, candidate Bush made clear that remaking and strengthening the U.S. military would be a top priority. Hence, increased military pay and increased military spending would be key priorities for his administration. Perhaps the poster child for the Bush administration's commitment to military preparedness was a national missile defense system, which it committed to developing and deploying as a protection against rogue states or against groups with access to weapons of mass destruction.

What the Bush Administration Initially Opposed

Both candidate and President Bush also knew what foreign policy actions he opposed. Most fundamentally, the administration sought to narrow the number of U.S. actions around the world and focus only on strategically important ones. This position, too, is highly compatible with classical realism. First, the United States would not be as involved in trying to change other states internally or create political democracy within other countries. As candidate Bush stated, "America cherishes [its] freedom, but we do not own it. We value the elegant structures of our own democracy—but realize that, in other societies, the architecture will vary. We propose our principles, but we must not impose our culture" (Bush 1999a). In other words, the United States would invite other states to imitate its values and political structure, but it would not seek to impose them on other states.

Second, Bush opposed U.S. humanitarian interventions without a clear strategic rationale for being involved in such missions. Thus, U.S. involvement in communal and regional conflicts would be rare. Rice made the point forcefully: The U.S. military is neither "a civilian police force" nor "a political referee," in internecine and communal conflicts. "And it is most certainly not designed to build a civilian society" (Rice 2000, 53). The administration demonstrated its reluctance to become involved in regional and communal conflict early on. In the election campaign, candidate Bush proposed to bring U.S. military forces home from their peacekeeping duties in the Balkans if he was elected. Later, President Bush indicated that the administration would pull back from U.S. involvement in Middle East discussions. The administration also sought to move away from negotiations with the North Koreans during its first months in office. In all, there was a reluctance to engage the United States in important ethnic, communal, and regional conflicts that existed in the world.

Third, the Bush administration eschewed involvement with international institutions and opposed several key international agreements. For example, the administration rejected the Kyoto Protocol to control global warming, opposed the Comprehensive Test Ban Treaty as a means of stopping the spread of nuclear weapons to new nations, and indicated its willingness to withdraw from the 1972 ABM Treaty in order to deploy national missile defense. While the Bush administration endorsed efforts at freeing up global trade, it was undoubtedly more cautious about embracing environmental and labor standards within the World Trade Organization. More generally, the administration looked skeptically on the United Nations as a key instrument of U.S. foreign policy.

Fourth, and like past administrations, the Bush administration was not inclined to afford much influence to the Congress in the conduct of foreign policy or to U.S. allies. Despite winning the presidency by the narrowest of margins, the administration tended to pursue its foreign policy (and its domestic agenda) in a manner that suggested a wider mandate than it possessed. Similarly, and given Bush's general approach to foreign policy, he was more inclined to pursue an international agenda singularly—without being encumbered too greatly by the views of allies.

September 11, the American Public, and Its Policymakers

All Americans will always remember where they were, and what they were doing, when they first heard that American Airlines flight 11 had crashed into the north tower of the World Trade Center, or a few minutes later when United Airlines flight 175 crashed into the south tower. And few will forget where they were a little while later when American Airlines flight 77 crashed into the Pentagon and United Airlines Flight 93 crashed in a field in Pennsylvania after a vain attempt by the passengers to overpower their hijackers.

From an analytic point of view, the events of that day represent one of those rare and spectacular political events that can change the mindset or the image of the public and its leaders regarding foreign policy. Such "watershed" events are rare indeed, as one political scientist noted many years ago, but when they do occur, they can reverse or change the views toward the international system of a generation or more (Deutsch 1966). In an earlier period the Vietnam War—or the "searing effects of Vietnam," to use the words of a political scientist at the time—had a jarring effect on attitudes toward war and peace and toward the use of U.S. force abroad (Russett 1975, 8). More recently, the collapse of the Berlin Wall and the implosion of the Soviet Union—the ending of the Cold War—might be cited as similar spectacular events affecting foreign policy. Yet September 11 appears to rank near the top of these spectacular events because of its pervasive effect not only for the generation being socialized to politics at the time but also for the leveling effect it had on foreign policy beliefs across generations.

In this sense, September 11 has had a more profound effect than these other spectacular events—whether Pearl Harbor, the Vietnam War, or the Berlin Wall—for at least three reasons. First, it was the first substantial attack on the American continental homeland since the burning of Washington in the War of 1812. The U.S. public had always assumed the security of the homeland, and these events shattered that assumption. September 11 demonstrated that no state or person was secure from those determined to do them harm. Second, September 11 was fundamentally an attack on U.S. civilians, not military personnel (although, to be sure, military personnel were killed at the Pentagon). Even Pearl Harbor and its devastation had fundamentally been directed at military personnel. Third, and importantly, the terrorist attack was the deadliest in U.S. history—costing almost 3,000 lives and surpassing the death toll at Pearl Harbor by almost 1,000. In all, then, September 11 produced a profound and pronounced effect, whether measured by the changed attitudes among the U.S. public toward foreign policy, the changed agenda within Congress with new levels of support for the president on foreign policy issues, or the changed nature of the presidency itself.

Impact on the Public

The impact of September 11 on the American people was evident almost immediately after the attacks. Hosts of Americans were suddenly flying flags from their car windows, wearing them on their lapels, and pasting them to the front windows of their homes. People of all walks of life and from all parts of the country exhibited a huge outpouring of support for the victims and their families. Support, too, for President Bush and his foreign policy actions increased across party lines. Bush's approval went from 51 percent just prior to September 11 to 86 percent immediately after the event. The "rally 'round the flag" effect by the American public (35 points) was the largest ever recorded by the Gallup polling organization. Indeed, within a short-time, Bush's approval rating had reached 90 percent (Gallup Tuesday Briefing 2001; Murray and Spinosa 2004).

While the immediate outpouring of patriotism and support for the president by the public is not surprising given the gravity of the events of September 11, what has been unusual has been the lasting effect of this so-called rally effect. The average level of public support for Bush during the first four months after September 11 was 84 percent (Newport 2002). A year later, his public approval was still at 70 percent. After eighteen months in office, Bush's average approval over that time frame was 72 percent, the highest cumulative average of any post-Vietnam president, and the third highest for that time period (after Kennedy and Johnson) of any post–World War II president (Murray and Spinosa 2004). To be sure, his support began to decline prior to the war with Iraq in early 2003, rose with the outbreak of war (Saad 2003a), and began to decline as post-Iraqi reconstruction proved difficult (Saad 2003b; Moore 2003). Still, the lingering support for President Bush (even in the midst of recession and a weak economy) seemed tied to the residual impact of September 11.

After September 11, the American public's attitudes toward foreign policy took a sharp turn away from those that it had held as recently as the 1998 Chicago Council on Foreign Relations survey (Chicago Council 2002). Now, those attitudes supported a more robust American approach abroad. In particular, while the public continued to provide strong support for nonmilitary measures to address terrorism, the public was now willing to endorse a variety of military measures as well. The public supported the use of American air strikes and ground troops against terrorists and would even support the assassination of terrorist leaders, when such efforts were done with multilateral support. A large percentage of the public, too, favored sending U.S. troops to Iraq, although as part of a multilateral approach toward the invasion of that country. The public gave strong support for more spending on defense and intelligence gathering. Sixty-five percent of the public wanted to increase spending on homeland security. A majority of the public also supported maintaining U.S. military bases overseas. In all, then, the public was hardly a constraint on the president's foreign policy actions after September 11; instead, it appeared to be endorsing the actions that the administration was already pursuing or contemplating.

Impact on Congress

September 11 had a similar effect on Congress and its role in policymaking, especially when compared to Congress's role over the previous three decades. The end of the Cold War accelerated the pluralistic decision-making process that had emerged after the Vietnam War and enhanced the role of Congress. With the collapse of the and the ending of the Soviet Union, for instance, the United States' foreign policy agenda changed dramatically, and a broad array of new economic, environmental, sociocultural, and security issues now took center stage. Many of these issues allowed or required congressional action, and many of them did not immediately produce common positions among the American people or members of Congress. Instead, economic and environmental issues, for example, often affected constituencies differentially and exacerbated differences within Congress and between Congress and the White House. As a result, foreign policy issues became increasingly partisan and contentious. Indeed, the Clinton administration fought numerous difficult battles with the Republican-controlled Congress on foreign policy during its time in office, and it had a decidedly mixed record in this new political environment (McCormick 2000).

In large measure, the events of September 11 changed all that, and, much like the impact on public attitudes, these events served as a watershed in congressional-executive relations on foreign policy. In particular, September 11 seems to have resurrected an aphorism popular during the height of the Cold War: "Politics stops at the water's edge." Much as the public rallied behind the president after September 11, members of Congress appeared to put aside partisan divisions to confront international terrorism. Symbolically, President Bush's embracing Senator Tom Daschle, Senate Majority Leader at the time, after a speech in the House of Representatives, aptly portrayed this new sense of unity. Substantively, the impact of September 11 on congressional behavior manifested itself in the high degree of bipartisan support for legislation to combat international terrorism.

Within a week of the September 11 attack, Congress had enacted Senate Joint Resolution 23 authorizing the president to use force "against those nations, organizations, or persons he determines planned, authorized, committed, or aided the terrorist attacks." Just over a month later, Congress passed the U.S.A. Patriot Act that afforded the executive branch greater discretion in pursuing terrorist suspects and narrowed some previous civil liberty protections. Over the next several months, Congress passed several pieces of legislation that afforded the executive greater power in dealing with international terrorism, ranging from waiving previous restrictions on aid to Pakistan, enhancing border security and visa entry requirement to aiding the victims of terrorism, increasing intelligence authorization, and amending the immigration statute. As table 9.1 shows, some twenty-one pieces of legislation were passed as part of the congressional response to September 11.[2]

Table 9.1 also shows that these pieces of legislation were largely passed without much dissent by members of Congress. In all, only five pieces of legislation produced any significant opposition, and this opposition was confined to the House of Representatives. Even these five pieces of legislation—the Air Transportation Safety and System Stabilization Act, the U.S.A. Patriot Act, the Terrorist Bombings Convention Implementation Act, the Export-Import Bank Reauthorization Act, and the National Defense Authorization Act—drew only a modest amount of opposition. In two of the votes, 9 percent were opposed, and in the other three, 13, 16, and 18 percent, respectively, were opposed. In other words, Congress overwhelmingly supported the president in the first year after September 11.

This level of congressional support continued in the second year as well, albeit not quite at the same level. In October 2002, Congress passed a joint resolution authorizing the president to use force "as he determines to be necessary and appropriate in order to defend the national security of the United States against the continuing threat posed by Iraq and enforce all relevant United Nations Security Council Resolutions regarding Iraq," and it did so by a large margin in each chamber (in the House by a vote of 296–133, and in the Senate by a vote of 77–23). The Department of Homeland Security Act of 2002 passed by a wide margin in the House (295–133) but stalled in the Senate for a time. After the 2002 midterm elections, the Senate acted quickly, passing that measure by a 90–9 vote in November 2002 and establishing one of the largest governmental bureaucracies in the history of the American Republic. In all, then, despite occasional questioning of the administration's policy on terrorism by some members of Congress, there was now both bipartisan support and interbranch cooperation on this issue.

Impact on the President

Finally, and importantly, the events of September 11 appear to have profoundly affected Bush himself, as was evidenced at both a personal and policy level. On the night of the tragic events, Bush dictated for his diary that "the Pearl Harbor of the twenty-first century took place today" (Woodward 2002, 37). With that assessment, Bush appeared to realize

Table 9.1

Legislation Related to the Attack of September 11

	Date	*Public law no.*	*House vote*	*Senate vote*
Congressional Sentiment	9/18/01	107–39	Without objection	100–0
Authorization for Use of Military Force	9/18/01	107–40	Without objection	98–0
Public Safety Officer Benefits bill	9/18/01	107–37	413–0	Unanimous consent
Emergency Supplemental Appropriations Act	9/18/01	107–38	422–0	Unanimous consent
Air Transportation Safety and System Stabilization Act	9/22/01	107–42	356–54	Unanimous consent
A bill to amend the Immigration and Nationality Act	10/1/01	107–45	Without objection	Unanimous consent
U.S.A. Patriot Act	10/26/01	107–56	357–66	98–1
Foreign Assistance Waivers	10/27/01	107–57	Voice vote	Unanimous consent
Aviation and Transportation Security Act	11/19/01	107–71	410–9	Voice vote
Designating September 11 as Patriot Day	12/18/01	107–89	407–0	Unanimous consent
Afghan Women and Children Relief Act	12/21/01	107–81	Voice vote	Unanimous consent
National Defense Authorization Act for Fiscal Year 2002	12/28/01	107–107	382–40	96–2
Intelligence Authorization Act for Fiscal Year 2002	12/28/01	107–108	via Voice vote	100–0
Higher Education Relief Opportunities for Students Act	1/15/02	107–122	Voice vote	Unanimous consent
Victims of Terrorism Relief Act of 2001	1/23/02	107–134	418–0	Unanimous consent
Extended Unemployment Compensation bill	3/25/02	107–154	Voice vote	Unanimous consent
Enhanced Border Security and Visa Entry Reform Act	5/14/02	107–173	411–0	97–0
Bioterrorism Response Act of 2001	6/12/02	107–188	425–1	98–0
Export-Import Bank Reauthorization Act	6/14/02	107–189	344–78	Unanimous consent
Police and Fire Chaplains Public Safety Officers' Benefit Act	6/24/02	107–196	Without objection	Unanimous consent
Terrorist Bombings Convention Implementation Act	6/25/02	107–197	381–36	83–1

Source: Library of Congress, "Legislation Related to the Attack of September 11, 2001," available at http://thomas.loc.gov.

that he had new responsibilities. "He was now a wartime president," as Bob Woodward (2002, 37) noted, with all the implications of that judgment for his leadership.

Fred Greenstein (2004), a longtime student of presidents, provided an important window on how the president was affected by comparing Bush's leadership style before and after the events of that day. In particular, by assessing his leadership on six qualities—emotional intelligence, cognitive style, political skill, policy vision, organization capacity, and effectiveness as a public communication—Greenstein finds that Bush's cognitive style and his effectiveness with the public were the areas most affected and the other four leadership qualities were sometimes strengthened.

In the area of emotional intelligence, for example, the events of September 11 themselves strengthened Bush's ability to face the national tragedy, and the process of assembling a coalition against terrorism sharpened his political skills. While Bush had always had a fairly clear policy vision and could maintain a strong organizational team, September 11 strengthened his resolve in these areas. In the two other areas, September 11 had a greater effect. While Bush was routinely criticized during the 2000 campaign as lacking "intellectual curiosity" and not "drawn to the play of ideas," Bush appeared transformed by September 11. He had become more "thoughtful" and more "focused" in his thinking. Furthermore, and perhaps the most important leadership transformation, Bush became a more effective communicator to the American public and beyond. As Greenstein observes, "Bush has made himself a public presence." Through his visits to the World Trade Center and the Pentagon and with his eulogy at the National Cathedral, Bush conveyed his transformation in this area.

Two other scholars who focus on the role of personality in policymaking largely reach the same conclusion about the impact of September 11 on Bush's increased attention on foreign policy. As Thomas Preston and Margaret Hermann (2004, 370) note, "[Bush's] normal lack of interest in foreign affairs and desire to delegate the formulation and implementation of foreign policy to others, which had been the dominant pattern within his advisory system before the terrorist attacks, was forced to give way to his current, more active and involved pattern." In this sense, foreign policy became a real focal point for him. Nonetheless, Preston and Hermann also contend that Bush continued to see global issues in black-and-white terms (an approach that he used to convey a sense of moral clarity in the public arena), and he still relied on a "like-minded inner circle of advisers for policy guidance" (2004, 377). In this sense, his leadership style on foreign policy showed elements of continuity, even as it changed after September 11.

After September 11

The events on September 11 affected not only the president's leadership style but also the administration's approach to foreign policy content. Almost overnight, the administration changed its course in important ways. Although these events ironically confirmed some of the administration's assumptions about the world (such as the importance of hard power over soft power and the need for enhanced military preparedness), they also suggested the limitation of Bush's commitment to classical realism. While the administration did not do a *volte-face* in his policy, it appeared to change its approach from classical realism to defensive realism and incorporated a distinct form of idealism into its foreign policy actions.

Defensive Realism/Limited Idealism

While defensive realism makes many of the same assumptions as classical realism, it differs in one crucial aspect: defensive realism sees "insecurity" as the motivating force for state actions. Fareed Zakaria summarizes this fundamental difference: "While [classical realism] implies that states expand out of confidence, or at least out of an awareness of increased resources, [defensive realism] maintains that states expand out of fear and nervousness. For the classical realist, states expand because they can; for the defensive realist, states expand because they must" (Zakaria 1998, 8–9). The new threatening environment after September 11 thus propelled the Bush administration to change some of its foreign policy assumptions and actions—and eventually to create a new statement of its security strategy that incorporated elements of defensive realism rather than classic realism.

Along with this new defensive realism, the Bush administration also embraced a form of idealism in foreign affairs, especially as it related to combating international terrorism in the new era. A moral imperative shapes a nation pursuing an idealist foreign policy approach as it seeks to promote common values within and across states. In this sense, foreign policy becomes more than state-to-state relations among the strong and instead seeks to advance universal norms worldwide. In the post–September 11 period, the Bush administration sought to do just that as it promoted a worldwide campaign against terrorism. As such, it became increasingly concerned about the actions of all states (and groups) and the internal composition of many states, especially concerning their attitudes toward terrorism. Put somewhat differently, the administration appeared to embrace the Wilsonian idealist tradition in its foreign policy, albeit an idealism driven rather singularly toward combating international terrorism (for a critique, see Dorrien 2003).

Changes in Assumptions

After September 11, the Bush administration changed at least three foreign policy assumptions it had initially embraced.[3] First, and perhaps most significantly, the administration moved from a narrow or particularistic foreign policy approach to a more universal one, from a concern with narrowing national interests as compared to the Clinton years to broadening those interests to pursue universal security for all states threatened by international terrorism. Indeed, the administration, in various ways, equated American security with universal security.

Second, the Bush administration moved away from its rather narrowly defined unilateralist approach to foreign policy to a greater multilateral effort, albeit a multilateralism with a unilateralist option for the United States. Its involvement against terrorism with a broad array of states, with regional and international institutions, and with its multiple activities at home reflected this evident, but reluctant, multilateralism. In all of these arenas, the United States sought to pursue multilateral efforts, but Bush threatened to act unilaterally if multilateral support did not develop—as the war against Iraq ultimately demonstrated. In this sense, the depth of the administration's commitment to multilateralism has been rightly questioned by numerous critics.

Third, the administration moved from its reliance on a stark realist approach to foreign policy—without much concern with the internal dynamics of states—to a version of idealism—with a clear concern about the internal dynamics of some states. Put differently, the United States became more concerned with the attitudes and policies of some states regarding terrorism and less concerned with other internal conditions within those states. In this regard, humanitarian interventions, peacekeeping efforts, and peacemaking actions within states had now become part and parcel of the Bush foreign policy approach, not unlike his immediate predecessor.

Changes in Actions

President Bush's address to a joint session of Congress shortly after the terrorist attacks best captures the universal nature of the administration's post–September 11 foreign policy approach. Instead of embracing a policy of a "distinctly American internationalism," as he had done in the 2000 election campaign, Bush now adopted what we might call a "comprehensive American globalism," albeit narrowly defined and animated by the moral outrage against the attacks on the World Trade Center and the Pentagon. That is, Bush committed the United States to fighting terrorism, and states that support terrorism everywhere—and with all means. As he noted, "Our enemy is a radical network of terrorists, and every government that supports them. . . . Our war on terror begins with al Qaeda, but it does not end there. It will not end until every terrorist group of global reach has been found, stopped, and defeated" (Bush 2001e). In words reminiscent of the Truman Doctrine at the start of the Cold War, Bush outlined the dichotomous and stark nature of the global struggle—a struggle between the way of terror and the way of freedom, a struggle between those states who support terror and those who do not, and a struggle between the uncivilized and civilized world. Recall what he said:

> These terrorists kill not merely to end lives, but to disrupt and end a way of life. With every atrocity, they hope that America grows fearful, retreating from the world and forsaking our friends. They stand against us, because we stand in their way.
>
> We will pursue nations that provide aid or safe haven to terrorism. Every nation, in every region, now has a decision to make. Either you are with us, or you are with the terrorists. From this day forward any nation that continues to harbor or support terrorism will be regarded by the United States as a hostile regime.
>
> This is not . . . just America's fight. And what is at stake is not just America's freedom. This is the world's fight. This is civilization's fight. (Bush 2001e).

The president also conveyed the multilateral nature of this new foreign policy approach in his initial speech on the war on terrorism, and it was demonstrated by the actions that the administration immediately undertook. Bush declared:

> Our response involves far more than instant retaliation and isolated strikes. Americans should not expect one battle, but a lengthy campaign, unlike any other we have ever seen. . . . We will starve terrorists of funding, turn them one against another, drive them from place to place, until there is no refuge or no rest. . . . We ask every nation to join us. We will ask, and we will need, the help of police forces, intelligence services, and banking systems around the world. The United States is grateful that many nations and many international organizations have already responded—with sympathy and with support. Nations from Latin America, to Asia, to Africa, to Europe, to the Islamic world. (Bush 2001e)

What was most dramatic about the approach was the decision to embrace a coalitional effort, the speed with which it was put together, and the variety of participants it included—especially in light of the Bush administration's foreign policy assumptions when it took office. Table 9.2 lists some of the bilateral and multilateral actions taken by other nations in the first twenty days after September 11; the table captures the collective effort to assist the United States. In addition, of course, nations worked cooperatively to freeze financial assets of known or suspected terrorist organizations, to impose new security standards at airports, and to enhance law enforcement worldwide.

By the time a military operation was commenced in Afghanistan on October 7, 2001, several allied countries (Britain, Canada, Australia, Germany, and France, among others) pledged to assist with the operation. And by that time more than forty nations had approved American overflight and landing rights (U.S. Department of State, 2001a, b; U.S. Embassy Islamabad 2002). Furthermore, the military undertaking in Afghanistan, Operation Anaconda, eventually included contributions from some twenty countries.

A third dimension to this post–September 11 change was the administration's interests and actions regarding communal and regional conflicts. The administration's decision to focus on the internal situation in Afghanistan is hardly surprising given the September events, but

Table 9.2
Bilateral and Multilateral Efforts to Assist the United States Immediately after September 11

Russia was the first nation to call the United States; it offered to share information and the use of its airspace for humanitarian efforts.
China, India, and Pakistan immediately offered to share information and/or offered support.
Twenty-seven nations offered American overflight and landing rights for actions against Afghanistan.
Forty-six multilateral organizations declared support for the United States.
One hundred nations offered to provide intelligence support to the United States.
The UN Security Council adopted a resolution instructing all nations to pursue terrorists and their supporters.
Australia invoked Article IV of the ANZUS Treaty and declared that September 11, 2001, was an attack on Australia
NATO invoked Article V, thus viewing the September 11 attack as an attack on NATO.

Source: U.S. Department of State, "Operation Enduring Freedom Overview," available at http://www.state.gov/s/ct/rls/fs/2001/5194.htm.

what is surprising is the extent to which the administration committed itself to changing or assisting in changing the domestic situations in a number of other countries. These range from identifying Iran, Iraq, and North Korea as an "axis of evil," to supplying military training and advisory units to such countries as the Philippines, Yemen, and Georgia, to using U.S. naval power near Sudan to block possible escaping al Qaeda fighters.

The administration's efforts aimed at conflict resolution in the Middle East and between India and Pakistan and at opening up discussions with the North Koreans illustrated a newfound concern with the internal dynamics of various countries and regions. Almost immediately after September 11, the administration appointed a special envoy, General Anthony Zinni, to the Middle East, and Secretary of State Colin Powell traveled to India and Pakistan in an attempt to defuse the situation over Kashmir. President Bush reiterated his willingness to open discussions with the North Koreans over peace and stability on the Korean peninsula (although this was a position the administration adopted as early as the summer of 2001). At the same time, the administration was willing to look past some internal concerns about some nations (such as China, Russia, and Pakistan), especially their human rights conditions, since their cooperation on the war on terrorism was more important than anything else for the United States.

In sum, the new approach, quickly labeled the Bush Doctrine, sought to hunt down terrorists, and those who supported them, on a worldwide scale. While cooperation and support from other countries would be sought, the United States would go it alone if necessary.

Formalizing the Bush Doctrine

In September 2002, one year after the attacks on New York and Washington, the Bush administration issued a fuller statement and rationale for its foreign policy approach. This statement, *The National Security Strategy of the United States of America* (2002), postulated that the fundamental aim of U.S. foreign policy was "to create a balance of power that favors freedom."[4] To create such a balance, the administration asserted that the United States "will defend the peace by fighting terrorists and tyrants, . . . will preserve peace by building good relations among the great powers, . . . [and] will extend the peace by encouraging free and open societies on every continent." The statement demonstrates how much American actions would now be motivated by the new threatening environment—and how singularly important that environment would be in dictating U.S. actions—much as defensive realism would postulate. Yet also note the idealist and universal nature of this proposed foreign policy agenda with its concerns for the internal makeup and operations of states and groups. A summary and assessment of this statement provides a fuller understanding of the Bush administration's policy content (see also Daalder, Lindsay, and Steinberg 2002a, on which I draw).

First of all, the administration recognizes and accepts the fact that the United States "possesses unprecedented—and unequaled—strength and influence in the world" and acknowledges that "this position comes with unparalleled responsibilities, obligations, and opportunity." It also recognizes that the task of building this new balance of power for freedom would be much more difficult than in earlier eras, since the United

States "is now threatened less by conquering states than we are by failing ones, . . . less by fleets and armies than by catastrophic technologies in the hands of the embittered few."

The Bush administration outlines seven courses of action to promote this fundamental goal of promoting freedom and advancing the "non-negotiable demands of human dignity":

1. Strengthen alliances to defeat global terrorism and work to prevent attacks against us and our friends;
2. Work with others to defuse regional conflicts;
3. Prevent our enemies from threatening us, our allies, and our friends with weapons of mass destruction;
4. Ignite a new era of global economic growth through free markets and free trade;
5. Expand the circle of development by opening societies and building the infrastructure of democracy;
6. Develop agendas for cooperative action with other main centers of global power; and
7. Transform America's national security institutions to meet the challenges and opportunities of the twenty-first century.

Although these courses of action together constitute the effort to construct this new balance of power for freedom, some of them contribute directly to one of the three peace themes identified earlier. In order to provide a better sense of the direction of U.S. foreign policy and to identify the policy emphasis within the administration, I group these courses of actions under what appears to be the proper theme of either defending, preserving, or extending the peace.

Defending the Peace

The first three courses of action explicitly focus on defending the peace against terrorists and rogue states. Under the first course of action, the administration seeks to rally nations and alliances around the world to defeat terrorism. The new adversary is now "not a single political regime or person or religion or ideology." Instead, it is an "elusive enemy" who "will be fought on many fronts" and "over an extended period of time. Progress will come through the persistent accumulation of successes—some seen, some unseen." Moreover, a broad array of actions will be used to defeat terrorism—disrupting the funding of terrorists through various means, taking direct actions against terrorist and terrorist organizations, denying territorial sanctuaries to terrorist groups in failed countries, addressing domestic conditions that breed terrorism, and strengthening homeland security. While the national strategy statement makes clear that regional and international organizations would be used in pursuing this objective, it also states that the United States would act alone or through a "coalition of the willing" if necessary.

A second course of action to defend the peace is to address the regional conflicts in the world today. These conflicts "can strain our alliances, rekindle rivalries among the great powers, and create horrifying affronts to human dignity." The Bush administration therefore committed itself to taking a variety of actions to reduce the impact of these regional conflicts on global stability and, where possible, to aid in their resolution. The administration made clear, though, that there are limits to how much the United States can and will do: "The United States should be realistic about its ability to help those who are unwilling or unready to help themselves."

A third dimension of defending the peace focuses on those rogue states and terrorists who might gain access to weapons of mass destruction. That is, the Bush administration uses the threat of weapons of mass destruction as a way to link terrorists and rogue states and to identify both as the combined enemies of U.S. foreign policy. These rogue states, while small in number, are states "that brutalize their own people, " "display no regard for international law, " "are determined to acquire weapons of mass destruction, " "sponsor terrorism around the globe," and reject human values and hate the United States and everything for which it stands." A major policy imperative for the United States is thus to defend itself, its allies, and friends from these states and groups that would seek to acquire weapons of mass destruction.

In particular, the United States must be prepared to "deter and defend" against terrorists and rogue states, strengthen nonproliferation efforts against them, and have "effective consequence management" against the effects of weapons of mass destruction, if deterrence fails. In one of the most controversial sections of the national strategy statement, the United States must have available "the option of preemptive actions to counter a sufficient threat to our national security." The administration's argument is based on the view that the terrorists and rogue states that possess these weapons will not be deterred and will use acts of terrorism and weapons of mass destruction in any effort to achieve their ends. Under appropriate safeguards, then, the United States must be prepared to act preemptively against such adversaries.

Preserving the Peace

While the first three courses of actions would also contribute to preserving the peace, the sixth course of action—developing cooperation with other centers of power—is the one course of action explicitly focused on that goal. Under this course of action, the United States would seek to lead a broad coalition, "as broad as practicable," as the document puts it, to promote a balance of power in favor of freedom. This coalition, moreover, would thus join together as a means to achieve the first three courses of action—namely, defending the peace against terrorists and rogue states.

The coalition-building effort would involve America's traditional allies—NATO (and an expanded NATO), Japan, Australia, Korea, Thailand, and the Philippines—but it would also include Russia, India, and China. In this sense, the Bush administration advocates submerging differences that might exist between the United States and key countries (such as Russia, China, India, and Pakistan) in an effort to build a larger and nearly universal coalition against international terrorism. What is particularly noteworthy about this section of the document is its relative silence on the role of international organizations, save for some discussion of NATO and the European Union.

Extending the Peace

The fourth and fifth courses of actions—igniting global economic growth and expanding the number of open societies and democracies—reflect the economic and political components of the administration's foreign policy approach (as contrasted with the security dimension so evident in the other courses of action). They also reflect the administration's effort to bring more states into this balance of power for freedom and some of its idealistic underpinnings as well. In substance, these two courses of action share a considerable continuity of policy with the Clinton administration's effort to enlarge the number of market democracies, but they also convey the priorities of the Bush administration in these areas as well.

The Bush administration's view is that economic growth "creates new jobs and higher incomes. It allows people to lift their lives out of poverty, spurs economic and legal reform, and the fight against corruption, and it reinforces the habits of liberty." Thus, the United States is committed to "a return to economic growth in Europe and Japan" and "to policies that will help emerging markets achieve access to larger capital flows at lower costs." In particular, the Bush administration reaffirmed its commitment to global, regional, and bilateral free trade initiatives as the way to foster global economic growth and development. The protection of the environment should accompany this commitment to economic growth. As such, the administration pledged to reduce U.S. greenhouse gas intensity by 18 percent during the next ten years as its contribution to a better environment. (This commitment, however, would be accomplished outside the Kyoto Protocol.)

The Bush administration's development aims are closely tied to its economic growth goals. The national strategy statement recognizes that "a world where some live in comfort and plenty, while half ...live on less than $2 a day, is neither just nor stable." As such, development is "a moral imperative" for the United States. The administration thus pledges to increase its development assistance by 50 percent, work to reform the World Bank and its activities to help the poor, develop measures to document progress within countries, and increase the amount of funding in the form of grants, as opposed to loans. At the same time, the administration continued to view trade and investment as "the real engines of economic growth." Finally, the administration continues to emphasize basic needs within poor countries, such as improving public health, education, and agricultural development, as its top priorities.

The last course of action in the statement calls for transforming national security institutions at home. While such a transformation would have an impact on all three themes of defending, preserving, and expanding peace, the priorities listed focus primarily on improving the military and the intelligence communities and strengthening homeland security to meet the demands of defending peace at home and abroad. To be sure, there is a brief mention of improving diplomacy and the Department of State, but the emphasis is surely more on the "hard power" agencies than on the "soft power" ones.

Overall, then, Bush's national strategy statement outlines an approach to enlist a worldwide campaign to address the threats posed by terrorists and rogue states and to create a new balance of power favoring human freedom. The security threats posed by these groups and states seem paramount in the Bush administration's actions toward others. The responses of other states toward these threats will increasingly trump concerns about political differences on other issues and will likely dominate efforts to foster economic and political development as well. Increasingly, the United States will judge states on their commitment to addressing the dangers of terrorism and rogue states and will work to engage other states in a grand coalition against such threats. At the same time, the national strategy statement concludes by emphasizing the commitment of the Bush administration to act unilaterally if collective efforts fail: "In exercising our leadership, we will respect the values, judgment, and interests of our friends and partners. Still, we will be prepared to act apart when our interests and unique responsibilities require."

Iraq and the Bush Strategy

After Afghanistan, the first real test of the Bush Doctrine of pursuing terrorists and tyrants was, of course, the pursuit of Saddam Hussein's Iraq. Indeed, discussion of Iraq by the Bush administration occurred almost immediately after September 11. In the first set of meetings by policymakers after those events, Secretary of Defense Donald Rumsfeld "raised the question of Iraq," although the Pentagon "had been working for months on developing a military option for Iraq" (Woodward 2002, 49). At that time, however, President Bush wanted more attention directed toward Afghanistan—particularly al Qaeda and the Taliban. As such, Iraq was placed on the backburner for a time.

By early 2002, however, Iraq once again gained the attention of President Bush and key policymakers because Saddam Hussein's regime represented a state that had used chemical and biological weapons against its own people and had started the development of a nuclear weapons program as well. While its link to terrorists was still unclear to many, the possibility of a "rogue state" (in the administration's definition) joining together with nonstate terrorist groups was a lethal combination for the United States and the international community.

By the summer of 2002, the issue had set off a pitched debate within the administration. Some key advisers supported quick and unilateral action to remove Saddam Hussein, while others, most prominently Secretary of State Powell and his deputy, Richard Armitage, argued that this approach had "risks and complexities" that needed more analysis

(Purdom and Tyler 2002). In addition, the discussion of pursuing a war strategy against Hussein had alienated Republican allies in Congress and former officials from previous administrations, notably former secretary of state Henry Kissinger and former national security adviser Brent Scowcroft. While these officials supported the need to remove Saddam Hussein, they were concerned that the administration's approach had risked "alienating allies, creating greater instability in the Middle East, and harming long-term American interests."

By the fall of 2002, the Bush administration decided to challenge the international community, and the United Nations, to address the issue of weapons of mass destruction in Iraq by seeking a multilateral solution. In a speech to the General Assembly, President Bush challenged the United Nations to address this issue of Iraq and weapons of mass destruction:

> Our principles and our security are challenged today by outlaw groups and regimes that accept no law of morality and have no limit to their violent ambitions. . . . Our greatest fear is that terrorists will find a shortcut to their mad ambitions when an outlaw regime supplies them with the technologies to kill on a massive scale.
>
> In one place—in one regime—we find all these dangers, in their most lethal and aggressive forms. (Bush 2002)

After five weeks of negotiation, the UN Security Council passed Resolution 1441 unanimously on November 8, 2002 (Text of UN Resolution 2002). The resolution found Iraq in "material breach" of a previous UN resolution (Resolution 687, which was passed at the end of the Gulf War in 1991 and called for Iraq's disarmament of its weapons of mass destruction). In addition, Resolution 1441 required Iraq to report within thirty days on all aspects of its programs related to weapons of mass destruction and ordered that Iraq shall immediately allow UN and IAEA (International Atomic Energy Agency) inspectors back into the country. Significantly, too, the resolution stated "that the Council has repeatedly warned Iraq that it will face serious consequences as a result of its continued violations of its obligations."

In accordance with this resolution, Iraq provided a report to the UN in December 2002 on its weapons program and allowed the UN and IAEA inspectors back into the country. Over the next several months, the chief inspectors provided reports to the Security Council on the status of the inspections and the disarmament. In all, these reports indicated that Iraq was not fully complying with the resolution and with the inspectors, but the inspectors requested more time from the Security Council to continue their work.

By March 2003, the Bush administration's patience had run out on the failure of the Security Council to act against Iraq. At the urging of Prime Minister Tony Blair of Great Britain, the United States, Britain, and Spain circulated another draft resolution to once again find Iraq in "material breach" and to get implicit approval for military action to enforce UN Resolution 1441. This resolution never reached a vote, since several nations on the Security Council, led principally by France, which threatened to use its veto, indicated that they would not support it. Indeed, France indicated that it would not support any resolution that would lead to war.

As a result, President Bush (2003c) issued an ultimatum to Iraq and its leadership on March 17, 2003: "Saddam Hussein and his sons must leave Iraq within 48 hours. Their refusal to do so will result in military conflict, commenced at a time of our choosing." When the Iraqi leadership refused to do so, the United States attacked a command bunker in Baghdad, and the war, called Operation Iraqi Freedom, had begun. The president took this action without another UN resolution and instead relied on the congressional resolution passed in October 2002. To be sure, the administration put together a "coalition of the willing" (some forty-two nations initially), much as the national security strategy statement of a few months earlier had implied. Yet the United States and the United Kingdom carried out the principal military action, with some assistance from Australia and a few other countries. In all, the Bush administration was willing to act alone (or with an informal coalition) in addressing the issues of tyrants and terrorists and in implementing its national security strategy.

The war campaign went well and quickly for the United States and Great Britain, with the loss of relatively few lives. The United States gained control of Baghdad by April 9, only three weeks after the war's initiation, and Bush declared "major combat operations" over on May 1. Still, winning the peace and establishing a stable democratic government proved more difficult. Indeed, American lives continued to be lost over the following months as Iraqi resistance remained. Equally challenging was the effort to uncover clear evidence of the existence of weapons of mass destruction, the fundamental rationale for the war. As a result, the Bush administration's foreign policy came under greater scrutiny and greater criticism by summer 2003.

Critiquing the Bush Doctrine in the Post–September 11 Era

Reactions to the national security strategy statement provided the first careful evaluations of the Bush Doctrine, but the policy debates prior to and after the fall of Baghdad brought into sharp relief the key questions about the Bush approach to foreign policy and its implications for the United States' role in the world. None of these criticisms succeeded in altering the Bush administration's fundamental approach, but they highlight the issues surrounding the Bush Doctrine.

Daalder, Lindsay, and Steinberg (2002a,b) provided one of the earliest critiques of the national security strategy statement and framed their assessment around five major concerns with it. First, they noted that the goals of promoting freedom and liberty and opposing terrorism and rogue states are laudable, but they also pointed out that the statement does not spell out how to achieve these goals in any systematic way. In this sense, a strategy is largely missing. Second, the goals may lead to contradictory actions since some states that oppose terrorism fail to respect freedom within their own countries. Put somewhat differently, the document seems to imply that the administration places more value on a state's supporting antiterrorism than on its supporting internal freedoms—especially since the administration is willing to cooperate with states with questionable records on advancing freedom. Third, the national strategy statement places too much emphasis on preemption without specifying which circumstances would justify that course of action. As Daalder, Lindsay, and Steinberg noted, deterrence remains the fundamental strategy, but it is somewhat lost in the discussion within the document. Fourth, they disagreed with the emphasis on a "coalition of the willing" versus the use of formal international institutions, because the latter can assist American interests more than the former and creating a coalition of the willing appears to be more difficult than the Bush administration acknowledged. Finally, the efforts to promote global prosperity and development are commendable, but they do not go far enough in addressing the institutional needs of failed states. These kinds of states are unlikely to satisfy the conditions (that is, to "fight corruption, respect basic human rights, embrace the rule of law, invest in health care and education") that the administration set out to qualify for this new assistance. As a result, Daalder, Lindsay, and Steinberg argued, "There is a risk that the countries that need help the most will not be eligible for it, and the countries eligible for it will be the ones that need it least."

An assessment of the national security strategy by John Lewis Gaddis (2002) is more favorable than Daalder, Lindsay, and Steinberg's, but Gaddis, too, raised some similar concerns about it. Gaddis saw the approach as "a grand strategy" that "could represent the most sweeping shift in U.S. grand strategy since the beginning of the Cold War" (2002, 50, 55, 56). In that sense, he believed that the strategy has real possibilities for U.S. foreign policy, especially compared with the Clinton administration's. Yet the strategy also has "potential stresses," as he puts it. The first is what he calls "multitasking"—addressing terrorists at the same time as tyrants may create a problem by stretching attention, resources, and support from others. Other presidents in U.S. history have focused on several foreign policy tasks at once, but such an effort will be difficult and pose a serious challenge for the Bush administration. Second, will the United States be "welcomed" by people in those countries where we act to combat terrorism and tyrants? Put differently, Gaddis wondered whether there is domestic support in other countries for this grand strategy. There will need to be to have it succeed (and the postwar difficulties in Iraq obviously lend credence to Gaddis's concern). Third, will the United States have the "moral high ground" for this strategy? Implicitly, to make the Bush administration's grand strategy work will require multilateralism. As Gaddis readily acknowledged, the Bush administration has not always done a very good job of seeking the support of others. Too often the administration has "depleted the reservoir of support from allies it ought to have in place before embarking on such a high-risk strategy"(Gaddis 2002, 56). In short, unilateralism is simply unlikely to succeed.

Prior to and after the occupation of Baghdad, the Bush Doctrine was subject to additional criticism from several different quarters—both for its policy content and the policymaking process that produced it. All tended to focus on some common themes: the Bush approach was too unilateralist and too ideological in its policy content, and it was too secretive and too ideological in its policymaking. Several critics, for example, pointed to a strategic plan developed in the early 1990s by officials in the first Bush administration (and who are now in the second Bush administration) as evidence of the ideological underpinning of the current Bush Doctrine. That plan called for a "policy of U.S. global domination." In 1997 some of those same individuals (particularly Dick Cheney, Donald Rumsfeld, and Paul Wolfowitz) helped initiate the Project for a New American Century, an organization that "called for an aggressive American policy of global domination" as well (see www.newamericancentury.org). With these individuals now in prominent positions in the George W. Bush administration, the officials were simply carrying out the plans developed earlier. Further, the kind of "unipolarism" now pursued by the Bush administration, a critic wrote, is essentially "a nationalistic and militaristic version of the liberal international vision of world democracy," and "the U.S. makes a mockery of its democratic ideals when it bullies other nations to serve U.S. interests and pretends that its bullying deserves to be called justice or idealism" (Dorrien 2003, 30–31, 33). In short, to these critics, neither the unipolarism employed nor the values promoted in the Bush Doctrine serve the long-term interests of the United States.

As the number of American deaths in postwar Iraq continued to mount and as weapons of mass destruction were not found by the summer of 2003, criticism of Bush's policy arose from the bureaucracy and Capitol Hill. Some charged that the administration had skewed intelligence data to support its desire to pursue the war against Iraq or pressured intelligence analysts to provide supportive estimates. And the Pentagon was accused of developing its own "hard-line view of intelligence related to Iraq" to justify U.S. military actions there (see, for example, Schmitt 2003). While the Bush administration denied such charges, skeptics remained, and Congress initiated inquiries into these matters. By July 2003, foreign policy criticisms appeared to reach a crescendo when the administration was forced to admit that a passage in the president's 2003 State of the Union address regarding Iraq's efforts to obtain uranium from an African nation was not supported by U.S. intelligence. George Tenet, director of Central Intelligence, took formal responsibility for this error (Sanger and Risen 2003), but the episode reinforced the view that the administration was determined to find evidence to justify military action against Iraq. Furthermore, the integrity of the Bush administration's policymaking was called into question, and the Senate Intelligence Committee called hearings to investigate.

By this time, too, foreign policy arose in the incipient 2004 presidential election campaign. As Democratic candidates began to test the waters in early caucus and primary states, the Bush administration's foreign policy was now a legitimate subject of debate. Former Vermont governor Howard Dean and Representative Dennis Kucinich, who both opposed the war in Iraq, had voiced criticism for some time, but other presidential contenders (Representative Richard Gephardt and Senator John Kerry) who had supported the war followed suit by the summer and fall of 2003. Representative Gephardt, for example, charged the president with "stunning incompetence" in the area of foreign policy (Beaumont 2003, 1B). Senator Kerry accused the administration of failing to have a plan to win the peace in Iraq, pointing to the "arrogant absence of any major international effort to build what's needed" in Iraq (Balz 2003, A6). And another contender for a time, Senator Bob Graham, called for further investigations into Bush's policymaking. In this sense, foreign policy, and the Bush Doctrine in particular, were again sources of domestic debate after a long hiatus since September 11.

The Bush administration sought to deflect some of these criticisms both by engaging in some diplomatic initiatives on other pressing problems and by initiating some postwar policy in Iraq. It did not, however, alter its fundamental course on terrorism. Indeed, its initial action as the war in Iraq was ending was to hint at possible actions toward Syria and Iran over their policies toward terrorism and weapons of mass destruction. Still, the administration moved away from that approach somewhat by undertaking several significant actions to broaden its foreign policy agenda. First, and perhaps most importantly, the administration issued its "Roadmap for Peace" on April 30, 2003, regarding the Israelis and the Palestinians and promptly began to work on implementing it. A Palestinian prime minister had been appointed; Israeli prime minister Ariel Sharon agreed to pull back some settlements in the West Bank; and a cease fire was negotiated among Israel, the Palestinians, and the groups responsible for suicide bombings in the region (Hamas and Islamic Jihad). And Bush visited the Middle East as a further stimulus to supporting this roadmap. Second, the Bush administration was successful in gaining approval for UN Security Council Resolution 1483 lifting sanctions against Iraq and encouraging other nations and international institutions to assist with the reconstruction of that nation. In addition, the resolution established a Special UN Representative for Iraq to oversee the reconstruction process there. And in the fall of 2003 the administration also succeeded in getting UN Security Council Resolution 1511 passed. This resolution called for states to contribute to a multinational force in Iraq and directed the Iraqi Governing Council to develop a timetable and program for a new constitution and democratic elections. Third, Bush and President Putin of Russia exchanged instruments of ratification of another strategic arms reduction treaty, signaling continued cooperation between the United States and a nation that had opposed the war in Iraq. Fourth, Bush met with European leaders at the G-8 (most notably, with French president Jacques Chirac) to begin to repair the rift with alliance partners that the war against Iraq had created. Fifth, Bush went on a five-day trip to Africa, only the third U.S. president to visit that continent, to promote his AIDS/HIV initiative and to demonstrate a broader foreign policy agenda than the war on terrorism had connoted. Furthermore, the administration sent some U.S. peacekeeping forces to aid strife-torn Liberia, although that action was driven both by security (that is, failed states are likely havens for terrorists) and by humanitarian concerns. Finally, as Iraqi insurgent attacks against the American military peaked in late fall 2003, the administration appeared to accelerate its efforts to turn over more responsibilities to Iraqis and aim for the return of sovereignty to the Iraqi people by the summer of 2004.

None of these actions, though, reflected a fundamental shift in the policy approach the Bush administration adopted after September 11. Indeed, terrorist incidents in Saudi Arabia in the spring and fall of 2003 and in Morocco in the spring of that year (and attributed to al Qaeda) only reinforced the administration's stance. Still, the mounting criticism at home and abroad of the administration's unilateral and ideological approach appeared to introduce a more cautionary note in considering further military responses, whether against North Korea, Iran, or elsewhere. For the near term, then, the administration appeared determined to pursue its combination of defensive realism and limited idealism in shaping U.S. foreign policy—albeit at a more muted level than actions against Afghanistan and Iraq implied. The approach, moreover, will likely remain as long as the American public continues to be supportive, the Congress remains relatively acquiescent (as evidenced by its supporting $87 billion in military and reconstruction spending for Iraq and Afghanistan in the fall of 2003), and the international community fails to challenge American primacy successfully. An important unknown is the direction of reconstruction and reconciliation within Iraq. As attacks on Americans continued and the death toll exceeded the total killed during major combat operations in March and April 2003, opposition increased at home, and public and congressional criticism mounted. The capture of Saddam Hussein in December 2003, however, gave a political boost to the administration's efforts in Iraq. The situation is likely to remain an important crucible for Bush's foreign policy as well.

Implications of Bush's Foreign Policy Strategy

In all, the combination of defensive realism and idealism of the Bush administration represents a determined effort to restore a consistent, coherent, and universal foreign policy approach, something that largely eluded Bush's immediate predecessors, William Clinton and George H. W. Bush. Indeed, in practice Bush's approach closely resembles the early years of his father's immediate predecessor, Ronald Reagan. Although the contexts are markedly different, the actions, ideological and universal in nature, during each of these administrations—one staunchly anti-Communist, the other, staunchly anti-terrorist—bear striking resemblance to each other. Like Reagan, Bush is strongly committed to setting a clear course for U.S. actions abroad, to acting alone, and to using U.S. military capacity, if necessary. Moreover, the Bush administration remains committed to that course even in light of recent challenges at home and abroad.

The larger implication of Bush's foreign policy strategy, however, remains unclear. Will it usher in a new foreign policy consensus that the American public and policymakers will embrace for the foreseeable future? Or will it isolate the United States from the rest of the global community? On the one hand, the approach has an underlying moral content, so important to the American public in addressing foreign policy, and it is aimed at a threat that the American public can comprehend—unlike the diffuse set of threats identified by administrations at the end of the Cold War. Second, terrorism directly threatens people's lives and is thus readily understandable. Third, the administration's approach is comprehensive—much like the containment policy at the end of World War II—and thus everyone can contribute.

On the other hand, the approach may alienate the United States from the rest of the global community, an especially troubling outcome at this important time in global politics. As political analyst Zakaria (2003, 20) noted just prior to the initiation of the war against Iraq, "Never will [America] have waged a war in such isolation. Never will have so many of its allies been so firmly opposed to its policies. Never has it provoked so much public opposition, resentment, and mistrust."

Not only have America's traditional allies, France and Germany, opposed the unilateralism implicit in applying the Bush Doctrine, but America's many friends and supporters after September 11, notably Russia and China, have as well. In addition, the larger international community, including the United Nations, has raised serious doubts about this approach, largely through its inaction. Importantly, too, anti-Americanism among states, fueled by opposition to the war in Iraqi, has increased (Pew Global Project Attitudes 2003). And as the Iraqi occupation wore on with more Americans dying there and questions arose over intelligence analyses prior to that war, public support began to erode—an erosion partially reversed by the capture of Saddam Hussein. Overall, the Bush Doctrine may well produce the opposite of what the administration intended, and it may undermine international efforts to confront the many transnational threats, including international terrorism, that it initially sought.

10 THE PERSISTENT MANDATE
George W. Bush and Economic Leadership

Raymond Tatalovich and John Frendreis

The fact that George W. Bush lost the popular vote to Albert Gore and won the Electoral College thanks to the timely intervention of the U.S. Supreme Court preordained nothing about Bush's stewardship of the economy. Sam Kernell once persuasively argued that peace and prosperity are the twin pillars of presidential popularity (Kernell 1978), and more recently Theodore Lowi alleged that the new covenant between the president and the populace is service delivery—specifically, a healthy economy (Lowi 1985). So important is the economy for presidential reelection that some scholars, notably Edward R. Tufte, believe that there is a "political business cycle" that encourages the administration to manipulate fiscal and monetary policy to cultivate positive economic conditions pursuant to the president's reelection (Tufte 1978). These analysts do not subscribe to the assumption that presidents possess the policy tools to finely manipulate economic performance; however, there is amble evidence that presidents who fail to nurture economic health do so at their own political peril. Simply ask Richard Nixon about 1960, or Gerald Ford about 1976, or Jimmy Carter about 1980, and the celebrated case of George Herbert Walker Bush in 1992. The famous sign above the desk of Clinton campaign strategist James Carville—"It's the economy, stupid"—was no theoretical breakthrough. It was simply a warning to Carville not to stray from their focus on economic conditions—a no-brainer given that the United States was then experiencing a shallow and slow expansion from a brief recession of 1990–1991.

At first glance, there are superficial similarities between Bush-I and Bush-II. Both engaged the U.S. military against Iraq; both went to war with large majority support from the American people; both saw their approval ratings rise, especially the meteoric leap experienced by Bush-I; and both governed during a period of economic unease. Once Iraqi troops were driven from Kuwait and U.S. forces were home, the distraction of war ended and the public took note that economic conditions were less than grand. This situation fueled the long-standing perception that Bush-I had devoted too much attention to foreign policy at the expense of domestic politics, and his generally aloof demeanor clinched the argument—by Clinton—that President George Herbert Walker Bush lacked empathy for ordinary people.

Of course, President George W. Bush is his own man, a down-to-earth Texan who connects with the grass-roots, but the *big* difference between him and his father was September 11, 2001. The terrorist destruction of the World Trade Center transformed the Bush presidency, and America as well. "America's War on Terrorism" dominated the headlines, followed by the "Invasion of Iraq" on March 19, 2003, aimed at toppling the government of Saddam Hussein. However, economic performance remained uneven throughout 2002, with eerie parallels with what Bush-I experienced when he faced reelection. Although real gross-domestic product (GDP) somewhat rebounded over the first nine months of 1992, the unemployment rate actually rose from 7.4 percent during the first quarter to 7.6 percent during the second and third quarters of 1992, roughly a month before Election Day (table 10.1). President George W. Bush witnessed rising unemployment, from 5.8 percent to 6.2 percent over the first two quarters of 2003 despite six consecutive quarters of economic growth. Although the unemployment rate is a "lagging" indicator of business cycles—turning downward long after economic growth has resumed—the economy had been shedding jobs longer after the end of the 2001 recession than after the 1990–1991 contraction (Altman 2002). These ominous trends were not lost on the Bush White House as they looked forward to 2004, though perhaps a closer look will show that the differences between 1992 and 2004 outweigh the parallels.

TABLE 10.1
Comparing Bush-I and Bush-II on Economic Indicators

		Quarter			
	Economic indicator	*1st*	*2nd*	*3rd*	*4th*
Bush-I					
1989	Real GDP	5.0%	2.2%	1.9%	1.4%
	Consumer Price Index	121.7	123.7	124.7	125.9
	Unemployment rate	5.2%	5.2%	5.2%	5.4%
	Consumer Confidence Index	118.0	116.8	117.4	115.0
1990	Real GDP	5.1%	0.9%	–0.7%	–3.2%
	Consumer Price Index	128.0	129.3	131.6	133.7
	Unemployment rate	5.3%	5.3%	5.7%	6.1%
	Consumer Confidence Index	107.9	105.7	90.7	61.8
1991	Real GDP	–2.0%	2.3%	1.0%	2.2%
	Consumer Price Index	134.8	135.6	136.7	137.7
	Unemployment rate	6.6%	6.8%	6.9%	7.1%
	Consumer Confidence Index	65.2	77.9	75.6	55.1
1992	Real GDP	3.8%	3.8%	3.1%	5.4%
	Consumer Price Index	138.7	139.8	140.9	141.9
	Unemployment rate	7.4%	7.6%	7.6%	7.4%
	Consumer Confidence Index	51.3	69.9	59.2	66.1
Bush-II					
2001	Real GDP	–0.6%	–1.6%	–0.3%	2.7%
	Consumer Price Index	175.7	177.5	177.8	177.3
	Unemployment rate	4.2%	4.5%	4.8%	5.6%
	Consumer Confidence Index	113.9	115.0	109.1	88.3
2002	Real GDP	5.0%	1.3%	4.0%	1.4%
	Consumer Price Index	177.9	179.8	180.6	181.2
	Unemployment rate	5.6%	5.8%	5.8%	5.9%
	Consumer Confidence Index	101.2	108.4	95.2	81.7
2003	Real GDP	1.4%	3.3%	8.2%	
	Consumer Price Index	183.0	183.7	184.6	
	Unemployment rate	5.8%	6.2%	6.1%	
	Consumer Confidence Index	68.3	82.7	80.6	

Source: Real gross domestic product (GDP) is reported by the Bureau of Economic Accounts, U.S. Department of Commerce; Consumer Price Index and unemployment rate are reported by the Bureau of Labor Statistics, U.S. Department of Labor; Consumer Confidence Index is reported by the Conference Board. We calculated the average change in real GDP and the average change in the Consumer Confidence Index over each quarter and averaged the unemployment rates and the Consumer Price Index values over each three-month quarter.

The outcome of the 2002 midterm elections shows how national security fears can overwhelm concerns about the economy. Apart from the historical legacy—that the presidential party had lost House seats in all but three midterm elections since 1860—there was the economic record. Between Bush's inauguration and the midterm elections, the value of the Standard & Poor's 500 Stock Index suffered a steeper decline (-31.8 percent) than under any president except Herbert Hoover (-33.7 percent) during the Great Depression (Norris 2002). Twenty years earlier, the Democrats exploited the weak economy, attacked Reaganomics, and gained twenty-six seats in the House of Representatives, but this time the Democrats had difficulties getting any political traction from economic issues. And this was not due to the Democrats not trying to make economics the issue, since congressional Democratic candidates across the nation attacked GOP plans to privatize Social Security, claimed that the North American Free Trade Agreement (NAFTA) shifted jobs to Mexico, and promised more job growth. In the election aftermath, it was obvious that the Democrats made a strategic blunder by allowing President Bush and the GOP to monopolize the issue of domestic terrorism and homeland security.

Informed observers, however, argued that the Democrats failed for other reasons. First, the economy may have been lackluster, but it was hardly terminal. "By most standard measures, the economic downturn has not been acute," said Harvard political economist Benjamin M. Friedman (Rosenbaum 2002b). For example, the September 2002 unemployment rate was only 5.6 percent, whereas in September 1982 it was 10.1 percent, and in September 1992 it was 7.3 percent. Also, inflation was not a worry, as interest rates remained the lowest in decades, and both productivity and personal income were relatively high. The most publicized manifestation of economic malaise was the stock market. True enough, but investors are more sophisticated than the ordinary income earner, and due to historically low interest rates, the rise in home prices meant that middle- and upper-income Americans could take solace knowing that their real estate investment was gaining in value.

Second, even those people who expressed concern about the economy did not blame President Bush, nor the Republican Party, but rather the terrorist attacks of September 11, 2001, and the business cycle. Finally, Democrats could not gain political advantage because they failed to articulate an alternative economic vision for America. "Democrats have not unified on a common approach to the economy," said Leon E. Panetta, Clinton's director of the Office of Management and Budget. "They've beaten up on Bush, but they're afraid to take on his tax cut. They complain about the deficit, but they haven't said how they would pay for the new programs they want" (Rosenbaum 2002b).

In January 2003, *Washington Post/ABC News* polling showed that seven-in-ten Americans would give UN inspectors more time to search Iraq for weapons of mass destruction, with 57 percent opposed to military action to topple Saddam Hussein. More ominous was Bush's popularity slide, which, at 59 percent, had not been seen anytime since September 11, 2001. While 71 percent approved of his handling of the war on terrorism, his economic stewardship was coming into question. Fifty-three percent disapproved of his handling of the economy; only one-quarter of Americans viewed the economy as excellent or good; and most people believed his multibillion dollar tax cut would benefit the wealthy, not the middle class, and were opposed to eliminating the tax on stock dividends (Milbank and Morin 2003). Nonetheless, these pollsters noted that public ambivalence toward Bush's 2001 tax cuts did not stop their enactment, and indications were that Bush would prevail again—though not entirely. Indeed, the political map altered when the advent of military action against Iraq seemed imminent. The war in Iraq commenced on March 19, and a *CBS/New York Times* tracking poll on March 20–21 found that President Bush was now enjoying two-thirds approval for his job performance, that 53 percent (up from 35 percent in early February) believed the country was on the right track, and that almost half approved of his handling of the economy (Associated Press 2003). Combat gave Bush a popularity pump where he had suffered an erosion of popular support—the economy—but by July 2003 his approval ratings had fallen back to 59 percent in some surveys. The obvious question is whether history will repeat itself and Bush-II will suffer the fate of Bush-I.

The State of the Bush Economy

The five-member Business Cycle Dating Committee of the National Bureau of Economic Research (NBER), which tracks the business cycle, reported that the economy fell into recession in March 2001, but nearly two years later, in January 2003, NBER still could not confirm that the economic contraction had ended. It was not until the following July that NBER made its authoritative determination that the 2001 recession had ended, in November of 2001, and had endured for eight months. The 1990–1991 recession also lasted only eight months, but NBER did not issue its definitive ruling until December 1992, after Bush-I lost the election to Clinton. This Bush-II recession did not begin under President Clinton, although the projected economic growth rate of 4.1 percent for 2000 was revised downward to 3.8 percent, indicating a slowing of the economy in the last six months of 2000. For all of 2001, GDP grew by only 0.3 percent, also down from the preliminary 1.2 percent projection, but what complicated NBER's task in deciphering recent economic trends was that, although real GDP—its primary indicator of economic recovery—began rising after November 2001, unemployment has not fallen (but increased) due to workers' increased productivity and rose to a nine-year high of 6.4 percent in June 2003, one month before NBER made its announcement (Altman 2003b).

This lackluster performance had some unpleasant implications for many Americans. In September 2002 the Census Bureau reported that the proportion of Americans living in poverty rose to 32.9 million during 2001, or 11.7 percent as compared to 11.3 percent in 2000, the first increase in eight years and, moreover, that median household income fell to $42,228 in 2001, a 2.2 percent decline from 2000, the first such decline in middle-class incomes since the last recession ended in 1991 (Pear 2002). And although the U.S. jobless rate at the time hovered just below 6 percent, which is not excessive compared to recent European experience, one ominous trend reported in September 2002 by the Department of Labor was an increasing number of long-term unemployed. Nearly 3 million Americans were unemployed for at least fifteen weeks, up more than 50 percent from a year ago, and this despite the fact that a smaller share of the workforce was unemployed in the wake of the 2001 downturn than in the post-recession periods of the early 1980s and 1990s (Leonhardt 2002).

In February 2003 the University of Michigan's Index of Consumer Confidence fell to 79.2, its lowest level since September 1993 (when it stood at 82.4), a significant development because consumer spending accounts for two-thirds of U.S. economic activity. Since business investment had been lackluster for some time, what prevented the economy from falling into recession was sustained consumer spending. But the decline in consumer confidence was not a good signal for future spending, and it, in turn, was influenced partly by the dismal stock market. Since 1998 about 20 percent of the change in consumer confidence has been linked to movements in the stock market, mainly because more Americans than ever own stock. Between 1989 and 1998, the proportion of shockholders rose from 32 percent to 49 percent (Morin and Deane 2002).

Apparently fears about a pending war in Iraq, terrorism, and bleak economic prospects colored how Americans judged the economy at the time and in the long-term. A Gallup poll taken in March 2003 showed that declining public confidence in the future, which began in December 2001, reached a seven-year low, with 36 percent satisfied but 61 percent dissatisfied with the country's direction (Milbank 2003). As late as July 2002 the Bush administration resisted calls from liberal economists and Democrats for economic stimulus. "In terms of the state of the economy, I see nothing that would suggest the need for any change in policy," said R. Glenn Hubbard, Council of Economic Advisors chairman. "What the president has already done, plus the monetary policy stance, is an awful lot already at a time when the economy is doing reasonably well" (Milbank and Weisman 2002). Nonetheless, Bush was not about to tolerate a public image, like his father's, of being disconnected from everyday economics. Thus Bush convened the "President's Economic Forum" at Baylor University on August 13, 2002. No dissenting voices were heard to the overall theme that the fundamentals of Bush's economic policy were sound, though there were soft spots in the economy, but Democrats charged that the event was nothing more than a staged pep rally for the White House. Indeed, nothing memorable emerged from that assemblage of business leaders, economists, students, union leaders, professors, small business owners, and a few Democrats.

Economic Advisory Turnover

The sure-footed economic team Clinton assembled—notably Treasury Secretary Robert E. Rubin—was a point of real contrast with the economic advisors Bush recruited. Even judged by Bush's own standards of leak-proof loyalty, his economic advisors were uniformly less celebrated than was his sterling national security advisory system. Was it a bit paradoxical that, in mid-July 2002, Treasury Secretary Paul H. O'Neill should be taking a week-long trip to Romania, Ukraine, Uzbekistan, Kyrgyzstan, and Georgia, following his May trip to Africa with rock star Bono of the band U2, and which preceded his scheduled visit to South America—amidst falling Dow Jones averages and declining public economic confidence? Not paradoxical, argued some observers, but symptomatic of an administration with no strong economic voice. "We desperately need someone the business community, the financial community, the press, and the public can look to as the lead economic spokesman," commented Robert D. Hormats, vice chairman of Goldman Sachs International (Rosenbaum 2002a).

Quite a contrast from when Bush took office, when barely four months later Congress approved the largest tax cut in twenty years, a credit to his economic team. In the months since, Bush's economic agenda had stalled. That could not be entirely blamed on his advisory team, because after Senator James Jeffords (R-VT) became an Independent and the Democrats gained control of the Senate, key items on Bush's economic agenda could not secure approval. These items included making the 2001 ten-year tax cuts permanent, gaining fast-track trade authority, permitting oil and natural gas drilling in the Arctic National Wildlife Reserve, and allowing some privatization of Social Security investment accounts. On other issues, the economic advisers lost the debate to political operatives: the March 2002 decision to impose tariffs on imported steel and the May decision to sign an agricultural bill with huge new subsidies for farmers. Before the Council on Foreign Relations, Treasury Secretary O'Neill remarked that he opposed steel tariffs because the U.S. should be a leading free-trade nation, "an unusual indiscretion in an administration that prides itself on loyalty" (Rosenbaum 2002a). All this led to speculation that Bush would make changes in his economic team after the midterm elections.

Late in October Senator Paul S. Sarbanes (D-MD), who chaired the Banking Committee, stated on CNN's "Novak, Hunt, & Shields" that the Bush administration would have to consider replacing its economic team after the November 5 elections. "It's not just O'Neill. You've got Larry Lindsay rattling around and the Council of Economic Advisers," he added (J. Price 2002). The day before, Senator Sarbanes had called on Harvey L. Pitt, chairman of the Securities and Exchange Commission, to resign. Appointed by Bush, Pitt had been a lawyer representing accounting and securities firms for twenty years, but Sarbanes was unhappy that the SEC voted 3–2 to appoint former FBI and CIA director William Webster, now aged 78, to lead the new Public Company Accounting Oversight Board that Congress had created in response to the flurry of corporation scandals. Commented Sarbanes, "The real problem is Harvey Pitt, who completely mishandled this situation. He had a wonderful opportunity [to pick somebody knowledgeable about accounting], but he just blew it" (J. Price 2002).

When nominated by Bush and unanimously confirmed, Pitt was widely praised as one of the most experienced securities lawyers in the nation. But Pitt made several political missteps during his brief career, the latest furor erupting when Pitt apparently backed away from appointing John H. Biggs, a highly respected head of the TIAA-CREF investment plan, to head the new accounting oversight board and, to make matters worse, made no effort to find a candidate acceptable to all sides. Instead, he appointed Webster. His political demise accelerated with the disclosure days before the election that Pitt never notified the White House or the other SEC commissioners that he knew that Webster had headed the audit committee of U.S. Technologies, a company accused of fraud (Labaton 2002).

Sarbanes proved to be prophetic. On November 5, around 9:00 as the polls were closing, Pitt resigned his chairmanship. Then one month after the historic GOP victory in the 2002 midterm elections, Bush sacked his economic team on precisely the same day that the Department of Labor reported the November unemployment rate as having risen to 6 percent, a higher jump from the 5.7 percent October rate than many analysts expected. Six percent boosted the number of jobless workers to 8.5 million, up 300,000 from October 2002.

The resignations of Treasury Secretary O'Neill and National Economic Council Chairman Lindsey were welcomed by Wall Street and congressional leaders, who had been urging their departure ever since the stock market began its slide. O'Neill was criticized for statements that shook the faith of international bond markets, and he alienated Capitol Hill conservatives. Reportedly, O'Neill also disagreed with Lindsey about the need for a broad economic stimulus package, with Lindsey being supported by White House political operatives. Lindsey did not lose credibility for policy reasons but rather because he lacked the managerial skills to achieve a coherent economic message (Weisman 2002a). Every pundit read these developments as a signal that the Bush administration was concerned about the adverse impact of a struggling economy on the 2004 presidential election. Nor was it coincidental that opinion polls were beginning to blame Bush for the economic malaise.

Bush's quick dispatch of O'Neill and Lindsey upended the common view among inside observers that Bush's code of loyalty would not permit such gratuitous political firings. The decision apparently was made at a meeting two days earlier with Karl Rove, Bush's top political strategist, Chief-of-staff Andrew H. Card Jr., and Card's deputy, Joshua B. Bolten. "Give credit to Rove and the boys—it was a big move, it was necessary and they did it," exclaimed Scott Reed, campaign manager for Bob Dole's 1996 presidential campaign. "You can't afford to go into an election without an economic spokesman. As we learned during the stock market showdown this summer, Bush can't be his own economic spokesman. They're coming out with a new economic growth plan, and they need new spokesmen to sell that to Wall Street and Main Street" (Milbank 2002d).

Having heard so many laments that Bush's economic team lacked the star quality of Clinton's, Bush took a page from the Clinton playbook by nominating Stephen Friedman, a conservative Republican, to be director of the National Economic Council (NEC). The NEC post had been created in 1993 for Robert E. Rubin, who co-chaired the investment banking firm of Goldman Sachs & Company *with* Friedman, now Bush's choice for the position. While at Goldman Sachs, Friedman was the boss of Joshua Bolten, White House deputy chief of staff, who lobbied for Friedman. Supply-siders made moves to scuttle his nomination because they believed that Friedman—as vice chairman of the board of directors for the Concord Coalition—might not be able to stomach the federal deficits resulting from another round of tax cuts (Weisman 2002b,c). But Bush rejected those protests and Friedman expressed his support for a new economic-stimulus package, saying, "I strongly share your convictions, sir, that now is the time for a robust growth and jobs policy" (Crutsinger 2002).

For a successor to O'Neill, Bush turned to John W. Snow, CEO of CSX Corp., a giant railroad operator, who had served in the Transportation Department and headed the National Highway Traffic Safely Administration in the Ford White House. He also had experience heading the Business Roundtable, a prestigious policy forum representing corporate America, and the White House was counting on his having the political savvy O'Neill lacked (Blustein, Phillips, and Hilzenrath 2002).

Mindful that his father's 1992 loss to Clinton was attributed to the widespread perception that Bush-I was disconnected from the economic troubles of ordinary Americans, Bush-II took steps to showcase his hands-on approach to economic policymaking. In January and April of 2003, Bush invited academic and private-sector economists to two White House meetings designed to rally support for his third round of income tax cuts. But not all the leading economic minds were invited. "The Bush administration has counseled with economists at various times," observed Ethan S. Harris of Lehman Brothers. "Basically 90 percent of the people are kind of preaching to the choir, and maybe they have one or two middle-of-the-road people. They really don't seem to want to hear opposing views (Altman 2003a)."

In late February 2003, R. Glenn Hubbard, the architect of Bush's ambitious plan to slash taxes on corporate dividends, resigned, whereupon Bush nominated Harvard University economist N. Gregory Mankiw to be chairman of the Council of Economic Advisors. Hubbard was the only member of Bush's original economic team. Hubbard apparently left for personal reasons, but his departure occurred at a time when Congress began debating Bush's proposed economic stimulus package. Newly appointed Treasury Secretary Snow and NEC chairman Friedman faced the task of rallying legislative support for Bush's tax cuts, which neither had had a role in formulating. One news account made the point that "the current staff turnover has had little effect on the economic stimulus package Mr. Bush is to announce" because that "economic plan was hammered out months ago by a small core of still-in-place presidential advisers—Vice President Dick Cheney, Karl Rove, Andrew H. Card Jr., and Joshua Bolten—who control all domestic policy in an administration where power is ever more tightly held at the White House (Bumiller 2003a)."

Bush's original economic team not only was compared unfavorably to Bush's national security team—Defense Secretary Donald H. Rumsfeld, Secretary of State Colin L. Powell, and National Security Adviser Condoleezza Rice—but also had to compete for influence against that well-entrenched group of White House insiders. Completing the turnover among top White House economic policymakers was the resignation of Mitchell E. Daniels Jr. as OMB director in mid-2003, so he could launch his campaign for the Indiana GOP gubernatorial nomination. Daniels's successor was Joshua Bolten, who helped formulate Bush's first two tax cuts (Bumiller 2003c). Thus, in the end, President Bush had assembled an economic team that spoke with one voice on the need for tax cuts.

Economic Policies

Bush had successes with his economic game plan. During the summer of 2002 Bush signed two landmark bills, one restoring presidential authority over trade negotiations and the other addressing corporate fraud. The avalanche of corporate scandals began when the Houston-based energy-trading giant Enron filed for bankruptcy in December 2001, followed by the financial collapse of telecommunications conglomerate WorldCom in June 2002, as well as filings for bankruptcy protection by Adelphia Communications and Global Crossing. In this story of inside trading and accounting practices that hid corporate liabilities the Arthur Anderson Company, once the largest and most prestigious accounting firm in the nation, was indicted by the federal government and ultimately was dissolved. In the wake of loose and often fraudulent accounting practices that artificially inflated stock prices, allowing corporate executives to make obscenely high profits while ordinary investors, company employees, and pensioners faced financial near-ruin, President Bush publicly rebuked corporate greed. But his reform proposals were tame alongside the legislative reaction inside Congress. As one reporter observed, "Rarely has an issue caught such instant bipartisan fire in Washington. This one was fueled by nearly daily disclosures of corporate fraud, the plummeting stock market, and politicians' concerns that voters would hold them responsible" (Bumiller 2002b). Led by co-sponsors Senator Sarbanes (D-MD) and Representative Michael Oxley (R-OH), Congress overwhelmingly approved this legislation on July 25, 2002, with a vote of 423–3 in the House and 99–0 in the Senate. Congressional Republicans refused to defend corporate America as they joined with Democrats to pass legislation to overhaul corporate fraud, securities, and accounting laws, and to create a regulatory board with investigatory and enforcement powers to oversee the accounting industry and penalize wrongdoing by auditors, besides mandating long prison terms for business executives who knowingly defraud investors.

Fast-track trade authority was first given to President Ford in 1974 but lapsed in 1994 because President Clinton was unable to persuade Congress to approve this legislation. Bush won a major legislative victory when Congress reauthorized this presidential power in 2002. It allows the president to make trade deals through 2007 that Congress can approve or reject but not change, and Bush promised to use his newly won powers to aid the ailing economy. "Starting now, America is back at the bargaining table in full force," he said. "I will use trade promotion authority aggressively to create more good jobs for American workers, more exports for American farmers, and higher living standards for American families" (Bumiller 2002b). Bush added that his administration would move quickly to negotiation trade agreements with Chile, Singapore, and Morocco in addition to forging a Free Trade Area of the Americas, a thirty-four–nation agreement to integrate most North and South American economies into one free-trade bloc analogous to NAFTA. In fact, the first effects of his fast-track authority was legislation accepting Chile and Singapore as free-trading partners, legislation the House approved in July 2003 as did the Senate not long thereafter. As a precursor to an upcoming trip to Africa, Bush publicly declared in January 2003 that he wanted Congress to extend beyond 2008 the termination date of the African Growth and Opportunity Act that Clinton had signed in May of 2000, giving thirty-five African nations duty-free access to American markets (Bumiller 2003b).

For a long time the Republicans have been the free-trade advocates on Capitol Hill, and even Clinton was betrayed by the majority of congressional Democrats when he asked for legislative approval of NAFTA. For President Bush, however—who was trying to appeal to steelworkers and steel companies in electorally important states like West Virginia, Ohio, and Pennsylvania—those free-trade principles had to give way to political expediency. In March 2002 Bush took arguably the biggest protectionist action in decades by imposing tariffs of nearly 30 percent on many types of steel imported from Europe, Asia, and South America. While there is no doubt that the U.S. steel industry is in deep trouble, with more than thirty companies facing bankruptcy, protectionism is a double-edged sword. Other domestic industries like automobile manufacturing rely on cheaper steel imports and, most assuredly, other nations may begin a trade war. In reaction, the European Union petitioned the World Trade Organization (WTO), which, in July 2003, issued its preliminary ruling that those tariffs were illegal. In November the WTO issued its definitive ruling against the United States, meaning that the European Union now could retaliate unless the Bush administration backed down, which it did in early December. The Bush administration was expected to appeal that determination, but it had previously failed repeatedly in cases brought against the United States before the WTO, losing thirteen of fifteen cases since 2001 (Becker 2003). Another major setback came earlier, in August 2002, when the WTO ruled that the European Union could impose $4 billion in penalties on the United States for allowing tax breaks to businesses facilitating American exports. This action represented the largest penalty against any nation since the WTO was created in 1995 (Andrews 2002a).

Bush was also the first president to impose the eighty-day cooling off period under the Taft-Hartley Act of 1947 since President Nixon had imposed it to halt a 1971 longshoreman's strike (Sanger and Greenhouse 2002). One month before the 2002 midterm elections Bush invoked Taft-Hartley to open twenty-nine West Coast ports that were shut down for eleven days due to a labor-management dispute. With some economists estimating that the shut-down could cost the economy more than $10 billion, Bush indicated his reluctance to interfere but feared that its continuation would undermine economic recovery.

An extension of unemployment benefits for people who had exhausted their jobless aid was integrated into the White House's 2002 economic stimulus package. On January 8, 2003, Bush signed into law a second extension of unemployment benefits for roughly 2.5 million Americans; it ran through May, at which time Congress approved yet a third $7.4 billion extension for nearly a million unemployed people. In May, the unemployment rate was 6.0 percent, and this quick action by the GOP Congress was intended to deflect Democratic criticism of its $350 billion tax-cut package benefiting mainly middle- and upper-income Americans.

Unidimensional Fiscal Policy

After the turnover on Bush's economic team, everyone in his administration was now reading from the same page with respect to fiscal policy. The personnel changes resulted in a sort of groupthink supportive of tax cuts as the primary means for stimulating economic growth and lowering unemployment. On February 3, 2003, Bush sent Congress his thirteen-pound, 3,000 page budget for fiscal-year 2004 (which began October 1, 2003) that recommended total expenditures of $2.23 trillion, a projected $307 billion deficit, and a multibillion dollar economic growth plan based on eliminating individual taxes on dividends as well as accelerating and making permanent the 2001 tax cuts. To put this deficit in perspective, recall that the Bush administration announced in

October 2002 that the fiscal-year 2002 (ending September 30, 2002) deficit would be $159 billion, as compared to the $127 billion surplus recorded for fiscal-year 2001, ending September 30, 2001 (Stevenson 2002).

In early 2003 economists on the Left and Right joined the intellectual battle. In January, 110 economists, including conservative Nobel laureates Milton Friedman, James Buchanan, and Vernon Smith, signed a letter urging support for Bush's multibillion dollar tax cut and for making his 2001 tax cuts permanent as well as for restraining federal spending in order to aid the sluggish economy. "As a rule, government cannot create wealth or expand the economy. Only the private sector can do that," stated the letter addressed to all Representatives and Senators. "Government can, however, hinder economic growth through excessive taxes, high marginal tax rates, over-regulation, or unnecessary spending" (Lakely 2003). Barely a month later another group of more than 400 economists, with ten Nobel laureates, including Joseph Stiglitz (who served on Clinton's CEA), signed a statement sponsored by the Economic Policy Institute, a liberal think-tank in Washington, D.C. They counterargued that the Bush proposals would effect a permanent change in the tax code and will not spur job creation. Nor, they said, would the permanent dividend tax cut serve as a short-term economic stimulus.

Four days after the war in Iraq began—and three days after the House and Senate passed budget blueprints that included tax cuts without any cost estimates for that military conflict, President Bush told congressional leaders that the price tag for the war would be $74.8 billion. Even without that expenditure, or fiscal policy changes like enactment of Bush's proposed $726 billion economic stimulus package, the Congressional Budget Office said that the deteriorating fiscal condition of the federal government would yield a 2003 deficit of $246 billion (24 percent higher than the deficit the CBO had projected only two months earlier). If Bush's package of spending and tax cuts was approved, the deficit would rise to $287 billion in 2003 and $338 billion in 2004, and it would remain in the red through 2013. In total, the CBO estimated that Bush's fiscal policies would yield a $2.7 trillion debt through 2013.

The CBO's forecast of future red ink notwithstanding, the House voted 215–212, with a virtual party-line division, to adopt the $2.2 trillion budget including Bush's $726 billion tax cuts in its budget resolution in late March, but the situation was more fluid in the Senate where a few Republican moderates held the balance of power. First, the Senate passed 52–47 an amendment by Senator Russell Feingold (D-WI) to cut $100 billion to pay for the war in Iraq, and proceeded to defeat by 62–38 Democratic attempts to halve the tax cuts to $350 billion. But a week later—after Bush submitted his request for $74.7 billion to fund the war in Iraq—the Senate revisited the issue and reversed itself, voting 51–48 to chop $350 billion from the ten-year scheduled tax cuts (through 2013). In conference committee, the Senate prevailed in a deal brokered by Vice President Cheney, because Bush was now willing to accept any legislative deal, fearing the political fallout if Congress recessed for Memorial Day without acting on an economic stimulus package. In the end, though he originally proposed a $726 billion tax reduction and derided as "little bitty" the Senate's $350 billion tax cut, nonetheless in late May 2003 President Bush signed—and proudly hailed—legislation that allocated $20 billion to fiscally strapped states plus $12 billion to aid low-income families and afforded $318 billion in income tax cuts, increased child tax credits, reduced rates on capital gains and dividends, and increased tax breaks for small business. All told, the package would cost $350 billion over ten years, but its price tag may balloon to $870 billion if the various tax provisions are *not* allowed to expire. For example, the reduced capital gains tax rate of 15 percent is supposed to revert to its higher rate in 2008 and, that same year, dividend income again would be fully taxed as earned income (Rosenbaum and Firestone 2003).

Critics charged that this latest round of tax cuts would balloon the federal deficit and do little to stimulate the economy, but President Bush was undeterred. "By ensuring that Americans have more to spend, to save, and to invest, this legislation is adding fuel to an economic recovery," said Bush at the signing ceremony (Stevenson 2003b). If May had been July, one wonders if any triple-digit tax cut would have cleared Congress, because on July 15 the White House projected a $455 billion budget deficit for the current fiscal year (2003), $150 billion more than it had projected five months earlier. Much greater in dollars than the previous record of $290 billion during fiscal-year 1992, this shortfall also represents 4.2 percent of the GDP that, though smaller than the fiscal-year 1983 deficit under Reagan (at 6 percent of GDP), is still notable because in only six years since 1946 has the budget deficit exceeded 4.2 percent of GDP. According to OMB projections, the federal deficit would rise to $475 billion in fiscal-year 2004, then fall to $304 billion in fiscal-year 2005, $238 billion in fiscal-year 2006, $213 billion in fiscal-year 2007, and $226 billion in fiscal-year 2008—together, $1.9 trillion in new federal debt through 2008. Democrats charged that the unending red ink resulted from the Bush tax cuts, but the OMB estimated that 53 percent of the deficit could be attributed to the weak economy, another 24 percent to domestic security and war, and only 23 percent to tax cuts. It was left to newly installed OMB director Bolten to defend a deficit of this magnitude as being "manageable if we continue pro-growth economic policies and exercise serious spending discipline" (Rosenbaum 2003).

In fact, projected spending likely will exceed the OMB estimates because these forecasts did not include future peacekeeping costs for American troops in Afghanistan and Iraq, nor the added burden of a new drug prescription plan for Medicare. In November 2003, Congress passed and Bush signed a GOP-sponsored $400 billion new prescription drug benefit—the largest entitlement expansion since Medicare was established in 1965—to assist seniors in paying for drugs. The congressional Democrats, favoring a $900 billion expenditure over the next decade, tried to make political points while decrying the GOP drug benefit as being inadequate.

One key component of Bush's 2003 economic package never had a chance in Congress. Included in it was a proposal to create three new savings plans resembling 401(k) plans or individual retirement accounts (two for retirement and one for anything), to be funded with after-tax income so that future earnings and withdrawals would be tax free, and to allow higher contribution limits with no restrictions on contributors' income. Democrats and liberal critics have accused the Bush administration of shifting tax burdens from wealthy Americans to the less affluent. Bush countered that his critics were engaging in "class warfare," but even the House Republican leaders were cool to this idea and also irritated because the proposal was hatched by ousted treasury secretary O'Neill without any input from GOP lawmakers, including Speaker Hastert (VandeHei 2003). In sharp contrast, after the 2003 tax cuts became law, Bush did capitulate to Democratic demands that the working poor were deserving of the increased child credit given to middle- and upper-income taxpayers. On this issue, House Republicans were opposed to extending the tax credit (from $600 to $1,000) per child because the working poor do not pay federal income taxes, but President Bush reversed course (though his original proposal had also limited the credit to only taxpayers), urging Congress to send him corrective legislation so that the working poor would also receive child tax-credit checks from the Treasury.

Monetary Policy and the Fed

And what about the Federal Reserve Board? Where Democrat Clinton was entirely willing to accommodate Fed chairman Alan Greenspan, there was speculation over whether Bush would reappoint Greenspan as Fed chairman when his term expires on June 20, 2004. Although he supported Bush's $1.35 trillion ten-year tax cuts that Congress enacted in 2001, by early 2003 Greenspan was warning Congress that further tax cuts would be "premature" as an economic stimulant because uncertainty about war was the primary obstacle to economic growth. "I am one of the few people who still are not as yet convinced that stimulus is a desirable policy at this particular point," he told the Senate Banking, Housing, and Urban Affairs Committee (Berry and Weisman 2003). Greenspan testified that further tax cuts should be offset by spending reductions or tax increases. He also challenged the Bush administration's "deficits don't matter" argument, doubting that economic growth is sufficient to recover revenues lost from the tax cuts (Crutsinger 2003). Those candid remarks, said Senate Minority Leader Tom Daschle (D-SD), were the "kiss of death" for Bush's tax plans, and the resulting swirl of controversy caused Greenspan to backtrack when he appeared days later before the House Financial Services Committee, now affirming that the Bush package "does have some short-term stimulus." "It probably will increase the levels of stock prices and the wealth effect accordingly, and there are some small income effects," said Greenspan. The White House effort at damage control began with President Bush telling an audience of investors in Alexandria, Virginia, "If the economy needs a little oomph . . . why wait?" (Hill 2003). In light of later signals from the White House that his tenure would be extended, Greenspan subsequently equivocated by not unambiguously opposing Bush's proposed $726 billion tax cuts for 2003 and, before a congressional hearing in July, hedging his bets: "I would prefer to find the situation in which spending was constrained, the economy was growing, and that tax cuts were capable of being initiated without creating fiscal problems," said Greenspan (Weisman and Berry 2003).

Despite whatever misgivings Greenspan had about deficits, monetary policy has been entirely compatible with fiscal policy. The Bush administration has repeatedly advocated cutting taxes and, for its part, the Federal Reserve Board has undertaken an aggressive strategy of cutting interests rates to historic lows. On June 25, 2003, the Fed reduced its federal funds rate (the interest rate banks charge each other on overnight loans) from 1.25 percent to 1 percent, the lowest level since 1958. It was the thirteenth rate cut since January of 2001, when the Federal Open Market Committee under Greenspan began its rate-cutting campaign. Though historically the Fed has been more concerned about price stability than joblessness, now the Fed was less concerned about inflation than that the continued sluggish economy would yield falling price levels (deflation), something the United States has not experienced since the Great Depression.

Politics and Deficits

Will deficits do damage to the Bush reelection campaign? Probably not, because deficits—not surpluses—have been the norm of budgetary politics over three decades. Critics may point to the four budget surpluses we enjoyed during 1998–2001, but how many voters will recall that 1969 was the last year prior to 1998 that the federal government showed a surplus? More than a few commentators viewed this development as Reaganomics resurrected, and congressional Democrats quickly charged that the tax cuts were targeted to the wealthy whereas ordinary Americans would have to pay the price of record deficits and rising interest rates. What is unusual about this budgetary debate is that Republicans typically defend fiscal restraint and Democrats and liberal economists advocate deficit spending—particularly during economic downturns—but today we find Democrats railing against deficits, despite the sluggish economy. Recall the 1994 "Contract with America" whereby the GOP pledged a balanced budget and, ultimately, succeeded in pressuring President Clinton to accept a seven-year timetable for ending deficits.

The current partisan turnabout on deficits has been rationalized by some conservatives as a strategic ploy against bigger government. "In the 80s and 90s, the Democrats said, 'We're against deficits,' meaning 'We're against tax cuts,'" according to Grover Norquist. "And the Republicans said, 'We're against deficits,' meaning 'We're against spending increases" (Toner 2003a). Conservative economist Milton Friedman echoed that sentiment when he defended the projected $307 billion federal deficit in the *Wall Street Journal*. "Deficits will be an effective—I would go so far as to say, the only effective—restraint on the spending propensities of the executive branch and the legislature," wrote Friedman (Firestone 2003).

It seems incredible to label as "conservative" a president who embraces three-digit deficits over the next decade, the most massive reorganization of the federal government in sixty years (through the Department of Homeland Security), and the largest Medicare entitlement expansion in five decades (prescription drugs). By embracing tax cuts and new programmatic spending despite burgeoning red ink, Bush is not cowed by deficits the way his father was when Bush-I reneged on his 1988 "read my lips, no new taxes" campaign promise and two years later begrudgingly accepted higher taxes to restrain deficit spending. Even if deficits themselves are not a political liability, more important politically is the White House's orchestrating three huge tax cuts over three years as the cornerstone of countercyclical policy. No more can Bush imply that he inherited a sluggish economy from Clinton, meaning that Bush can be held accountable for economic performance in 2003 and 2004.

Comparing Bush-I and Bush-II

A review of important economic indicators suggests that George W. Bush may escape the political fate of his father. Putting aside the common view that Bush-II and his chief political operative Karl Rove learned the lesson of Bush-I and, furthermore, that Bush-II in the wake of military victory in Iraq has refocused his energies on economic policy, the larger reality is that U.S. economic performance may show enough improvement by November 2004 for Bush to claim bragging rights.

This latest recession is indicated by the negative growth rates in real GDP during the first three quarters of 2001 (table 1). Afterward, real GDP grew unevenly over the four quarters of 2002, showing that a vigorous recovery has not been sustained. Unemployment during the first three months of 2001 was generally under 5 percent but rose during 2002 as the economy continued to slough off jobs. But the 5.8 percent quarterly highs, which extended into 2003, still compare favorably with the jobless rates during the 1991–1992 recession. During the third and fourth quarters of 1990 plus the first quarter of 1991—when the United States suffered negative growth rates—the unemployment rate surpassed 6 percent and rose to over 7 percent from the fourth quarter of 1991 through all of 1992, an election year. If unemployment even marginally eases as it began to do at the end of 2003, Bush-II will be decidedly better positioned to defend his record than Bush-I was. Inflation is not a problem today, nor was it a problem in 1992, since increases in the consumer price index during both periods hovered around the 2–3 percent annual rate.

Nor was Bush-I helped by consumer sentiment, as measured by the Consumer Confidence Index (CCI). The CCI fell below 100 during the third quarter of 1990 and slowly deteriorated during 1991 and 1992. For Bush-II, the CCI was quite robust during the first three quarters of 2001 but then dropped during the fourth quarter, the fallout from the economic slowdown and the September 11 terrorist attacks. It exceeded the 100 mark during the first two quarters of 2002 then steadily declined over the next three quarters as the nation prepared for the war in Iraq. The CCI of 68.3 during the first quarter of 2003, however, would not be stellar by any measure except when compared with the 59.2 CCI during the third quarter of 1992 that ended on September 31—five weeks before the electorate voted against President George H. W. Bush. The second quarter of 2003 showed an improvement in consumer confidence, with the CCI averaging 82.7, suggesting that Americans anticipated better economic conditions, but then shocked analysts by plunging to 76.6 in July 2002. "The rising level of unemployment and sentiment that a turnaround in labor market conditions is not around the corner have contributed to deflating consumers' spirits this month," explained Lynn Franco, director of the Conference Board's Consumer Research Center (D'Innocenzio 2003). Yet the stock market appeared optimistic about future economic activity as reflected in the Dow Jones Industrial Average (DJIA). The DJIA stood at nearly 10,000 at the end of 2001 but dropped to just above the 7,000 mark in October 2002, before it began moving upward again. The rally, which began in March 2003 and drove the DJIA above 90,000 in December, signaled that investors believed that an economic recovery was underway.

By the end of 2003, the U.S. economy was beginning to rebound. It is not exactly an albatross around Bush's neck because there is time for these indicators to show a pronounced recovery before November 2004. If they do, it would seem unlikely that any Democratic presidential candidate will perceive that "it's the economy, stupid" and thus wage the kind of one-issue campaign against Bush-II that Clinton did against Bush-I.

CONCLUSION
George W. Bush's Project

Steven E. Schier

The presidency of George W. Bush is unusual in the wide scope of its ambitions. The Bush administration's redefinition of foreign policy, spurred by the events of September 11, 2001, led to an audacious doctrine of preempting likely terrorist threats overseas and prosecution of a successful war with Iraq in 2003. At home, the Bush administration tacked toward the center in its approach to education, prescription drug benefits for seniors, and stem-cell research. Meanwhile, the White House voiced the agenda of its partisan base in pressing for repeated tax cuts, even in the face of growing budget deficits. Just as Bush's innovations in foreign policy have altered basic parameters of international relations, his approach to taxing and spending is reshaping the politics of fiscal policy. These far-reaching changes are broadly consistent with his administration's major project: the entrenchment of a Reagan-style conservative regime of military hawkishness and supply-side economics within the major institutions of national politics.

Can this ambitious project succeed? The administration has proved to be more successful in achieving its policy and electoral goals than most observers predicted at the time of Bush's inauguration. Still, many impediments stand in Bush's way. Several features of contemporary politics—particularly characteristics of "institutional thickening," to use

Stephen Skowronek's phrase—may yet serve to frustrate Bush's ambitions, as they did Clinton's. In this situation, according to Skowronek, "more has to be changed to break from the past, and those adversely affected by the changes will be able to put up more formidable resistance" (Skowronek 1997, 56).

Three aspects of institutional thickening were very prominent when Bush took office. First, party power is weaker than during times of successful regime reconstruction (Lincoln and FDR) or orthodox innovation (Polk and Theodore Roosevelt). At the beginning of the twenty-first century, it is much more difficult to install a durable political regime through long-term changes in mass party identification. The lasting success of any party's "governing team" is less electorally certain now. Though parties remain important sources of campaign resources (Herrnson 1998), congressional elections remain primarily candidate-centered, loosening the authority of parties over their elected office-holders (Schier 2000). Second, the even partisan balance in the House and Senate impedes ambitious legislative programs. Clinton's health-care debacle of 1993–1994 and Bush's problems in 2003 passing his faith-based initiative and getting approval for oil drilling in the Arctic National Wildlife Refuge illustrate these difficulties. Third, the proliferation of thousands of interest groups in Washington (Rauch 1999) complicates presidential initiatives in domestic policy to no end. Interest group battles over oil drilling and faith-based initiatives stymied Bush's progress on these fronts.

Given these impediments, the scale of Bush's early political and policy successes is impressive. He benefited, as Kevin S. Price and John J. Coleman note in their chapter, from several GOP electoral victories beginning in 1994 that created an opportunity for a realignment into majority party status in the early twenty-first century. The GOP's regaining control of the Senate in 2002 gave the party control of both houses of Congress (albeit narrowly). As Bertram Johnson notes in his chapter, Bush made much of this opportunity, gaining passage of a Medicare prescription drug benefit in late 2003. The military, an institution long sympathetic to the GOP's national security agenda, prospered under GOP rule. Bush's sway over the military and Congress, arguably, was broader than that Clinton ever enjoyed. Though Clinton in 1993–1994 had a Democratic Congress, his relationships with Democratic lawmakers and the Pentagon were continually rocky during his presidency. Several authors here attest to the Bush administration's strategic and tactical dexterity at extending its political control in Washington. Nicol C. Rae notes how the administration successfully dismissed any questions about its legitimacy early on. James L. Guth explains how the administration's promotion of selected social policies maintained the allegiance of cultural conservatives. John J. Pitney Jr. notes the administration's ability to parry various political attacks well. Peri E. Arnold describes the administration's prowess with the "crafted message." John Kenneth White and John J. Zogby note the careful cultivation of Bush's image as a "likeable partisan," appealing to the GOP base and swing voters on carefully selected issues and through personal appeal.

The Bush presidency frequently has been tactically preemptive. According to Coleman, "The preemptive president seeks to occupy a middle ground largely defined by the priorities of his opponents, but with enough independence from these opponents and his own party to put his distinctive stamp on policy" (Coleman 2000, 153). But Bush's tactical preemption has always been partisan, not personal like Clinton's. Moreover, it follows a series of GOP preemption tactics in election campaigns in recent years in which the party effectively "fuzzed" differences with Democrats on key electoral issues like health care, the environment, and education. GOP candidates fought on the other party's turf because swing voters care about certain Democratic issues. By presenting their own answers to education reform and Medicare prescription drug coverage for seniors, Republican congressional candidates effectively neutralized their vulnerability on these issues with key voting groups. Bush has done the same as president, proposing his own education and health-care initiatives and thus blunting Democratic attacks.

Such tactics, however, are not central to the Bush project of conservative regime restoration. Rather, they are tactical concessions made to win the wider war over the role of government. The strategically vital initiatives of the Bush presidency concern this project. A repeated resort to tax cuts fuels the GOP base. It also deprives the national government of funds for further spending expansion, a strategy attributed to the Reagan administration in the early 1980s (Schick 2003, 6). And it reflects the supply-side economic thinking that characterized much of the Reagan administration's economic policymaking. By pressing for additional tax cuts in a time of growing budget deficits, George W. Bush seeks even more alignment with supply-side economics than either his father or Reagan sought. Bush's aggressive new foreign policy based on military power reflects Reagan's consistent emphasis on "peace through strength." By tactically appealing to groups of swing voters and keeping the conservative GOP base energized over the fundamentals of economic and foreign policy, the Bush presidency seeks lasting conservative dominance of national politics. This is no small task and one that can only succeed when the broader context of national issues is favorable.

The Issue Context

Economic issues pose serious risks for the Bush presidency. At the end of Clinton's time in the White House, it seemed that balanced budgets had become the unquestioned basis of domestic economic policy, reducing policy debate to middle-level regulatory issues regarding health care, trade, and the environment (Schier 2000; Coleman 2000). The Bush presidency has turned that conventional wisdom upside down. Sluggish economic growth spawned budget deficits early in the Bush presidency. As Raymond Tatalovich and John Frendreis note in their chapter, Bush responded not by making budget balance the signal goal, as Bush's father did, but by focusing on economic growth through supply-side tax cuts. The great likelihood, however, is that additional tax cuts will perpetuate lasting budget deficits. Such deficits pose three major problems for Bush.

First, it seems just a matter of time before enduring deficits splinter the administration's support among congressional Republicans. Negotiations over the fiscal-year 2004 budget came perilously close to collapsing in 2003 because of the differing views of House and Senate Republicans over the size of a tax cut. A small group of moderate Senate Republicans demanded that cuts be limited to a maximum of $350 billion in lost revenue through 2013. House Republicans wanted at least $550 billion; they eventually settled for $326 billion and passed their budget resolution by a scant three-vote margin, amid widespread complaints by fiscal conservatives that the large deficits it would produce were unacceptable. This intraparty turbulence represents but a foretaste of what fiscal politics might resemble for the GOP.

Second, large deficits hand the Democrats an issue for future elections. Bush's partisan opponents found some rhetorical traction in 2003. Senate Minority Leader Tom Daschle (D-SD), for example, decried the administration's proposed fiscal-year 2004 budget, with its projected deficit of $304 billion, as the product of "the most fiscally irresponsible administration in history" entailing "more of the same failed economic policies and misplaced priorities that have weakened our economy now and are undermining it for the future" (Daschle 2003). The tax cut also proved a hard sell with voters, with majorities in polls preferring a much smaller tax cut and many opposed to any tax cut at all (*Los Angeles Times* poll, January 2–February 2, 2003; *ABC News/Washington Post* poll, March 27–28, 2003). Whether Democrats, with their image of imperfect fiscal rectitude, will be able to take advantage of this during the 2004 elections is not clear. The large deficits in 1991–1992 did give Bill Clinton and Ross Perot a leg up in their campaigns against Bush's father.

Third, persistent large deficits endanger the spending prospects for other policies the Bush administration has advocated. Perhaps the war on terrorism will serve to maintain political support for expansive defense spending, but the longer large deficits persist, the more pressure will build on all federal spending, even by the Pentagon. The Bush administration's ambitious and expensive plan to partially privatize Social Security is all but politically impossible in an era of growing deficits (Fletcher 2002).

Orthodox innovators like Bush run the risk of innovating in a fashion that disrupts the partisan coalition that brought them to power: "The characteristic challenge is to mitigate or assuage that factional ruptures within the ranks of the establishment that will inevitably accompany even the most orthodox of innovations and agenda adaptations" (Skowronek 1997, 41). Bush's second round of tax cuts might at first glance seem among the "most orthodox" of innovations, deriving from the supply-side theories in vogue during the Reagan administration. The Republican coalition, however, includes many traditional fiscal conservatives for whom budget balance is a primary goal. The Newt Gingrich–led Republican revolution in the 1995 Congress strongly pushed budget balance, coming within one Senate vote of sending a balanced-budget amendment to the Constitution to the states for ratification. Those sentiments will die hard if deficits persist. In this instance, Bush's big ambitions portend serious problems down the road for his governing coalition.

September 11 permanently altered the issue context of American foreign policy and, as crises do, handed President Bush a great political opportunity. The immediate response to the crisis made partisanship temporarily unfashionable in Washington and lessened institutional combat between the White House and the then-Democratically controlled Senate over how to address the threat of international terrorism. Bush used this opportunity to define threats to national security and how to address them, an undertaking Clinton avoided during his eight years in power (McCormick 2000). Much of what Bush articulated remains widely accepted in Washington politics—his views on the gravity of the threat and the need for enhanced domestic security and increased military spending. More controversial, however, is the administration's emphasis on preempting potential terrorist threats in other nations, epitomized by the invasion of Iraq in 2003. James McCormick in his chapter terms this approach "defensive realism," protecting America's national security interests through unprecedented military initiative.

Unilateralist premises underlie this approach to national security. Ivo Daalder and James Lindsay define the core assumptions of the administration's foreign policy: "American primacy in the world is the key to securing America's interests—and that it is both possible and desirable to extend the unipolar moment of the 1990s into a unipolar era" (Daalder and Lindsay 2003, 6). The administration's unipolar orientation has not proved to be domestically unpopular for Bush, but international diplomatic costs are quite evident. The administration received international disparagement for its abandonment of the Kyoto global warming agreement, International Criminal Court, and Anti-Ballistic Missile Treaty. Opposition to the war in Iraq by France, Russia, and Germany reflected their rejection of the administration's expansive foreign policy doctrine. The "coalition of the willing" in Iraq contained only three nations with significant military forces—the United States, the United Kingdom, and Australia—and worldwide opinion polls revealed that Bush's approach to the war was widely unpopular (Pew Research Center 2003).

Orthodox innovators often tap "the strength of the established regime most effectively when asserting American power in international affairs" (Skowronek 1997, 245). So it has proved in Bush's case. The public has long viewed Republicans as more competent in the stewardship of foreign and defense policy, and Bush strengthened the conservative regime by "playing to type" after September 11. The administration recognized that prosecuting the war on terrorism not only was crucial for regime legitimacy but also offered great political opportunities.

Hence, during the 2002 congressional elections the administration raised national security issues, on which Republicans had a great polling advantage, with impressive results. Bush, with his disciplined focus on the war on terrorism, played to the favorable GOP stereotype. As John Harris notes in his chapter, the Bush administration's consistent focus on this and other important issues contrasts sharply with the Clinton administration's far-flung approach. Ultimately, though, tactics alone will not determine the overall success of this very ambitious administration. Instead, whether it succeeds in restoring the conservative regime will depend on how well it negotiates new fundamentals in the international and domestic economic environment.

The Two Pillars

In 2000, I identified two pillars undergirding the American political situation: global geopolitical hegemony and domestic economic prosperity (Schier 2000). Since that time, both pillars have been shaken, rearranging America's politics. Though I mentioned terrorism and rogue nations as potential threats, the events of September 11 have shown these to be greater threats than I or most commentators ever imagined. It is now clear that the international politics of American security are far more central to presidential governance than they appeared to be under Clinton. With terrorism the greater threat, the Bush administration has deemphasized the multilateralist approach of the Clinton administration. This pattern predated September 11, as illustrated by the administration's lack of support for the Kyoto accord and the International Criminal Court (Daalder and Lindsay 2003).

Will the administration's deemphasis of multilateralism be a lasting approach? That depends on Bush's domestic political success and the course of the war on terrorism, two entangled variables. By 2003, the Bush administration had achieved considerable public approval through its aggressive handling of Afghanistan and Iraq. The troublesome military occupation of Iraq, however, began to erode popular support for Bush's foreign policy—a slide somewhat reversed by the capture of Saddam Hussein in December 2003. Whatever the costs in terms of international diplomacy and domestic public opinion, Bush has nevertheless solidified his domestic political coalition around this approach. Given this experience, it seems safe to assume that disinclination toward multilateralism will last as long as his presidency does. The new risks to domestic security produced a large political opportunity that Bush adroitly seized.

The second pillar, domestic economic prosperity, is far less stable that it appeared to be in 2000. Then, healthy levels of economic growth produced a booming stock market and a federal government bulging with budget surpluses. Real GDP growth slowed after 2000 (from 3.8 percent to 0.3 in 2001 and 2.4 in 2002), and unemployment rose to over 6 percent by mid-2003. Bush has been as bold in his response to the U.S. economy as he was toward international terrorism. In his recurrent advocacy of tax cuts, he seeks to rearrange parameters of fiscal policy discussion as dramatically as he transformed foreign policy. Prioritizing tax cuts promises to downgrade balancing the budget as a hallowed policy goal. It is true that in recent decades Washington politicians have been at best uneven in their operational devotion to a balanced budget. Nevertheless, the goal has always had a privileged place in budget debates. Bush, unlike Clinton or his father, hopes to push concern about deficits into the future in return for immediate economic growth through tax cuts. Reagan did this in 1981, and then reverted to balanced budget gospel, at least rhetorically. Bush seems unlikely to do so. Stimulating the economy by cutting taxes may prove tactically brilliant for the 2004 election, as economic growth rebounded late in 2003. The ensuing deficits, however, may well split Bush's coalition wide open (Schick 2003). And this may pose a considerable threat to his regime restoration project.

The presidency of George W. Bush will ultimately be judged by how well it took control of the events that transpired on Bush's watch. His administration's definition of control is very expansive, and its goal is to resurrect "political time" by installing a lasting conservative political regime. This sort of restoration has not achieved completion since FDR entrenched the New Deal coalition during the 1930s. The enormous undertaking runs the risk of fracturing Bush's own coalition as many regime articulators have done before—Lyndon Johnson and his father among them. At this writing, the greatest threat to the project lies in Bush's approach to domestic economic policy, probably because the domestic political implications of Bush's audacious foreign policy may be slow in appearing.

Is Bush on top of his time? If he is, his coalition will grow and strengthen, and he will depart a successful incumbent after two terms. Moreover, he will have accomplished a lot by the historical standards of the presidency. If he is not, he will depart in early 2005 or have a bad second term, a fate all too frequent for recent presidents. In any event, his presidency is far more consequential than anyone foresaw on January 20, 2001.

† Notes †

2. Political Warfare during Wartime

1. In light of recent controversies over Confederate symbolism, it is ironic that a Democratic leader used that phrase. It started with a Confederate soldier at Gettysburg: "We'll fight them, sir, 'til hell freezes over, and then, sir, we will fight them on the ice" (Foote 1963, 577). Two other things should have given Andrew pause about using the line. First, the rebel soldier uttered it right after Pickett's charge, a blunder that had set his side on the road to defeat. Second, Pat Buchanan often quoted it during his presidential campaign.

2. The political community started referring to Democratic territory as the "blue states" after the 2000 election. Broadcast networks had used blue in their graphics for the states Gore had won and red for those Bush had won. In this light, we could refer to Clinton haters and Gore haters as "red-hots."

3. The Party Base of Presidential Leadership and Legitimacy

1. Formally, one might think of political signals (such as election results) as "informative" when and to the extent that such signals lead a receiver to engage in behavior that the receiver views as welfare-enhancing.

2. Prospective candidates will come up with more than one such blueprint, of course. Think of the Democratic response to Jimmy Carter's loss in 1980. In 1984, Walter Mondale, Gary Hart, and Jesse Jackson represented three divergent impulses in the Democratic coalition, each of which represented some mix of sincere ideology and strategic calculation. Our point is not that the political information provided by elections leads inevitably to a unified party response, but that it encourages individual party elites to select what they consider the most promising response among several plausible alternatives.

3. Truman won 49.6 percent of the popular vote in 1948, Republican Thomas Dewey won 45.1 percent, Dixiecrat Strom Thurmond won 2.4 percent, and Progressive Henry Wallace won 2.3 percent.

4. The chronically low turnout in the South may have contributed to Wilson's anemic popular vote totals in 1912, but the central political lesson of his election—that Roosevelt's insurgency made Wilson's triumph much more likely—clarified the new president's plurality status. Notwithstanding the idiosyncrasies of southern turnout, Wilson won a textbook plurality victory. After all, if Democratic-leaning

Southerners did not turn out in 1912, they would provide little assurance to Wilson as he looked ahead to 1916. It is also important to note that Wilson had taken the measure of his political circumstances prior to 1912. In other words, Wilson had begun to develop a progressive identity before he received the information implicit in the 1912 returns, but those returns still played an enormously important role in confirming the political utility of the new president's reformist ambitions for his party. This is precisely the point: Plurality elections do not reveal startling new conditions in the political system; instead, they crystallize the very conditions that have kept the winning party from winning recent presidential elections.

5. The alleged deal between Adams and Clay had the former agreeing to appoint the latter as Secretary of State. When Adams did so, he added substantial fuel to Jackson's political fire.

6. One might also include the following presidents (and their respective percentages of the popular vote) in the plurality category: James Buchanan (45 percent) in 1856, Abraham Lincoln (40 percent) in 1860, Woodrow Wilson (42 percent) in 1912, and Richard Nixon (43 percent) in 1968.

4. The Likeable Partisan

1. To settle the contest Congress created a special electoral commission to review the disputed electoral votes of Florida, Louisiana, and South Carolina. By promising to remove federal troops from the Old Confederacy, Hayes won crucial southern support from each of these state's electors.

2. Jimmy Carter was the lone Democratic victor in 1976. Nixon prevailed in 1968 and 1972, Ronald Reagan won back-to-back victories in 1980 and 1984, and George H. W. Bush won in 1988.

3. The House vote was 296 in favor and 133 against. The Senate vote was 77 in favor and 23 against.

4. The U.S.A. Patriot Act passed by votes of 357 to 66 in the House and 98 to 1 in the Senate.

6. George W. Bush and Religious Politics

1. This survey was conducted by the Survey Research Center at the University of Akron, sponsored by the Ethics and Public Policy Center, and funded by a generous grant from the Pew Charitable Trusts. Here we focus primarily on actual voters from the post-election interviews ($N = 1{,}520$). The large number of voters allows us not only to classify members of the major religious traditions into culture war categories, using the extensive batteries of religious questions, but also to consider religious minorities. The relatively small numbers in these latter categories does suggest caution in interpretation, however.

2. The four questions involved the respondent's assessment of Bush's conduct of the war on terror, overall foreign policy, the war against Iraq, and the war in Afghanistan. The scale produced has an alpha reliability coefficient of 0.78.

3. For the questions making up this social traditionalism scale, see Conover and Feldman (1986). We have divided the full scale into quartiles for analysis.

7. One President, Two Presidencies

1. My characterization of a conventional presidency and a war presidency should not be confused with the "two presidencies" research tradition that hypothesizes, and seeks to find, a difference in congressional responses to presidential initiatives in domestic legislation and foreign relations related legislation (Shull 1991). My distinction relates more narrowly to the presidency's characteristics in a context of international crises and war. And regarding the effects of each presidency, I refer not only to the likely response of Congress to the president in these different contexts but the likely responses from other elites and the public.

8. A Stake in the Sand

1. Bush's success in pushing for legislation to deal with terrorism may be a unique case due to the unprecedented 2001 terrorist attacks. For this reason, in this chapter I consider Bush's other legislative successes for the most part.

2. Author's analysis of 2002 National Election Study (University of Michigan). A Republican "activist" is defined as someone who tried to convince someone else to vote a particular way, attended a party event, gave money to a political candidate or group, or displayed a campaign button or sign. Opinion is measured by "feeling thermometers" on a scale from zero to 100. Significant differences in standard deviations are measured using F-tests. Standard deviations are as follows: Big business: 18.0; poor people: 20.7; Christian fundamentalists: 24.3. A fourth thermometer referring to those receiving "welfare" had a standard deviation of 19.26, higher than that of big business, but not so different as to achieve standard levels of statistical significance.

3. A comparison of these two groups, of course, can only be suggestive, and not definitive. The two organizations may use very different rating systems. Also, the NTU and the Christian Coalition may focus on particular economic and social policies that are not representative of the full range of such policies on the public agenda.

4. National Taxpayers Union ratings are from the organization's Web site, http://www.ntu.org/features/congress_by_numbers/ntu_rates_congress/rates_congress.php3. Christian Coalition Ratings are from the *Almanac of American Politics*.

5. This power to minimize the impact of isolated dissenters should not be confused with the power to silence an organized bloc of dissenters, which I argue arises more often on social issues.

9. The Foreign Policy of the George W. Bush Administration

I have benefited from discussions with colleagues Christopher Ball, Sumit Ganguly, Brian Girvin, Alan Kessler, and Steven Schier. I thank them for their comments and suggestions.

1. Clinton argued that American actions in Kosovo were motivated by a "moral imperative" to aid the persecuted people in this province (and hence were consistent with principles of liberal internationalism), but he also contended that Ameri-

can actions involved "protecting our interests" and demonstrating the continued effectiveness of NATO (McCormick 2000).

2. This table was constructed from information available on THOMAS: Legislative Information on the Internet, http://thomas.loc.gov/.

3. In another recent analysis, Daalder and Lindsay (2003) argue that the events of September 11 enabled the administration to institute a foreign policy design they already embraced. In this sense, the administration's foreign policy was less changed, than actualized, by September 11.

4. Interestingly, the phrase, "distinctly American internationalism" remains in this document, but it now takes on a different meaning from what it meant at the beginning of the administration.

† References †

Abrams, Jim. 2001. "Armey Wants to Meet with NAACP Head." *Associated Press,* February 22.

Ackerman, Spencer, and John B. Judis. 2003. "The Selling of the Iraq War." *New Republic,* June 30, 14–28, 23–25.

Aldrich, John H. 1995. *Why Parties? The Origins and Transformation of Party Politics in America.* Chicago: University of Chicago Press.

Aldrich, John H., and David W. Rohde. 1997. "The Transition to Republican Rule in the House: Implications for Theories of Congressional Politics." *Political Science Quarterly* 112 (4):541–67.

——. 2000. "The Consequences of Party Organization in the House: The Role of the Majority and Minority Parties in Conditional Party Government." In *Polarized Politics: Congress and the President in a Partisan Era,* edited by J. R. Bond and R. Fleisher, 31–72. Washington, D.C.: CQ Press.

Allen, John L. 2003. "In Rome, Novak Makes Case for War." *National Catholic Reporter,* February 21.

Allen, Mike. 2001. "For Bush, Politics in the Fast Lane." *Washington Post,* January 10.

Allen, Mike, and Alan Cooperman. 2003. "Bush Backs Religious Charities on Hiring." *Washington Post,* June 25.

Altman, Daniel. 2003a. "Divided Economic Advice and the Lure of Politics." *New York Times,* April 12.

——. 2003b. "Recession Is Over; Jobs Aren't Trickling Down." *New York Times,* July 18.

Andrews, Edmund L. 2002a. "Steel Tariffs Put G.O.P. on the Spot in Campaigns." *New York Times,* August 24.

——. 2002b. "White House Aides Push for 50% Cut in Dividend Taxes." *New York Times,* December 25, A1.

Apple, R. W., Jr. 2001. "President Seen to Gain Legitimacy." *New York Times,* September 16.

Associated Press. 2003. "Poll: Public Optimistic About Quick War." *Yahoo! News,* March 22.

Auster, Elizabeth. 2002. "Bush Aide Always Rushing, but Job Gives Him a Rush." *Cleveland Plain Dealer,* 3.

Aversa, Jeannine. 2003. "Fiscal 2003 Deficit Has Hit $193.9 Billion." *Washington Post,* March 21, A35.

Ayres, Edward L. 1992. *The Promise of the New South: Life after Reconstruction.* New York: Oxford University Press.

Baer, Kenneth S. 2000. *Reinventing Democrats: The Politics of Liberalism from Reagan to Clinton.* Lawrence: University of Kansas Press.

Bai, Matt. 2003. "Party of One." *New York Times Magazine,* March 23, 32.

Balz, Dan. 2001. "Gore Pledges to Back Bush, Calls for Unity." *Washington Post,* September 30, A3.

——. 2003. "Kerry Raps Bush Policy on Postwar Iraq." *Washington Post,* July 11, A1, A6.

Balz, Dan, and Bob Woodward. 2002. "America's Chaotic Road to War." *Washington Post,* January 27.

Barber, James David. 1992. *The Presidential Character: Predicting Performance in the White House,* 4th ed. Upper Saddle River, NJ: Prentice-Hall.

Barone, Michael. 2001. *The Almanac of American Politics.* Washington, D.C.: National Journal Group.

——. 2002. "Who's Majority?" *National Review* 54 (December 9):30–34.

Barr, Stephan. 2001. "Bush Initiative Has Employees Feeling Exposed at Interior." *Washington Post,* November 28.

——. 2002. "Agencies Look into Outsourcing." *Washington Post,* August 9.

Barshay, Jill. 2001. "Bush Starts a Strong Record of Success with the Hill."

——. 2003a. "Can Tax Cuts Pay Their Way?" *CQ Weekly,* January 11, 67.

——. 2003b. "Democrats Splinter on Stimulus Alternative as Daschle's Plan Fails to Unite Caucus." *CQ Weekly,* January 25, 199.

Barshay, Jill, and Alan K. Ota. 2003. "White House Tax Cut Package Gets a Wary Reception." *CQ Weekly,* January 11, 68.

Bartels, Larry. 1998. "Where the Ducks Are: Voting Power in a Party System." In *Politicians and Party Politics,* edited by John Geer, 43–79. Baltimore, MD: Johns Hopkins University Press.

Bash, Dana. 2002. "Daschle Says 'Shrill' Talk Radio Spurs Threats." *CNN.com,* November 25.

Beaumont, Thomas. 2003. "Gephardt Takes Aim at Bush." *Des Moines Register,* July 14, 1B.

Becker, Elizabeth. 2002. "A Nation Challenged: Domestic Security; Bush Is Said to Consider a New Security Department." *New York Times,* April 12.

——. 2003. "W.T.O. Rules against U.S. on Steel Tariff." *New York Times,* March 27.

Benedetto, Richard. 2003. "Democrats Keep 'Misunderestimating' Bush." *USA Today,* April 21.

Bennet, James. 2001. "The Bush Years: C.E.O., U.S.A." *New York Times Magazine,* January 14, 26.

Berggren, D. Jason, and Bonnie K. Levine-Berggren. 2000. "Recapping the Role of Religion in the 2000 Presidential Primaries." *Religion Matters* 1 (July):1–15.

Berke, Richard L. 2001. "Florida G.O.P. Sees Bush Visit as Latest Slight." *New York Times,* June 14.

Berke, Richard, and Frank Bruni. 2001. "Crew of Listing Bush Ship Draws Republican Scowls." *New York Times,* July 2, A11.
Berke, Richard L., and David E. Sanger. 2002. "Some in Administration Grumble as Aide's Role Seems to Expand." *New York Times,* May 13.
Berlin, Sir Isaiah. 1993. *The Hedgehog and the Fox.* Chicago, IL: Elephant Paperback.
Bernstein, Elizabeth, and Eleanor Daspin. 2003 "A House Divided." *Wall Street Journal,* February 21.
Berry, Jeffrey M. 1999. *The New Liberalism: The Rising Power of Citizen Groups.* Washington, D.C.: Brookings Institution Press.
Berry, John M., and Jonathan Weisman. 2003. "Greenspan Says Tax Cuts Are Premature." *Washington Post,* February 12.
Binder, Sarah A., and Steven S. Smith. 1997. *Politics or Principle: Filibustering in the United States Senate.* Washington, D.C.: Brookings Institution Press.
Black, Earl, and Merle Black. 2002. *The Rise of Southern Republicans.* Cambridge, MA: Belknap Harvard.
Blanton, Dana. 2002. "Bush Bests Gore in Rematch." Foxnews.com, November 22.
Blustein, Paul, Don Phillips, and David S. Hilzenrath. 2002. "Former CEO Comes with Some Baggage." *Washington Post,* December 10.
Bolton, Alexander. 2002. "Members Hit White House Secrecy." *The Hill,* August 7.
Brant, Martha. 2002. "West Wing Story: More Than a War of Words." *Newsweek* online, April 12, available at http://www.msnbc.com/news/NW-front_Front.asp.
Broder, David. 2003a. "Tipping the Republicans' Hand?" *Washington Post,* June 18.
——. 2003b. "Black Thursday for Bush." *Washington Post,* July 15, A19.
Brooks, David. 2003. "Democrats Go off the Cliff." *Weekly Standard,* June 30.
Brownstein, Ronald. 2001. "Bush's Legislative Strategy: No Concessions Upfront; Style Mirrors the Approach He Used with Lawmakers in Texas." *Milwaukee Journal Sentinel,* January 8, 4A.
——. 2002. "Loyal to the Core, Bush Knows How to Play to the Crucial Outsiders." *Los Angeles Times,* May 27.
——. 2003. "Bush Moves by Refusing to Budge." *Los Angeles Times.* March 2, A1.
Bruni, Frank. 2000. "Bush Says Government Should Help Fathers Be Responsible." *New York Times,* July 19.
——. 2001a. "Accused of Moving Right, Bush Team Seeks to Secure Middle Ground." *New York Times,* May 31.
——. 2001b. "After Six Months, Bush Team Plans Change of Focus." *New York Times,* August 5.
——. 2001c. "For Bush, a Mission and a Defining Moment." *New York Times,* September 22, A1.
Bumiller, Elisabeth. 2002a. "Enron Contacted Two Cabinet Officers Before Collapsing." *New York Times,* January 10, A1.
——. 2002b. "Bush Signs Bill Aimed at Fraud in Corporations." *New York Times,* July 31.
——. 2002c. "Bush Signs Trade Bill, Restoring Broad Presidential Authority." *New York Times,* August 7.
——. 2003a. "The President's Team Changes Some Players but Not Its Game Plan." *New York Times,* January 5.

——. 2003b "Bush Says He Will Ask Congress to Extend Africa Trade Benefits." *New York Times,* January 16.
——. 2003c "Bush Chooses White House Adviser as Budget Director." *New York Times,* May 23.
Bumiller, Elisabeth, and Eric Schmitt. 2002. "On the Job and at Home, Influential Hawks' 30-Year Friendship Evolves." *New York Times,* September 11.
Burden, Barry C. 2001. "The Polarizing Effects of Congressional Primaries." In *Congressional Primaries and the Politics of Representation,* edited by Peter F. Galderisi, Marni Ezra, and Michael Lyons, 95–115. Lanham, MD: Rowman & Littlefield.
Burger, John. 2002. "A Bruising Year: Pro-Lifers Assess Bush." *National Catholic Register,* January 20–26.
Burke, John P. 2002. "The Bush Transition in Historical Perspective." *Political Science and Politics* 35 (1):23–26.
Burnham, Walter Dean. 1970. *Critical Elections and the Mainsprings of American Politics.* New York: Norton.
——. 1982. *The Current Crisis in American Politics.* New York: Oxford.
——. 1996. "Realignment Lives: The 1994 Earthquake and Its Implications." In *The Clinton Presidency: First Appraisals.* Chatham, NJ: Chatham House.
Bush, George H. W. 1992. Remarks to the Federalist Society in Philadelphia, Pennsylvania, April 3, 1992. In *Public Papers of the Presidents—George Bush.* Washington, D.C.: Government Printing Office.
Bush, George W. 1999a. "A Distinctly American Internationalism." Address delivered at the Ronald Reagan Presidential Library, November 19.
——. 1999b. "A Period of Consequences." Address delivered at The Citadel, September 23.
——. 2000. "Address at Austin, Texas." *New York Times,* December 14.
——. 2001a. "Inaugural Address." *New York Times,* January 21, 13.
——. 2001b. "Remarks by the President in Tax Cut Bill Signing Ceremony." *Weekly Compilation of Presidential Documents,* June 7.
——. 2001c. "Address to the Nation on the Terrorist Attacks, September 11, 2001." *Weekly Compilation of Presidential Documents,* September 17, 1302.
——. 2001d. "Remarks at the National Day of Prayer and Remembrance Service." *Weekly Compilation of Presidential Documents,* September 17, 1309.
——. 2001e. "Address to a Joint Session of Congress and the American People." *Weekly Compilation of Presidential Documents,* September 24.
——. 2002. "President's Remarks at the United Nations General Assembly." *Weekly Compilation of Presidential Documents,* September 12.
——. 2003a. Remarks at the 2003 President's Dinner. *Weekly Compilation of Presidential Documents,* May 21.
——. 2003b. "Address Before a Joint Session of the Congress on the State of the Union." *Weekly Compilation of Presidential Documents,* February. 3, 107–48.
——. 2003c. "President Says Saddam Hussein Must Leave Iraq Within 48 Hours." Remarks to the Nation, March 17, available at http://www.whitehouse.gov/news/releases/2003/03/20030317-7.html.
——. 2003d. "President Applauds Supreme Court for Recognizing Value of Diversity." White House press release, June 23.

Caldwell, Robert J. 2000. "History Offers Gore a Guide for Doing the Right Thing." *San Diego Union-Tribune*, November 12, G1.

Cannon, Carl M., and Alexis Simendinger. 2002. "The Evolution of Karl Rove." *National Journal*. April 27.

Carnes, Tony. 2000. "A Presidential Hopeful's Progress." *Christianity Today*, October 20.

Carter, Jimmy. 1996. Interview with Bill Moyers, November 13, 1978. In *The Columbia World of Quotations*. New York: Columbia University Press.

Carville, James, Stan Greenberg, and Robert Shrum. 2001. "Politics after the Attack." Democracy Corps memorandum, November 13, available at http://www.democracycorps.com/reports/analyses/Politics_after_the_Attack.pdf.

——. 2002. "Re: Enron." Democracy Corps memorandum, January 28, available at http://www.democracycorps.com/reports/analyses/Enron.pdf.

Ceaser, James W. 1979. *Presidential Selection: Theory and Development*. Princeton, NJ: Princeton University Press.

Ceaser, James W., and Andrew E. Busch. 2001. *The Perfect Tie: The True Story of the 2000 Presidential Election*. Lanham, MD: Rowman & Littlefield.

Center for Responsive Politics. 2002. "Top House Recipients of Enron Contributions 1989–2001." Available at http://www.opensecrets.org/news/enron/enron_house_top.asp.

Chicago Council on Foreign Relations. 2002. "A World Transformed: Foreign Policy Attitudes of the U.S. Public after September 11th." Key Findings, September 4, available at http://www.worldviews.org/key_findings/us_911_report.htm.

Clausewitz, Carl von. 1976. *On War*. Trans. and eds. Michael Howard and Peter Paret. Princeton, NJ: Princeton University Press.

Clinton, William. 1991. "A New Covenant for American Security." Address at Georgetown University, December 12.

——. 1992. "Remarks of Governor Bill Clinton." *Los Angeles World Affairs Council*, August 13.

Cochran, John. 2002. "Bush Readies Strategies for Legislative Success in 2003." *CQ Weekly*, December 14, 3235–39.

Cohn, D'Vera. 2001. "Married-with-Children Still Fading." *Washington Post*, May 15, A1.

Coile, Zachary. 2001. "Clinton Pal Wins Chair of Demo Party." *San Francisco Chronicle*, February 4, A3.

——. 2003. "Rep. Stark Blasts Bush on Iraq War." *San Francisco Chronicle*, March 19, A16.

Coleman, John J. 2000. "Clinton and the Party System in Historical Perspective." In *The Postmodern President: Bill Clinton's Legacy in U.S. Politics*, edited by Steven E. Schier, 145–66. Pittsburgh, PA: University of Pittsburgh Press.

CQ Weekly. 2002. Various dates. Washington, D.C.: Congressional Quarterly.

Conn, Joseph L. 2003. "Faith-Based Fiat." *Church and State* 56 (1):4–7.

Conover, Pamela Johnston, and Stanley Feldman. 1986. "Morality Items on the 1985 Pilot Study." *A Report to the 1985 National Election Study Pilot Study Committee*. May. Ann Arbor, MI: University of Michigan, Center for Political Studies.

Cook, Charles. 2001. "The Phases of Bush." *National Journal*, 18 December.

——. 2003a. "By Many Gauges, GOP Hold Only a Slim Edge." *National Journal* 35 (3):199–200.

——. 2003b. "After War, New Problems for Bush." *National Journal* online, March 18.

Cooperman, Alan. 2003. "Paige's Remarks on Religion in Schools Decried." *Washington Post,* April 9.

Crabtree, Susan. 2003. "Rove Vows to GOP: No Triangulation." *Roll Call,* 3 February.

Crutsinger, Martin. 2002. "Bush Names Friedman as Top Economist." *Washington Post,* December 12.

——. 2003. "Speculation Rises on Greenspan's Future." *Washington Times* online, February 16, available at http://customwire.ap.org/dynamic/fronts/HOME.

D'Innocenzio, Anne. 2003. "Rising Unemployment Sends Consumer Confidence Plunging." *Washington Post,* July 29.

Daalder, Ivo, and James M. Lindsay. 2003. "The Bush Revolution: The Remaking of America's Foreign Policy." Revised version of paper prepared for presentation at The George W. Bush Presidency: An Early Assessment Conference, April 25–26. Available at http://www.wws.princeton.edu/bushconf/DaalderLindsayPaper.pdf.

Daalder, Ivo H., James M. Lindsay, and James B. Steinberg. 2002a. "The Bush National Security Strategy: An Evaluation." Policy Brief No. 109. Washington, D.C.: Brookings Institution. Available at http://www.brookings.edu/comm/policybriefs/pb109.htm.

——. 2002b. "Hard Choices: National Security and the War on Terrorism." *Current History* 101 (December):409–13.

Dahl, Robert A. 1990. "The Myth of the Presidential Mandate." *Political Science Quarterly* 105 (4):355–72.

Darilek, Richard E. 1976. *A Loyal Opposition in Time of War.* Westport, CT: Greenwood.

Daschle, Tom. 2003. "Statement of Senator Tom Daschle on the President's Proposed Budget for Fiscal Year 2004."

Davies, Philip John. 2003. "A New Republican Generation?" *Contemporary Review* 282 (March):139–46.

DeGregorio, William A. 1997. *The Complete Book of U.S. Presidents,* 5th ed. New York: Random House.

Democratic Leadership Council. 2003. "The GOP Keeps Whistlin' Dixie." *New Dem Daily,* January 21.

Deutsch, Karl W. 1966. "External Influences on the Internal Behavior of States." In *Approaches to Comparative and International Politics,* edited by R. Barry Farrell, 5–26. Evanston, IL: Northwestern University Press.

Dewar, Helen. 2001. "A Serious Breach in Bipartisanship; Democrats Fire 'Shot Across the Bow.'" *Washington Post,* February 2, A6.

——. 2002. "Votes on Homeland Security Department Blocked." *Washington Post,* October 18, A9.

——. 2003a. "Bush's Use of Clout Intensifies Senate Split." *Washington Post,* March 2, A4.

——. 2003b. "Senate Passes Homeland Security Bill." *Washington Post,* November 20.

Dewar, Helen, and Dan Balz. 2001. "Democrats Fault Bush Tactics on Tax Cut." *Washington Post,* March 10, A4.

Dionne, E. J. 2001. "Harder Than McKinley." *Washington Post,* April 2.

——. 2003. "A Wartime Leader Can't Be Partisan as Usual." *Washington Post,* January 26, B1.

Dionne, E. J., Jr., and William Kristol, eds. 2001. *Bush v. Gore: The Court Case and Commentary.* Washington, D.C.: Brookings Institution.

Dorrien, Gary. 2003. "Axis of One." *Christian Century* 120 (March 8):30–35.

Douglas, Stephen. 1858. "First Debate with Stephen A. Douglas, Ottawa, Illinois." August 21. Available at http://speaker/house.gov/library/texts/lincoln/debate1.asp.

Dubose, Lou, Jan Reid, and Carl Cannon. 2003. *Boy Genius: Karl Rove, the Brains Behind the Remarkable Political Triumph of George W. Bush.* New York: Public Affairs.

Eagleburger, Lawrence. 1993. "Charting the Course: U.S. Foreign Policy in a Time of Transition." *Dispatch* 4 (January 11):16–19.

Edsall, Thomas B. 2002a. "GOP Eyes Jewish Vote with Bush Tack on Israel." *Washington Post,* April 30.

——. 2002b. "Lott Decried for Part of Salute to Thurmond." *Washington Post,* December 7, A6.

——. 2003. "GOP Outpaces Democrats in Fundraising with New Restrictions." *Washington Post,* March 21, A3.

Edsall, Thomas B., and Dana Milbank. 2003. "White House's Roving Eye for Politics." *Washington Post,* March 10.

Edwards, George C. III. 1989. *At the Margins: Presidential Leadership of Congress.* New Haven, CT: Yale University Press.

Eilperin, Juliet. 2001. "Bush Team Veteran Returns to the Court; Calio to Sell President's Agenda on Hill." *Washington Post,* January 31, 19.

——. 2002. "Democrat Implies Sept. 11 Administration Plot." *Washington Post,* April 12, A16.

Eisner, Marc A. 2000. *From Warfare State to Welfare State: World War I, Compensatory State Building, and the Limits of the Modern Order.* University Park, PA: Pennsylvania State University Press.

"Election 2000 Presidential Debate II with Republican Candidate Governor George W. Bush and Democratic Candidate Vice President Al Gore." 2000. Wait Chapel, Wake Forest University, Winston, NC, October 11. Available at http://www.c-span.org.

Elhauge, Einer. 2001. "Florida 2000: Bush Wins Again." *Weekly Standard,* November 26.

Evans, Roland, and Robert D. Novak. 1968. *Lyndon B. Johnson: The Exercise of Power.* New York: New American Library.

Federal Document Clearing House. 2000. "Vice President Gore and Governor Bush Participate in Second Presidential Debate Sponsored by the Presidential Debate Commission." *Federal Document Clearing House Political Transcripts,* October 11.

Federal News Service. 2001. "Remarks by President George W. Bush to a Joint Session of Congress." February 27.

Fenno, Richard. 1997. *Learning to Govern: An Institutional View of the 104th Congress.* Washington, D.C.: Brookings Institution.

Fineman, Howard. 2003. "Bush and God." *Newsweek*, March 10.

Firestone, David. 2003. "Conservatives Now See Deficits as a Tool to Fight Spending." *New York Times,* February 11.

Fisher, Louis. 2000. *Congressional Abdication on War and Spending.* College Station, TX: Texas A&M University Press.

Fleisher, Richard, and Jon R. Bond. 2000. "Partisanship and the President's Quest for Votes on the Floor of Congress." In *Polarized Politics: Congress and the President in a Partisan Era*, edited by J. R. Bond and R. Fleisher, 154–85. Washington, D.C.: CQ Press.

Fletcher, Michael A. 2002. "Social Security Changes Put on the Back Burner." *Washington Post,* November 11.

Foote, Shelby. 1963. *The Civil War: A Narrative—Fredericksburg to Meridian.* New York: Random House.

Fortier, John C., and Norman J. Ornstein. 2003. Congress and the Bush Presidency. Paper presented at "The Bush Presidency: An Early A, Princeton, NJ.

Fournier, Ron. 2003. "Dems Call Bush Credibility into Question." Associated Press, June 12.

Fram, Alan. 2003. "Lott's Ability to Lead Questioned." Associated Press, December 19.

From, Al. 2001. "Bush's No Moderate—He's to the Right of Reagan." *Christian Science Monitor*, April 26.

Frum, David. 1994. *Dead Right.* New York: Basic Books.

———. 2003a. "It's His Party." *New York Times,* 5 January.

———. 2003b. *The Right Man: The Surprise Presidency of George W. Bush.* New York: Random House.

Gaddis, John Lewis. 2002. "A Grand Strategy." *Foreign Policy* (November/December):50–57.

Gall, Carlatta. 2003. "In Afghanistan, Violence Stalls Renewal Effort." *New York Times,* April 26.

Gallup Tuesday Briefing. 2001. "Rallying Behind the Country's Leaders and Institutions." Tuesday Briefing, September 25, available at http://gallup.com/.

Geertz, Clifford. 1983. "Centers, Kings, and Charisma: Reflections on the Symbolics of Power." In *Local Knowledge, Further Essays in Interpretive Anthropology,* edited by Clifford Geertz, 121–46. New York: Basic Books.

George, Robert. 2003. "Sandra and George's Diversity Garden Party." *Reason* online, June 24.

Ginsberg, Benjamin, and Martin Shefter. 2003. *Politics by Other Means: Politicians, Prosecutors, and the Press from Watergate to Whitewater*, 3rd ed. New York: W.W. Norton.

Glaberson, William. 2001. "In New Senate, New Scrutiny of Judicial Nominees." *New York Times,* May 30.

Goodstein, Laurie. 2000. "Bush Uses Religion as Personal and Political Guide." *New York Times,* October 22.

——. 2001. "Abortion Foes Split over Plan on Stem Cells." *New York Times,* August 12.

——. 2002. "Evangelical Figures Oppose Religious Leaders' Broad Antiwar Sentiment." *New York Times,* October 5.

——. 2003. "Divide among Jews Leads to Silence on Iraq War." *New York Times,* March 15.

Green, John C. 2003. "The Undetected Tide." *Religion in the News* 6 (1): 4–6.

Green, Joshua. 2002. "The Other War Room: President Bush Doesn't Believe in Polling—Just Ask His Pollsters. *The Washington Monthly,* April.

Greenstein, Fred I. 2000. *The Presidential Difference: Leadership Style from FDR to Clinton.* New York: Free Press.

——. 2002. "The Changing Leadership of George W. Bush: A Pre- and Post-9/11 Comparison." *Presidential Studies Quarterly* 32 (2):387–96.

——. 2004. "The Changing Leadership of George W. Bush: A Pre- and Post-9/11 Comparison." In *The Domestic Sources of American Foreign Policy: Insights and Evidence,* 4th ed., edited by Eugene R. Wittkopf and James M. McCormick, 353–62. Lanham, MD: Rowman & Littlefield.

Grove, Lloyd. 2000. "The Reliable Source." *Washington Post,* October 27, C3.

Guth, James L. 2000. "Clinton, Impeachment, and the Culture Wars." In *The Postmodern President: Bill Clinton's Legacy in U.S. Politics,* edited by Steven E. Schier, 203–22. Pittsburgh, PA: University of Pittsburgh Press.

——. 2003. "The Political Activity of Evangelical Clergy in the Election of 2000: A Case Study of Five Denominations." *Journal for the Scientific Study of Religion* 42:4.

Hamilton, Alexander, John Jay, and James Madison. n.d. *The Federalist.* New York: Modern Library.

Hamilton, Alexander, and James Madison. 1976. *The Letters of Pacificus and Helvidius with the Letters of Americus.* Delmar, NY: Scholars' Facsimiles and Reprints.

Hargreaves, Mary W. M. 1985. *The Presidency of John Quincy Adams.* Lawrence, KS: University Press of Kansas.

Harris, John F. 2000a. "A Clouded Mirror: Bill Clinton, Polls, and the Politics of Survival." In *The Postmodern President: Bill Clinton's Legacy in U.S. Politics,* edited by Steven E. Schier, 87–105. Pittsburgh, PA: University of Pittsburgh Press.

——. 2000b. "Politics and Policy by the Numbers." *Washington Post,* December 31.

——. 2001a. "Mr. Bush Catches a Washington Break." *Washington Post,* May 6.

——. 2001b. "Clintonesque Balancing of Issues, Polls; Role of Politics Evident in Bush's White House." *Washington Post,* June 24.

Harris, John F., and Dan Balz. 2001 "A Question of Capital." *Washington Post,* April 29.

Harwood, John. 2003. "Bush Faces Republican Fire on Postwar Costs for Iraq." *Wall Street Journal.* March 19.

Hecht, Marie B. 1972. *John Quincy Adams: A Personal History of An Independent Man.* New York: Macmillan.

Heclo, Hugh. 1999. "The Changing Presidential Office." In *The Managerial Presidency,* 2nd ed., edited by James Pfiffner, 23–36. College Station, TX: Texas A& M University Press.

Heineman, Kenneth J. 1998. *God Is a Conservative: Religion, Politics, and Morality in Contemporary America.* New York: New York University Press.

Henning, Chuck. 1992. *The Wit and Wisdom of Politics,* expanded ed. Golden, CO: Fulcrum Publishing.

Herrnson, Paul. 1998. "National Party Organizations at the Century's End." In *The Parties Respond: Changes in American Parties and Campaigns,* 3rd ed., edited by L. Sandy Maisel, 50–82. Boulder, CO: Westview Press.

Hill, Patrice. 2003. "Fed Chief Tempers Stimulus Criticism." *Washington Times,* February 13.

Hinckley, Barbara. 1990. *The Symbolic Presidency.* New York: Routledge.

Hines, Crystal Nix. 2001. "Lag in Appointments Strains the Cabinet." *New York Times,* June 14.

Hirschfeld-Davis, Julie. 2002. "Quick Action Expected on Tax Package: Dividend Tax Cut Is Viewed as High on White House Agenda." *Milwaukee Journal-Sentinel,* December 8, 9A.

History News Network. 2003. "Quotes from History Relevant to Today's News." April 17.

Holland, Keating. 2000. "Poll: African-Americans Lack Confidence in Bush." *CNN.com,* December 18, http://www.cnn.com/.

Hoogenboom, Ari. 1995. *Rutherford B. Hayes: Warrior and President.* Lawrence, KS: University Press of Kansas.

Hook, Janet. 2003a. "Bush Plan to End Dividend Tax in for Changes." *Los Angeles Times,* February 2, 30.

——. 2003b. "Senate Limits Tax Cut, Triggers GOP Feud." *Los Angeles Times,* April 12, A1.

——. 2003c. "GOP's Go-To Guy Might Pose Risks for President." *Los Angeles Times,* June 16.

Hughes, Emmet John. 1973. *The Living Presidency.* New York: Coward, McCann, Geoghegan.

Hunter, James D. 1991. *Culture Wars: The Struggle to Define America.* New York: Basic Books.

Hurt, Jeanette. 2000. "Jesse Jackson Speaks at Rally to Get Out the Vote for Gore." *Milwaukee Journal-Sentinel,* October 29, 4Z.

Ignatieff, Michael. 2003. "The Burden." *New York Times Magazine,* January 5.

"The Incredible Shrinking President." 1992. *Time,* June 29, 50.

Ivins, Molly, and Lou DuBose. 2002. *Shrub: The Short but Happy Political Life of George W. Bush.* New York: Vintage Books.

Jacobs, Lawrence, and Robert Y. Shapiro. 2000. *Politicians Don't Pander: Political Manipulation and the Loss of Democratic Responsiveness.* Chicago, IL: University of Chicago Press.

Jacobson, Gary C. 2000. "Party Polarization in National Politics: The Electoral Connection." In *Polarized Politics: Congress and the President in a Partisan Era,* edited by Jon R. Bond and Richard Fleisher, 9–30. Washington, D.C.: CQ Press.

Johnson, Glen. 2003. "Kerry Says the U.S. Needs Its Own 'Regime Change.'" *Boston Globe.* April 3, A1.
Jones, Charles O. 2003. Capitalizing on Position in the George W. Bush Presidency: Partisan Patterns and Congress in a 50–50 Government. Paper presented at "The George W. Bush Presidency: An Early Assessment," April 25–26, Woodrow Wilson School, Princeton University, Princeton, NJ.
Jones, Jeffrey M. 2003. "Bush's Second-Year Approval Rating One of the Best Ever." *Gallup News Service,* January 17.
Judis, John. 2002. "Soft Sell." *New Republic,* November 11, 12.
Judis, John B., and Ruy Teixeira. 2002. *The Emerging Democratic Majority.* New York: Scribner.
Keller, Bill. 2003a. "The Radical Presidency of George W. Bush." *New York Times,* January 26.
——. 2003b. "God and George W. Bush." *New York Times,* May 17.
Kennedy, Helen. 2001. "Senate Confirms Ashcroft but 42 Democrats Oppose Nominee." *New York Daily News,* February 2, 8.
Kerbel, Matthew Robert. 1995. *Remote and Controlled: Media Politics in a Cynical Age.* Boulder, CO: Westview Press.
Kernell, Samuel. 1978. "Explaining Presidential Popularity: How Ad Hoc Theorizing, Misplaced Emphasis, and Insufficient Care in Measuring One's Variables Refuted Common Sense and Led Conventional Wisdom Down the Path of Anomalies." *American Political Science Review* 72 (June):506–22.
——. 1993. *Going Public.* Second edition. Washington, D.C.: CQ Press.
——. 1997. *Going Public: New Strategies of Presidential Leadership,* 3rd ed. Washington D.C.: CQ Press.
Kessler, Glenn. 2001. "House Panel Approves Key Part of Bush Tax Cut Plan." *Washington Post,* March 2, A1.
Kessler, Glenn, and Juliet Eilperin. 2001. "Congress Passes $1.35 Trillion Tax Cut." *Washington Post,* May 27.
Kessler, Glenn, and Dana Milbank. 2001. "Tax Cut Compromise Close Enough, Bush Says." *Washington Post,* April 7, A9.
Kettl, Donald F. 2003. *Team Bush: Leadership Lessons from the Bush White House.* New York: McGraw-Hill.
Key, V. O. 1955. "A Theory of Critical Elections." *Journal of Politics* 17: 3–18.
——. 1959. "Secular Realignment and the Party System." *Journal of Politics* 21:198–210.
Kiefer, Francine. 2001. "Bush Plans 2004 Wedding with Hispanics." *Christian Science Monitor,* May 14, 1.
Kilgore, Ed. 2001. "The Loyal Opposition during Wartime." *Blueprint,* November/December.
Kleppner, Paul. 1979. *The Third Electoral System, 1853–1892: Parties, Voters, and Political Cultures.* Chapel Hill, NC: University of North Carolina Press.
Koh, Harold. 1990. *The National Security Constitution.* New Haven, CT: Yale University Press.
Kornblut, Anne. 2001a. "Tax Cut Bill Wins Final Approval." *Boston Globe,* May 27, A1.
——. 2001b. "Year One, Resolve Steady Bush." *Boston Globe.* December 30.

Krehbiel, Keith. 1998. *Pivotal Politics: A Theory of U.S. Lawmaking.* Chicago, IL: University of Chicago Press.

——. 2000. "Party Discipline and Measures of Partisanship." *American Journal of Political Science* 44 (2):206–21.

Labaton, Stephen. 2002. "S.E.C.'s Embattled Chief Resigns in Wake of Latest Political Storm." *New York Times,* November 6.

Lacy, Mark. 2001. "Bush Deploys Charm on Daschle in Pushing Tax Cut." *New York Times,* March 10, A7.

Lakely, James G. 2003. "110 Economists Back Bush Tax Plan." *Washington Times,* January 18.

Lakely, James G., and Stephen Dinan. 2003. "Democrats Rally Behind U.S. Troops." *Washington Times,* March 18, A1.

Lancaster, John. 2001. "Senate Republicans Try to Regroup." *Washington Post,* May 26, A18.

Lawrence, Jill. 2000. "Aggressive NAACP Urged African Americans to Polls." *USA Today.* December 8, A8.

Layman, Geoffrey. 2001. *The Great Divide: Religious and Cultural Conflict in American Party Politics.* New York: Columbia University Press.

Leaming, Jeremy. 2003. "Born-Again Voucher Booster." *Church and State* 56 (3, March):12–13.

Lee, Christopher, and Stephen Barr. 2002. "New Agency, New Rules." *Washington Post,* November 14.

Leege David C., Kenneth D. Wald, Brian S. Krueger, and Paul D. Mueller. 2002. *The Politics of Cultural Differences.* Princeton, NJ: Princeton University Press.

Lemann, Nicholas. 2003. "The Controller." *New Yorker,* 12 May, 68–83.

Leonhardt, David. 2002. "Long-Term Jobless Rose by 50 Percent over the Last Year." *New York Times,* September 9.

Lewis, John. 2003. "Bush's Strategy of Racial Innuendo a Telling and Troubling Sign." *Atlanta Journal-Constitution,* January 20: A11.

Lewis, Neil. 2003. "Judicial Nominee Advances Amid Dispute over Religion." *New York Times,* July 24.

Lieberman, Robert C. 2000. "Political Time and Policy Coalitions: Structure and Agency in Presidential Power." In *Presidential Power: Forging the Presidency for the Twenty-First Century,* edited by Robert Y. Shapiro, Martha Joynt Kumar, and Lawrence R. Jacobs, 274–310. New York: Columbia University Press.

Lisi, Clemente. 2002. "Hill: Republicans Still Have Lott of Explaining to Do." *New York Post,* December 21: 4.

Lopez, Kathryn Jean. 2001. "On the Same Page? Assessing Bush's Outreach to Catholics." *National Catholic Register,* July 22–28.

Lorant, Stefan. 1951. *The Presidency.* New York: MacMillan Company.

Lowi, Theodore J. 1985. *The Personal President: Power Invested, Promise Unfulfilled.* Ithaca, NY: Cornell University Press.

Mann, Thomas, and Norman J. Ornstein, eds. 2000. *The Permanent Campaign and Its Future.* Washington, D.C.: American Enterprise Institute and Brookings Institution.

Marcus, Robert D. 1971. *Grand Old Party: Political Structure in the Gilded Age 1880–1896*. New York: Oxford University Press.

Mayer, Kenneth R. 2001. *At the Stroke of a Pen: Executive Orders and Presidential Power*. Princeton: Princeton University Press.

Mayer, William G. 1998. "Mass Partisanship, 1946–1996." In *Partisan Approaches to Postwar American Politics*, edited by Byron E. Shafer, 186–219. Chatham, NJ: Chatham House.

——. 2001. "The Presidential Nominations." In *The Election of 2000*, edited by Gerald Pomper. New York: Chatham House.

Mayhew, David R. 2002. *Electoral Realignments: A Critique of an American Genre*. New Haven, CT: Yale University Press.

McCormick, James M. 1998. *American Foreign Policy & Process*, 3rd ed. Itasca, IL: F.E. Peacock Publishers.

——. 2000. "Clinton and Foreign Policy: Some Legacies for a New Century." In *The Postmodern President: Bill Clinton's Legacy in U.S. Politics*, edited by Steven E. Schier, 60–84. Pittsburgh, PA: University of Pittsburgh Press.

McCormick, Richard P. 1975. "Political Development and the Second Party System." In *The American Party Systems: Stages of Political Development*, 2nd ed, edited by William Nisbet Chambers and Walter Dean Burnham, 90–116. New York: Oxford University Press.

McDonald, Forrest. 1994. *The American Presidency: An Intellectual History*. Lawrence, KS: University Press of Kansas.

McGerr, Michael E. 1986. *The Decline of Popular Politics: The American North, 1996–1928*. New York: Oxford University Press.

McManus, Doyle. 2003. "The World Casts a Critical Eye at Bush's Style of Diplomacy." *Los Angeles Times*, 3 March.

McQueen, Anjetta. 2001. "Education Bill Gives Both Parties Achievements to Tout, Concessions to Explain." *CQ Weekly*, December 22, 3086.

Mercer, Joshua. 2002. "Bush Names Mother Teresa Aid to Faith Post." *National Catholic Register*, February 10–16.

Meyerson, Harold. 2002. "Dems in the Dumps." *The American Prospect* 13 (December 16):22–24.

Mieckzkowski, Yanek. 2001. *The Routledge Historical Atlas of Presidential Elections*. New York, Routledge.

Milbank, Dana. 2001. "Serious Strategery: As Rove Launches Elaborate Political Effort, Some See Nascent Clintonian 'War Room.'" *Washington Post*, April 22.

——. 2002a. "Congress, White House Fight over Ridge Status." *Washington Post*, March 21.

——. 2002b. "A Hard-Nosed Litigator Becomes Bush's Policy Point Man." *Washington Post*, April 30.

——. 2002c. "Democrats Question Iraq Timing; Talk of War Distracts from Election Issues." *Washington Post*, September 16.

——. 2002d. "With '04 in Mind, Bush Team Saw Economic, Political Peril." *Washington Post*, December 7, available at http://washingtonpost.com/wp-dyn/articles/A20816-2002Dec6.html.

——. 2003. "Bush's Political Future Hinges on Quick War." *Washington Post,* March 15.

Milbank, Dana, and Mike Allen. 2002. "White House Claims Election Is Broad Mandate." *Washington Post,* November 7, A27.

Milbank, Dana, and Richard Morin. 2003. "Support for a War with Iraq Weakens." *Washington Post,* January 22.

Milbank, Dana, and Jonathan Weisman. 2002. "Bush Resists Taking New Economic Steps." *Washington Post,* July 18.

Milkis, Sidney M., and Michael Nelson. 1999. *The American Presidency: Origins & Development, 1776–1998.* Washington, D.C.: CQ Press.

Moe, Terry. 1999. "The Politicized Presidency." In *The Managerial Presidency,* 2nd ed., edited by James Pfiffner, 144–61. College Station, TX: Texas A & M University Press.

Mollison, Andrew. 2001. "House Finds 'Common Ground' on Education." *Atlanta Journal and Constitution,* March 23, 12A.

Moore, David W. 2001. "Top Ten Gallup Presidential Approval Ratings." Gallup press release, September 24, available at http://www.gallup.com/poll/releases/pr030701.asp.

——. 2003. "Fewer Say Iraq Worth Going to War Over." Gallup press release July 1 available at http://www.gallup.com/content/?ci=8761.

Morgan, Dan. 2003. "Congress Passes $78.5 Billion Emergency Spending Bill for War." *Washington Post,* April 13.

Morin, Richard, and Claudia Deane. 2002 "Democratic Majority Say No Gore in 'O4." *Washington Post,* July 18, available at http://www.washingtonpost.com/wp-dyn/articles/A24208-2002Jul18.html.

Morris, Dick. 1999. *Behind the Oval Office.* Los Angeles: Renaissance Books.

——. 2003. "W's Triangulation." *FrontPageMagazine.com,* June 25, available at http://www.frontpagemag.com/articles/printable.asp?ID=8564.

Murray, Shoon Kathleen, and Chrisopher Spinosa. 2004. "The Post-9/11 Shift in Public Opinion: How Long Will It Last?" In *The Domestic Sources of American Foreign Policy: Insights and Evidence,* 4th ed., edited by Eugene R. Wittkopf and James M. McCormick, 97–115. Lanham, MD: Rowman & Littlefield.

Nagel, Paul C. 1997. *John Quincy Adams: A Public Life, a Private Life.* New York: Knopf.

Nagourney, Adam. 2003a. "Bush, Looking to His Right, Shores Up Support for 2004." *New York Times,* June 30, A1.

——. 2003b. "The Rubber Dagger." *New York Times,* July 17, A1.

Nagourney, Adam, and Richard W. Stevenson. 2003. "Bush's Aides Plan Late Sprint in '04." *New York Times,* April 22.

Nather, David. 2001a. "Conferees Make Little Headway on Biggest Issues in Education Bill." *CQ Weekly,* August 4, 1926.

——. 2001b. "Education Bill Passes in House with Strong Bipartisan Support." *CQ Weekly,* May 26, 1256.

——. 2001c. "Student-Testing Drive Marks an Attitude Shift for Congress." *CQ Weekly,* June 30, 1560.

Nather, David, with John Cochran. 2002. "Still-thin Edge Leaves GOP with a Cautious Mandate." *CQ Weekly,* November 9, 2888–93.
National Journal. 2003. "2003 Polling on President Bush's Cabinet." National Journal.com, available at http://nationaljournal.com/members/polltrack/2003/national/03cabinet.htm.
National Security Strategy of the United States of America. 2002. September 17. Available at http://www.whitehouse.gov/nsc/nss.html.
Neustadt, Richard E. 1990. *Presidential Power and the Modern Presidents: The Politics of Leadership from Roosevelt to Reagan.* New York: Free Press.
Newport, Frank. 2002. "Terrorism Fades as Nation's Most Important Problem." News release, January 14, available at http://www.gallup.com/poll/releases/pr020114.asp.
Nie, Norman H., Sidney Verba, and John R. Petrocik. 1979. *The Changing American Voter,* enlarged ed. Cambridge, MA: Harvard University Press.
Nieves, Evelyn. 2003. "Short-Fused Populist, Breathing Fire at Bush." *Washington Post,* July 6, A1.
Nitschke, Lori. 2001a. "The Elusive Middle Ground." *CQ Weekly,* March 3, 467.
——. 2001b. "Tax Cut Bipartisanship Down to One Chamber." *CQ Weekly,* March 10, 529.
Nixon, Richard M. 1968. *Six Crises.* New York: Pyramid Books.
——. 1991. *In the Arena.* New York: Pocket Books.
Norquist, Grover. 2003. "Step-by-Step Tax Reform." *Washington Post,* June 9.
Norris, Floyd. 2002. "Bush Facing Twp Challenges: S.E.C. Choice and Economy." *New York Times,* November 7.
Novak, Robert D. 2001. "Bush Gives in on Education." *Eagle Forum Capitol Alert,* May 14.
Office of Management and Budget. 2001. "The President's Management Agenda."
Office of Senate Democratic Leader. 2003. "Democratic Leaders Daschle and Pelosi Provide Prebuttal to State of the Union Address." January 27.
Office of the Press Secretary. 1995. "Transcript of Press Conference by the President." Washington, D.C., April 18.
Oliphant, Thomas. 2002. "Bush's Security Flip-Flop." *Boston Globe.* June 9.
Online Newshour with Jim Lehrer. 1999. "Senator McCain on the Trail." September 1. Available at http://www.pbs.org/newshour/bb/election/july-dec99/mccain_9-1.html.
Ornstein, Norman J. 2001. "Relations with Congress." *Political Science and Politics* 35, (1):47-50.
Ota, Alan K. 2003a. "Tax Cut Package Clears Amid Bicameral Rancor." *CQ Weekly,* May 24, 1245–49.
——. 2003b. "Congressional Fine-Tuning Ahead for Bush Economic Stimulus Plan." *CQ Weekly,* February 8, 334.
Parmet, Herbert S. 1997. *George Bush: The Life of a Lone Star Yankee* (New York: Simon & Schuster.
Patterson, James T. 1972. *Mr. Republican: A Biography of Robert A. Taft.* Boston, MA: Houghton Mifflin.

Pear, Robert. 2002. "Number of People Living in Poverty Increases in U.S." *New York Times,* September 25.

——. 2003. "Sweeping Medicare Change Wins Approval in Congress." *New York Times,* November 26, A1.

Peters, Ronald M., Jr. 1990. *The American Speakership: The Office in Historical Perspective.* Baltimore, MD: Johns Hopkins University Press.

Peterson, Mark. 1990. *Legislating Together: The White House and Capitol Hill from Eisenhower to Reagan.* Cambridge, MA: Harvard University Press.

Pew Center. 2003. "Different Faiths, Different Messages." *Pew Forum on Religion and Public Life,* March 19.

Pew Global Project Attitudes. 2003. *Views of a Changing World June 2003.* Washington, D.C.: Pew Research Center for the People and the Press.

Pew Research Center for the People and the Press. 2003. Questionnaire: America's Image Further Erodes, Europeans Want Weaker Ties. March 18. Washington, D.C.

Pfiffner, James. 1996. *The Strategic Presidency,* 2nd ed. Lawrence, KS: University Press of Kansas.

Phillips, Kevin. 2001. "His Fraudulency the Second? The Illegitimacy of George W. Bush." *The American Prospect,* January 29.

Pianin, Eric. 2001. "Tax Cut May Bust Budget." *Washington Post,* May 26.

Pious, Richard M. 1979. *The American Presidency.* New York: Basic Books.

——. 1996. *The Presidency.* New York: Allyn and Bacon.

Pitney, John J., Jr. 2000a. *The Art of Political Warfare.* Norman, OK: University of Oklahoma Press.

——. 2000b. "Clinton and the Republican Party." In *The Postmodern Presidency: Bill Clinton's Legacy in U.S. Politics,* edited by Steven E. Schier, 167–82. Pittsburgh, PA: University of Pittsburgh Press.

Political Staff of the Washington Post. 2001. *Deadlock: the Inside Story of America's Closest Election.* New York: Public Affairs.

Pollich, Diana. 2002. "A Divided Electorate." *CBSNews.com,* November 6, available at http://www.cbsnews.com/stories/2002/11/06/politics/main528295.shtml.

Polsby, Nelson W., and Aaron Wildavsky. 1996. *Presidential Elections: Strategies and Structures in American Politics,* 9th ed. Chatham, NJ: Chatham House.

Powell, Stewart M. 2003. "Bush Hopes to Win by Compromising; He's Cutting Deals on Domestic Legislation." *Milwaukee Journal Sentinel,* June 22, A14.

Preston, Thomas, and Margaret Hermann. 2004. "Presidential Leadership Style and the Foreign Policy Advisory Process." In *The Domestic Sources of American Foreign Policy: Insights and Evidence,* 4th ed., edited by Eugene R. Wittkopf and James M. McCormick, 363–80. Lanham, MD: Rowman & Littlefield.

Price, Joyce Howard. 2002. "Sarbanes Wants New Bush Financial Team." *Washington Times,* October 27, available at http://www.washingtontimes.com/national/20021027-1510760.htm.

Price, Kevin S. 2002. "The Partisan Legacies of Preemptive Leadership: Assessing the Eisenhower Cohorts in the U.S. House." *Political Research Quarterly,* 55 (September): 609–32.

Purdom, Todd S., and Patrick E. Tyler. 2002. "Top Republicans Break with Bush on Iraq Strategy." *New York Times,* August 16, available at http://www.nytimes.com.

Rae, Nicol C. 1998. *Conservative Reformers: The Republican Freshmen and the Lessons of the 104th Congress.* Armonk:, NY: M. E. Sharpe.

——. 2000. "Clinton and the Democrats: The President as Party Leader." In *The Postmodern Presidency: Bill Clinton's Legacy in U.S. Politics,* edited by Steven E. Schier, 183–200. Pittsburgh, PA: University of Pittsburgh Press.

Rae, Nicol C., and Colton C. Campbell. 2001. "Party Politics and Ideology in the Contemporary Senate." In *The Contentious Senate: Partisanship, Ideology, and the Myth of Cool Judgment,* edited by Colton C. Campbell and Nicol C. Rae, 1–18. Lanham, MD: Rowman & Littlefield,.

——. 2003. *Impeaching Clinton: Partisan Strife on Capitol Hill.* Lawrence, KS: University Press of Kansas.

Lyn Ragsdale. 1996. *Vital Statistics on the Presidency, Washington to Clinton.* Washington, D.C.: CQ Press.

Rauch, Jonathan. 1999. *Government's End: Why Washington Stopped Working.* New York: Public Affairs.

Remini, Robert V. 1999. *Andrew Jackson.* New York: HarperCollins.

Rice, Condoleezza. 2000. "Promoting the National Interest." *Foreign Affairs* 79 (January/February):45–62.

Rohde, David W. 1991. *Parties and Leaders in the Postreform House.* Chicago, IL: University of Chicago Press.

Rosenbaum, David E. 2001a. "Bush Rules." *New York Times,* January 28.

——. 2001b. "Congress Agrees on Final Details of Tax Cut Bill." *New York Times,* May 26, A1.

——. 2001c. "On Party Lines, Panel Approves Lower Tax Rate." *New York Times,* March 2, A1.

——. 2002a. "No Strong Voice Is Heard on Bush's Economic Team." *New York Times,* July 21.

——. 2002b. "But It's *Not* the Economy, So Far." *New York Times,* October 12.

——. 2003. "White House Sees a $455 Billion Gap in '03 Budget." *New York Times,* July 16, A1.

Rosenbaum, David E., and David Firestone. 2003. "$318 Billion Deal Is Set in Congress for Cutting Taxes." *New York Times,* May 22.

Rosenberg, Joel C. 2003. "Political Buzz from Washington." *World* 18 (March 22):10.

Rosin, Hanna. 2000. "Personal Faith and Public Policy." *Washington Post National Weekly Edition,* September 11.

Rossiter, Clinton. 1957. *The American Presidency.* London: Hamish Hamilton.

Rove, Karl. 2002. Remarks at the Bush Library, Texas A&M University, College Station, TX, December 13. C-SPAN broadcast.

Rumsfeld, Donald H. 2002. "Secretary Rumsfeld Press Conference at NATO Headquarters, Brussels Belgium." U.S. Department of Defense, June 6, available at http://www.defenselink.mil/news/Jun2002/t06062002_t0606sd.html.

Russell, Gordon. 2001. "Convention Opens with Blast on Bush." *New Orleans Times-Picayune,* July 9, 1.

Russett, Bruce. 1975. "The Americans' Retreat from World Power." *Political Science Quarterly* 90 (Spring):1–22.

Saad, Lydia. 2003a. "Iraq War Triggers Major Rally Effect." Gallup news release, March 25, available at http://www.gallup.com/poll/releases/pr030325.asp.

——. 2003b. "Bush's Job Rating Still Above 60%." Gallup news release, July 2, available at http://www.gallup.com/poll/releases/pr030702.asp.

Sack, Kevin. 2001. "Blacks Who Voted Against Bush Offer Support to Him in Wartime." *New York Times*, December 25, A1.

Sailer, Steve. 2002. "Analysis: GOP Beats Dems by about 53–47." *United Press International*, November 6.

Sammon, Bill. 2001. *At Any Cost: How Al Gore Tried to Steal the Election.* Washington, D.C.: Regnery.

Sandalow, Marc. 2003. "Rep. Stark Takes Swipe at Bush over His Past Alcohol Use." *San Francisco Chronicle*, February 7, A3.

Sanger, David. 2000. "The 43rd President." *New York Times*, December 14.

——. 2003. "Bush Claim on Iraq Had Flawed Origin." *New York Times*, July 8.

Sanger, David E., and Steven Greenhouse. 2002. "President Invokes Taft-Hartley Act to Open 29 Ports." *New York Times*, October 9.

Sanger, David E., and James Risen. 2003. "C.I.A. Chief Takes Blame in Assertion on Iraqi Uranium." *New York Times*, July 12, A1, A5.

Scammon, Richard M., and Ben J. Wattenberg. 1970. *The Real Majority.* New York: Coward-McCann.

Schick, Allen. 2003. "Bush's Budget Problem." Paper presented at "The George W. Bush Presidency: An Early Assessment," April 25–26, Woodrow Wilson School, Princeton University, Princeton, NJ,.

Schier, Steven E. 2000. *By Invitation Only: The Rise of Exclusive Politics in the United States.* Pittsburgh, PA: University of Pittsburgh Press.

Schlesinger, Arthur M., Jr. 1973. *The Imperial Presidency.* Boston, MA: Houghton Mifflin.

Schlesinger, Robert. 2001. "Senate Committee Puts Bush's Education Plan on Fast Track." *Boston Globe*, March 7, A6.

Schmitt, Eric. 2003. "Aide Denies Shaping Data to Justify War." *New York Times*, June 5, available at http://www.nytimes.com.

Schrader, Ann, and Mike Soragher. 2001. "Initial Reviews Strong for Bush Speech." *Denver Post*, September 23.

Scott, James. 1998. *Seeing Like A State: How Certain Schemes to Improve the Human Condition Have Failed.* New Haven, CT: Yale University Press.

Seegers, Mary C., ed. 2002. *Piety, Politics, and Pluralism: Religion, the Courts, and the 2000 Election.* Lanham, MD: Rowman & Littlefield.

Seelye, Katharine Q. 2001. "Panel Tells Bush Global Warming Getting Worse." *New York Times*, June 7.

Shapiro, Walter. 2002. "Democrats' Crummy Sales Pitch Gets Them the Boot." *USA Today*, November 13, 5A.

Shepard, Scott. 2001. "Bush, GOP Fight for Tax Cut." *Atlanta Journal and Constitution*, April 6, A1.

Shull, Steven, ed. 1991. *The Two Presidencies: A Quarter-Century Assessment.* Chicago, IL: Nelson-Hall.

Sievers, Harry J. 1968. *Benjamin Harrison, Hoosier President: The White House and After.* Indianapolis, IN: Bobbs-Merill.

Silbey, Joel H. 1991. *The American Political Nation, 1838–1893* Stanford, CA; Stanford University Press.

Sinclair, Barbara. 1995. *Legislators, Leaders, and Lawmaking: The House of Representatives in the Postreform Era.* Baltimore, MD: Johns Hopkins University Press.

Skcopol, Theda. 1997. *Boomerang: Clinton's Health Security Effort and the Turn Against Government in U.S. Politics,* rev. ed. New York: W. W. Norton.

Skowronek, Stephen. 1997. *The Politics Presidents Make: Leadership from John Adams to Bill Clinton.* Cambridge, MA: Harvard University Press.

——. 2003. "Presidential Leadership in Political Time." In *The Presidency and the Political System,* 7th ed., edited by Michael Nelson, 111–57. Washington, D.C.: CQ Press.

Smith, Mark A. 2000. *American Business and Political Power: Public Opinion, Elections, and Democracy.* Chicago, IL: University of Chicago Press.

Smith, Richard Norton. 1984. *Thomas E. Dewey and His Times.* New York: Simon and Schuster, Touchstone.

Socolofsky, Homer E., and Allan B. Spetter. 1987. *The Presidency of Benjamin Harrison.* Lawrence, KS: University Press of Kansas.

Sparrow, Bartholomew. 1996. *From the Outside In: World War II and the American State.* Princeton, NJ: Princeton University Press.

Sproat, John G. 1968. *"The Best Men": Liberal Reformers in the Gilded Age.* New York: Oxford University Press.

Stanley, Harold W., and Richard G. Niemi. 2000. *Vital Statistics on American Politics, 1999–2000.* Washington, D.C.: CQ Press.

Stevenson, Richard W. 2001. "Bush Projections Show Sharp Drop in Budget Surplus." *New York Times,* August 23.

——. 2002. "Budget Deficit Is Said to Be $159 Billion." *New York Times,* October 25.

——. 2003a. "To Save Tax Cuts, Bush Banks on Political Capital." *New York Times,* April 21.

——. 2003b. "Bush Signs Tax Cut Bill, Dismissing All Criticism." *New York Times,* May 29, A18.

Stonecash, Jeffrey M. 2000. *Class and Party in American Politics.* Boulder, CO: Westview Press.

Stonecash, Jeffrey M., Mark D. Brewer, and Mack D. Mariani. 2003. *Diverging Parties: Social Change, Realignment, and Party Polarization.* Boulder, CO: Westview Press.

Strahan, Randall. 1998. "Thomas Brackett Reid and the Rise of Party Government," in *Masters of the House: Congressional Leadership Over Two Centuries,* edited by Roger H. Davidson, Susan Webb Hammond, and Raymond W. Smock, 33–62. Boulder, CO: Westview Press.

Sullivan, Andrew. 2001. "Who's Your Daddy?" *Time,* June 18, 92.

Suskind, Ron. 2003. "Why Are These Men Laughing?" *Esquire,* January.

Taylor, Humphrey. 2003. "Successful War Lifts Many (Republican) Boats and Their Ratings Surge." Harris Interactive, April 18, available at http://www.harrisinteractive.com/harris_poll/index.asp?PID=371.

Teixeira, Ruy. 2003. "Deciphering the Democrats' Debacle." *Washington Monthly*, May.

Text of UN Resolution on Iraq. 2002. November 8. Available at
http://www.cnn.com/2002/US/11/08/resolution.text/.

Thomma, Steven. 2001. "McAuliffe to lead Democrats; He Vows to Confront, Not Work with, Bush White House." *Milwaukee Journal-Sentinel*, February 4, 22A.

Toner, Robin. 2000. "Differing Sides on Abortion Issue See Stark Contrasts in Candidates." *New York Times*, October 27.

——. 2003a. "Role Reversal: Now, the G.O.P. Insists Deficits Aren't So Bad." *New York Times*, February 9.

——. 2003b. "Accusation of Bias Angers Democrats." *New York Times*, July 27, 1:18.

Toner, Robin, and Robert Pear. 2003. "Compromise Seen as Harder to Find on Medicare Drugs." *New York Times*, July 13.

Toobin, Jeffrey. 1999. *A Vast Conspiracy*. New York: Random House .

——. 2002. "Ashcroft's Ascent." *New Yorker*, April 15, 61.

Transcript of Debate between Vice President Gore and Governor Bush. 2000. *New York Times*, October 4, A30.

Tufte, Edward R. 1978. *Political Control of the Economy*. Princeton, NJ: Princeton University Press.

Tulis, Jeffrey J. 2003. "The Two Constitutional Presidencies." In *The Presidency and the Political System*, 7th ed., edited by Michael Nelson, 79–110. Washington, D.C.: CQ Press.

Tumulty, Karen. 2003, "I Want My Al TV." *Time Magazine*, June 30.

U.S. Department of State, Office of the Historian. 2001a. "Operation Enduring Freedom Overview." October 1. Available at http://www.state.gov/s/ct/rls/fs/2001/5194.htm.

——. 2001b. "The United States and the Global Coalition Against Terrorism, September–December 2001: A Chronology." December 31. Available at http://www.state.gov/r/pa/ho/pubs/fs/5889.htm.

U.S. Embassy Islamabad. 2002. "Fact Sheet: Coalition Contributions to the War on Terrorism." May 25. Available at http://usembassy.state.gov/posts/pk1/wwwh02052502.html.

U.S. National Archive and Records Administration. "Executive Order Disposition Tables: George W Bush." Available at www.archives.gov/federal_register/executive_orders/executive_orders.html.

Van Natta, Don, Jr. 2001. "The Sporting Life at the White House." *New York Times*, September 9.

VandeHei, Jim. 2003a. "GOP Not Backing Savings Changes." *Washington Post*, February 7.

——. 2003b. "Clinton Develops into a Force in the Senate." *Washington Post*, March 5.

——. 2003c. "GOP to Hammer Democratic War Critics." *Washington Post*, March 20, A14.

——. 2003d. "Decision on Tax Cut Left Open in GOP Budget Deal." *Washington Post,* April 11, A2.
Victor, Kirk. 2003. "Congress in Eclipse as Power Shifts to Executive Branch." *GovExec.com,* April 7, available at http://www.govexec.com/.
Wagner, Donald E. 2003. "Marching to Zion: The Evangelical-Jewish Alliance." *Christian Century* 120 (June 28):20–24.
Washington, Wayne. 2002. "Black Lawmakers See Retreat on Civil Rights, Justice Dept.'s Boyd Accused of Inaction." *Boston Globe,* June 20, A3.
Wattenberg, Martin P. 1984. *The Decline of American Political Parties: 1952–1980.* Cambridge, MA: Harvard University Press.
Wayne, Stephen J. 2001. *The Road to the White House: The Politics of Presidential Elections,* post-election ed. Boston, MA: Bedford/St Martin's.
Weber, Max. 1970. *From Max Weber: Essays in Sociology,* edited by H. H. Gerth and C. Wright Mills. London: Routledge and Kegan Paul.
Weisman, Jonathan. 2002a. "Treasury Secretary O'Neill Announces Resignation." *Washington Post,* December 6.
——. 2002b. "Battered Economic Team May Soon Feel Relief." *Washington Post,* December 7.
——. 2002c. "Bush's Economic Pick under Fire from Right." *Washington Post,* December 11.
——. 2003a. "Thomas Questions Dividend Tax Cuts." *Washington Post,* January 28, A1.
——. 2003b. "Chronic Budget Deficits Forecast; CBO Bases Estimate on Cost of President's Budget Plan." *Washington Post,* March 8.
——. 2003c. "White House Foresees 5-Year Debt Increase of $1.9 Trillion." *Washington Post,* July 16, A1.
Weisman, Jonathan, and John M. Berry. 2003. "As Budget Deficit Grows, Greenspan Speaks Softly." *Washington Post,* July 20.
Welch, William, and Judy Keen. 2001. "Tax Cut Battle Goes to Senate; Bush Plan Passes Easily in House." *USA Today,* March 9, 1A.
Westbrook, Robert. 2000. "Dubya-ism: Tender Is the Right." *Christian Century.* 117 (September 13–20): 912–16.
White, Ben. 2000. "Bush Administration Picks Transition Chiefs." *Washington Post,* December 21.
White, John Kenneth. 2002. *The Values Divide: American Politics and Culture in Transition.* New York: Chatham House.
Wildavsky, Aaron. 1966. "The Two Presidencies." *Transaction* December 23-31.
——. 1975. "The Two Presidencies." In *Perspectives on the Presidency,* edited by Aaron Wildavsky, 448–61. Boston: Little, Brown.
Williams, Rhys H., ed. 1997. *Cultural Wars in American Politics.* New York: Aldine de Gruyter.
Wood, Gordon S. 1992. *The Radicalism of the American Revolution.* New York: Knopf.
Woodward, Bob. 2002. *Bush at War.* New York: Simon & Schuster.
Yardley, Jim. 2002. "Enron, Our Story." *Essence,* July, 110.
York, Byron. 2002. "The Enron List." *National Review* online, January 11, available at http://www.nationalreview.com/york/york011102b.shtml.

Zakaria, Fareed. 1998. *From Wealth to Power: The Unusual Origins of America's World Role.* Princeton, NJ: Princeton University Press.
———. 2003. "Why America Scares the World and What to Do about It." *Newsweek* (March 24):18–33.
Zeleny, Jeff. 2002. "Chicago Tale? Bush Camp Can't Verify It." *Chicago Tribune*, July 14.

Contributors

Peri E. Arnold is Professor of Government at the University of Notre Dame. He is the author of *Making the Managerial Presidency* (Princeton University Press, 1986), for which he won the Louis Brownlow Award of the National Academy of Public Administration. He also won their 1996 Marshall Dimock Award for an article published in *Public Administration Review*. His current work focuses on the presidency of the Progressive Era.

John J. Coleman is Professor and Associate Chair of the Political Science Department at the University of Wisconsin, Madison. He is the author of *Party Decline in America: Policy, Politics, and the Fiscal State* (Princeton University Press, 1996) and articles on party organizations, elections, Congress, the presidency, campaign spending, and international trade. In 1997, he received the "Emerging Scholar Award" from the Political Organization and Parties section of the American Political Science Association.

John Fendreis is Professor of Political Science and Vice Provost at Loyola University, Chicago. He is co-author, with Raymond Tatalovich, of *The Modern Presidency and Economic Policy* (Peacock, 1994) and has written for such leading journals as the *American Political Science Review* and *Political Research Quarterly*.

James L. Guth is William Kenan Jr. Professor of Political Science at Furman University. He has written extensively for scholarly and popular publications on religion's role in American and European politics. His current project is an assessment of religious divisions as a source of American party cleavages.

John F. Harris is a political reporter on the national staff of the *Washington Post* who covered the Clinton presidency from 1995 to its conclusion in 2001. He received the Aldo Beckman and Gerald R. Ford Presidential Library awards for his White House coverage. His history of the Clinton presidency is forthcoming from Random House in 2004.

Bertram Johnson is Lecturer on Government at Harvard University. He has written on campaign finance, intergovernmental relations, and state and local politics.

James M. McCormick is Professor and Chair of the Political Science Department at Iowa State University. He is the author of *American Foreign Policy and Process* (Peacock, third edition, 1998) and numerous journal articles on U.S. foreign policy. He has twice received Fulbright fellowships, to New Zealand in 1990 and the Philippines in 2003.

John J. Pitney Jr. is Professor of Government at Claremont McKenna College in Claremont, California. He is the author of *The Art of Political Warfare* (University of Oklahoma Press, 2001), among other books.

Kevin S. Price is Assistant Professor of Political Science at the University of Washington, where he works in the fields of presidential and party politics, with emphasis on American political development.

Nicol C. Rae is Professor of Political Science at Florida International University. He is the author of *The Decline and Fall of Liberal Republicans* (Oxford, 1989), *Southern Democrats* (Oxford University Press, revised edition, 1994) and *Conservative Reformers: The Republican Freshmen and the Lessons of the 104th Congress* (Sharpe, 1998), among other books.

Steven E. Schier is Dorothy H. and Edward C. Congdon Professor of Political Science at Carleton College in Northfield, Minnesota. He has written or edited nine books, including *The Postmodern President: Bill Clinton's Legacy in U.S. Politics* (University of Pittsburgh Press, 2001), which won an "outstanding academic book" award from *Choice* magazine. He was Fulbright Senior Lecturer at York University in Toronto in 2002.

Raymond Tatalovich is Professor of Political Science at Loyola University, Chicago. He specializes in the American presidency, co-authoring with John Fendreis *The Modern Presidency and Economic Policy* (Peacock, 1994). Most recently, he co-authored with Thomas S. Engeman *The Presidency and*

Political Science: Two Hundred Years of Constitutional Debate (Johns Hopkins University Press, 2003).

John Kenneth White is Professor of Politics at The Catholic University of America. He has written extensively on the presidency and American politics. His most recent books include *New Party Politics: From Hamilton and Jefferson to the Information Age* (Wadsworth, 2003) and *The Values Divide: American Politics and Culture in Transition* (Chatham House, 2002).

John J. Zogby is President and CEO of Zogby International. He has polled for Reuters News Agency, *NBC News,* MSNBC, *Fox News,* Gannett News Service, the *New York Post, Atlanta Journal and Constitution,* and many other newspapers. He has taught at the State University of New York, Utica College, and Hamilton College's Arthur Levitt Public Affairs Center.

Index